JOHN MARSDEN'S WILL

John Marsden's Will

The Hornby Estate Case 1780–1840

Emmeline Garnett

THE HAMBLEDON PRESS

LONDON AND RIO GRANDE

Published by The Hambledon Press, 1998

102 Gloucester Avenue, London NW1 8HX (UK)
PO Box 162, Rio Grande, Ohio 45674 (USA)

ISBN 1 85285 158 9

A description of this book is available from
the British Library and from the Library of Congress

Typeset by Carnegie Publishing, Chatsworth Road, Lancaster

Printed on acid-free paper and bound in
Great Britain by Cambridge University Press

Contents

Illustrations

Text Illustrations

Preface

The long-running lawsuit of *Tatham* v. *Wright* was a legal cause célèbre of the early nineteenth century. Between 1826 and 1838 its outcome was discussed at London clubs and dinner-parties almost as eagerly as in the north. Its twists and turns were lengthily reported in *The Times*. The verbatim report of the 1834 trial was published not only in Lancashire but in London and Edinburgh as well. William IV himself sent messages of support to the plaintiff.

Public imagination was caught and held by a story which on the surface might have come straight from a contemporary novel. A feeble-minded landowner was imprisoned in his castle, his person and wealth in the clutch of a wicked steward, whose triumph was complete until there sprang up to challenge him a character beloved by a generation which remembered Nelson: a brave, open-hearted sailor with no resources but his indomitable courage.

A hundred years later the whole thing had been all but forgotten even in the Lune Valley where it originated, largely because the families on one side had died out, and those on the other had become pillars of the establishment, whom it would have been impolite to remind of the cause of their prosperity. Very faint echoes were still in the air in the author's childhood, but these had quite vanished when, in 1990, the acquisition of a rare copy of Fraser's printed verbatim report aroused new interest. The story was fascinating in its details, and even more so in the fact that from the printed evidence it was impossible to decide, had one been on that jury, which way one's vote would have gone.

The next step was the discovery that all the material gathered by the plaintiff's side during the twelve years of litigation, together with a small amount from the solicitor's office on the other side, was preserved in eight large tin boxes in Hornby Castle, which, by the generosity of the present owner, was made available. Each box contained a number of brown paper parcels, many of which had hardly been disturbed since being packed away in the 1850s, and there was no sort of catalogue.

The reference numbers given in the notes, therefore, belong to a working list of which a copy is now held with the collection.

The parts of this collection which were most valuable in the reconstruction of the story fall into three categories. First, the purely legal: briefs given to counsel, counsels' opinions, schedules of material needed in the trials, copies of judgements, printed reports, copy wills and so on. Many of these are in numerous copies.

Secondly, there are the depositions of witnesses and possible witnesses: these provide the basis for most of the first half of the book, and appear in every form, from the first brief and often wildly spelt notes of the field workers, through the successive amplifications and tidyings necessary to make them strong enough for court appearance. Some appear finally in printed form in Fraser's verbatim account, but many of them there have lost something of the original racy zest, because the shorthand writer often failed to understand the speakers' accent or dialect. Among the depositions one should also list Admiral Tatham's account, which he wrote to prove that he was indeed John Marsden's heir at law, and which includes a great deal of personal and family detail not available anywhere else.

Thirdly, there are the letters. Fortunately for the historian, the two mainstays of the case against the will, the Admiral himself and his cousin and most important supporter, Pudsey Dawson, met comparatively rarely throughout the twelve years, but corresponded roughly once a week. The Admiral was usually in the midlands; Pudsey had his house in Sidmouth, his business in London, his estates in Yorkshire. Other important characters were similarly scattered: John Higgin junior the attorney was based in Lancaster, Dr Lingard in Hornby, Thomas Gorst in London. All their letters are preserved (Dr Lingard's to John Higgin are in the Lancashire Record Office), and at some time a certain number between George Wright and his attorney, William Sharp, were also added to the collection. The first half of the book depends heavily on the depositions, the second half on the letters.

In quoting from original sources, I have taken the liberty of adding or altering or modernising punctuation where the meaning seemed to be obscured, but with as light a hand as possible.

Acknowledgements

I am most grateful to David Battersby of Hornby Castle for allowing me free access over eighteen months to the *Tatham* v. *Wright* material. Many others helped with advice, information, access, loans or permission to photograph. They include Robert Bassenden of Wray, Robert Bell of Langcliffe Hall, the late Antony Bent, Dr David Bentley QC, Professor Lloyd Bonfield, Geoffrey Bowring of Halton Park, the Reverend Martin Bull of Gargrave, Mrs Coghlan of Bretherton, Clive Lamb of Hornby, the staff of the Lancashire and Cumbria Record Offices, the staff of the Lancaster Reference Library, Olivia Ley of Burrow, the Reverend Nicholas McArdle of Hornby Catholic Church, Miss S. V. Pearson, the Reverend Iain Rennie of Hornby, the Reverend Canon David Rhodes of Giggleswick, Julian Roskill of London, Peter Sharp of Borwick, Professor A.W. Brian Simpson, Professor David Sugarman of Lancaster University, Mrs Edith Tyson of Lancaster, Hugh van Asch of Havelock North, New Zealand, Ushaw College Library, Dr Andrew White of Lancaster Museums, John Wilson of Tatham and the late Christopher Wright of Australia.

For permission to use portraits and photographs in their possession, I would like to thank David Battersby, Robert Bell, Geoffrey Bowring, Olivia Ley, Peter Sharp, Edith Tyson and Hugh van Asch; Gargrave Parochial Church Council, Hornby Catholic Church, Lancashire Record Office and the National Portrait Gallery. For almost all the actual photographs I have to thank Sara Mason.

Every person, however, is presumed to be of perfect mind and memory unless the contrary is proved: and therefore, if any one attempt to call in question, or overthrow the Will, on account of the supposed madness or want of memory in the testator, he must prove such impediment to have existed previous to the date of the Will: but people of mean understanding and capacity, neither of the wise sort, nor the foolish, but indifferent betwixt both, even though they rather incline to the foolish sort, are not hindered from making their Will. The law will not scrutinize into the depths of a man's capacity, particularly after his death, if he was able to conduct himself reasonably in the common course of life: as it might be opening a wide door to support pretensions of fraud or imposition on the testator.

Tomlin, *The Law Dictionary* (1820)

1

John Marsden

From Lancaster at its mouth to its source in the high Pennines, the River Lune runs almost due north. In its first twenty miles its course is through a mild and fertile valley scattered with small stone villages. It was always a country of small estates and modest prosperity based on the fattening of Scotch black cattle on their way to the southern markets, on the timber trades from woods that clothed the hillsides and on the sheep that ran on the fells. For most of its history it was a quiet place.

John Marsden, whose will sparked off the long-running case of *Tatham* v. *Wright* in 1826, belonged to a Lune Valley family of some distinction. The Marsdens were not great landowners, but their money and their property were older by a hundred years than that of most of the neighbouring estates. When Lancaster began to flourish as a port and a manufactory for the West Indian trade, in the mid eighteenth century, a great deal of money flowed into the Lune Valley, and a great many families began to climb into gentrydom, to be joined by many more in the great age of cotton. At the beginning of this era the Marsdens were already well established.

A seventeenth-century Henry Marsden made money from that perennial source of prosperity, the law. The name is frequently found in east Lancashire. His family was probably from Pendleton, but little is known of him except that he was a member of Gray's Inn in 1655, 'one of the six attorneys in the exchequer', and Member of Parliament for Clitheroe, briefly, in the last years of Charles I; and that about 1660, in the time-honoured English fashion, he came back from London to his roots and bought land.[1]

He acquired the manor of Bradford, Gisburn Hall and other property in Craven, and began to use a coat of arms conveniently borrowed from the ancient Shropshire family of Marston: *Sable, a fesse dancettée ermine, three fleurs-de-lis argent*, and *a demi-greyhound rampant* for a crest. So it was as an established gentleman, though not as long established as the family later claimed, that in 1674 he bought the manor of Wennington on the Wenning, a tributary of the Lune, from the Morleys. This family had held it for at least 300 years, and had managed to survive (but only just) the crippling embarrassments of being both Catholic and Royalist. The Robert Morley who inherited as a minor in 1666 sold it as soon as he was legally able.

It was not a great estate. The family house, standing where the present mansion stands, was known as Nether Hall. There were a few farms, a corn mill on the River Wenning, and Wennington village, which was no more than a scatter of cottages round a green. The church was at Melling, more than a mile away, and the advowson was in the gift of neighbouring Hornby Castle. There was another farm, another corn mill and a limekiln, in neighbouring parishes; altogether, about a thousand modern acres: a comfortable country gentleman's estate of no very great importance in the scheme of things.[2]

Nothing now remains of the original Nether Hall. Everything was swept away in the 1850s and replaced by the present rather endearing pile, all castellation and Gothic knick-knacks, from the hands of Austin and Paley. We know that it paid tax on eight hearths in 1664, which put it at the time among the top dozen or so of Lonsdale houses, but Lonsdale was a poor area: even its best houses were small compared with many in the West Riding, or south-east Lancashire.

At some time in the 1720s, Henry Marsden, the third of Wennington but the first actually to move there from Gisburn, rebuilt to suit a more modern taste. Not only his grandfather, who had bought the estate, but also his father, the second Henry, and his bachelor uncle Charles, had been successful lawyers of Gray's Inn, so he had benefited. He rebuilt in the economical fashion adopted by many in this area, attaching a large new section to the front of the old house, exactly as the neighbours were modernising Hornby Castle at about the same time. Sixty years later the 'old hall stairs' at Wennington were said to be still in place but unusable because filled up with rubbish.

This Henry Marsden died in 1742 at the age of forty-seven, and in his will left the considerable sum of £1000 to each of his four daughters, as well as a proper provision for his wife; but his main property to his son, another Henry.[3] The inventory of his possessions lists all the rooms of Wennington Hall. It makes it abundantly clear that the handsome country house stretched back to a rabbit warren of services and out-houses belonging to the older building: parlour, hall, green room, servants' little room, passage, kitchen, larder, common kitchen, laundry, still house, dairy, cellars, brewhouse, low dairy, 'grainery', stable, blue room upstairs, room over the hall, little room over the hall, parlour chamber, Mr Marsden's room, closet, linen closet, little garret, garret passage, great garret, gallery, first kitchen chamber, closet, second kitchen chamber, dressing room, 'Great Blew Chamber', closets, servants' garret, servants' rooms over the coach house.

Perhaps typical also of the time and place is the listing of goods and furnishings, which combines an element of wealth with a remarkable lack of luxury. Beds and bedding, chairs and tables there were in profusion; looking-glasses in several bedrooms; three long-case clocks, in the gallery, parlour and kitchen, and a smaller one in the parlour chamber; one bookcase in the 'Great Blew Chamber' but no mention of any books in it. Some 'black and white cutts' in the gallery and hall were the only pictures mentioned. There was plate valued at £125 but only 25s. worth of 'china ware', so when it was not appropriate to eat and drink from silver the family were still using wood or pewter. There is no evidence at all of the comforts and small elegancies of life which were common in more sophisticated parts of the country – of carpets, draperies, musical instruments, writing desks, portraits, maps or globes, nor of kitchen equipment which would indicate progress beyond the basic provision of meat, oatcake, cheese and home-brewed ale. As one might expect from such a hybrid building, it was riddled with rats. Fifty years later they kept people awake by cantering among the rafters.

The only items of real prestige in 1743 were the 'old Coach and chariot' in the coach house, not at all common in Lonsdale, the usual form of transport being still by saddle and pack horse. These vehicles were in use, for the 'coach mares' were listed among the horses, so at least the road to Lancaster, where the Marsdens had their town house in Market Street, was passable to wheeled traffic in some states of the weather.

This Henry Marsden had married appropriately, as had his two sisters, into the local squirearchy. It was a small society, and scattered: 'local' involving parts of Cumberland, Westmorland and West Yorkshire as well as north Lancashire. Travelling was difficult, but people undertook more of it than one might suppose, and long stays in friends' houses made up for the difficulty of getting there. Such visits allowed young people to become acquainted, so that most of these families were interrelated in complicated ways. Henry himself married Eliza Sandford of Askham in Westmorland. His sisters were married closer to home: Elizabeth to William Dawson of Langcliffe near Settle, and Jane to Charles Nowell of Cappleside in Rathmell. Through a daughter, the Nowell family became the Listers of Bell Hill in Giggleswick.

When Henry Marsden the third died in 1742, his widow had an

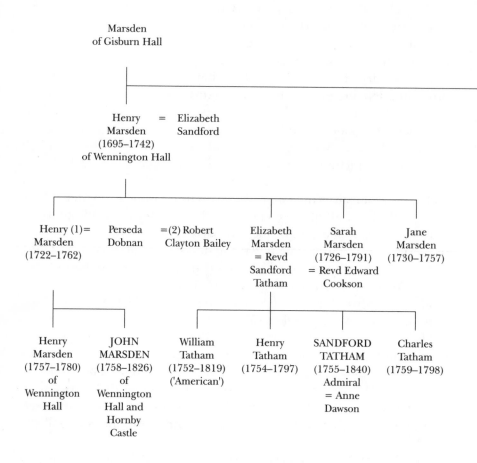

Marsden
of Gisburn Hall

Henry = Elizabeth
Marsden Sandford
(1695–1742)
of Wennington Hall

Henry (1)= Perseda =(2) Robert Elizabeth Sarah Jane
Marsden Dobnan Clayton Bailey Marsden Marsden Marsden
(1722–1762) = Revd (1726–1791) (1730–1757)
Sandford = Revd Edward
Tatham Cookson

Henry JOHN William Henry SANDFORD Charles
Marsden MARSDEN Tatham Tatham TATHAM Tatham
(1757–1780) (1758–1826) (1752–1819) (1754–1797) (1755–1840) (1759–1798)
of of ('American') Admiral
Wennington Wennington = Anne
Hall Hall and Dawson
Hornby
Castle

The Marsden, Tatham, Dawson and Lister families

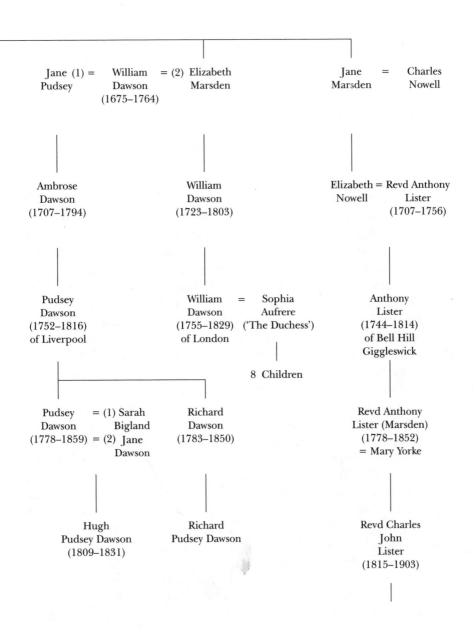

Jane (1) = William = (2) Elizabeth Jane = Charles
Pudsey Dawson Marsden   Marsden   Nowell
    (1675–1764)

Ambrose   William   Elizabeth = Revd Anthony
Dawson   Dawson   Nowell   Lister
(1707–1794)   (1723–1803)   (1707–1756)

Pudsey   William = Sophia   Anthony
Dawson   Dawson   Aufrere   Lister
(1752–1816)   (1755–1829) ('The Duchess') (1744–1814)
of Liverpool   of London   of Bell Hill
                 Giggleswick
           8 Children

Pudsey = (1) Sarah Richard   Revd Anthony
Dawson Bigland Dawson   Lister (Marsden)
(1778–1859) = (2) Jane (1783–1850)   (1778–1852)
     Dawson   = Mary Yorke

Hugh   Richard   Revd Charles
Pudsey Dawson Pudsey Dawson   John
(1809–1831)   Lister
                 (1815–1903)

elegant stone with a long and graceful Latin inscription put up in Melling church chancel. She and her daughters continued to live with her son Henry Marsden the fourth at Wennington, until he married in about 1755 Perseda Dobnan of Doncaster. Then his mother and her two unmarried daughters, Dorothy and Jane, retired to the family house in Lancaster. None of these three women lived very long: all were dead by 1760.

The other daughters had both married. Sarah married in 1752 the Reverend Edward Cookson, Vicar of Leeds, a cousin of some degree, by whom she was left a childless widow after five years, returning to her mother's house in Lancaster. This marriage seems to have been approved, but that of Elizabeth was not, although her husband, Sandford Tatham, was also a parson, and a cousin as well. They made a runaway match of it in 1751, though running no further than Ellel Chapel in Cockerham, three miles south of Lancaster, and seem to have been accepted by 'Madam Marsden' once the deed was done. Money, or the lack of it, may have been the original obstacle. Sandford Tatham was appointed to Hutton-in-the-Forest in Cumberland in 1752, but this benefice was worth only £50 a year. Even when he was further appointed to St Laurence, Appleby, in 1758, it was reckoned that he never had more than £200 a year. The situation was not improved by the rapid arrival of four little boys, all of whom survived.

Meanwhile Henry Marsden the fourth of Wennington and his wife Perseda also had children. Two girls died in infancy, two boys survived. The elder, born on 21 March 1757, was naturally christened Henry; the younger, born a year later to the day, was christened John.

The Marsdens were of that rank in society which automatically handed its babies to wet nurses to rear. So many babies were born, and so many died young, that it was not difficult to find a healthy working woman with milk to spare, and a strong relationship was often built up between the child and its surrogate mother. Henry Marsden called Mrs Denny, whose husband kept the Wennington alehouse, 'mother' to the day he died, and called in to see her nearly every day even as a grown man, taking his friends to visit her and introducing his relations when they came to stay. She in her turn took a special interest in everything that concerned him and his family, and felt quite at liberty to tell him what she thought of his behaviour if it did not please her.

Henry was a bright, strong child – 'a particularly handsome lad' according to his mother's old maid. The same was not true of his younger brother John, who was 'not quite so bright'. Whether anything went wrong at the birth – trauma, lack of oxygen – we do not know, but when the baby was handed to his nurse it was with little expectation that he would live. Perhaps she had lost her own child; she showed a strong determination to save this one. He would make no attempt to suck, so she dripped food down his throat from a teaspoon at short intervals by day and by night. For the whole of his first two years it seemed likely that the battle would be lost, but in the end he showed an intention to survive. From that moment, in physical health he never looked back, living longer than anyone in the family except his aunt Sarah Cookson.

During his childhood it became apparent that mentally he was not the same as other children, who quickly noticed the difference and christened him 'Silly Jack'. Henry Marsden the father died in 1762, perhaps unexpectedly, certainly intestate, when the children were aged five and four. Mrs Marsden lived sometimes in Lancaster, sometimes at Wennington, with them, until she remarried in 1768, when she seems to have moved permanently to Lancaster. Few details of John Marsden's first seven or eight years have survived, but he was always a difficult, restless, noisy child with no concentration. His mother found him very difficult to control and no doubt lost her patience frequently. Later on a rumour was prevalent that she had battered him. But this seems to have started with Sarah Cookson, whose relations with her sister-in-law deteriorated to the point of open warfare. Long afterwards Admiral Tatham repeated a story of his Aunt Cookson,

> who says J.M.'s mother almost stupefied him by her treatment of him. There was a story, probably invented or propagated by Mrs C., that Mrs Bailey had irrecoverably injured his Brain by violent application of the Heel of her Shoe to his Cranium – Ladies' Heels in those Days being a wooden Block about two inches in thickness. I don't exactly believe all about this ill-usage, though Probably the Old Lady might have used him roughly.[4]

In 1768 Mrs Marsden remarried, her second husband being Robert Clayton Bailey of Lancaster, Major, then Colonel, in the Militia. Thereafter they lived in Church Street, on the corner of China Lane, just below the Judges' Lodging. Bailey seems to have been an exemplary stepfather: at least, no one ever suggested anything against him, which in the later atmosphere of attack and counter-attack, in which personal descriptions ranged from the merely overheated to the wildly inventive, must be counted as high praise. One Thomas Townson, who knew John at school and remembered him chiefly for his habit of eating the turnip parings from the trough where a neighbouring gardener prepared his vegetables for market, said that 'Colonel Bailey took great pains with him and brought him round a little, but he was always a person of very defective intellect'.

Sarah Cookson, however, although she had been on good enough terms to stand witness at her sister-in-law's second wedding, within a year brought a lawsuit in Chancery against her and her husband, on the grounds that the late Henry Marsden's estates were being fraudulently estranged from the children. She sought an injunction against Bailey and his wife and the appointment of a guardian with 'a competent yearly sum of money'. With hindsight this is evidence of something more than zeal on behalf of her innocent nephews. She was a greedy woman, and a slightly unbalanced one. The court's decision, after three expensive years, to grant the injunction, but to make the boys' mother their guardian rather than the aunt, caused deep anger and enmity. It is probably not fanciful to say that she felt cheated and that the feeling did not fade away.

While young Henry Marsden went through the Lancaster grammar school and then to Eton, it is not easy to unravel the timetable of his brother John's schooldays. He started at a dame school – the scene of the turnip-eating – and then another 'petty school' before going, it would seem, to Slaidburn for a while, and then aged fifteen back to Lancaster, to the 'free school'. Not apparently to the 'grammar' department, presided over by the Reverend James Watson, which dealt in Latin and Greek, but to the less demanding 'writing school' on the floor above, where Mr Cockin dispensed a plainer form of education. This did not answer well either, so he was sent instead to the Kirkby Lonsdale free school, and boarded there, until he was nineteen.

It has to be remembered that everything known about John Marsden's boyhood, and nearly everything known about his life, is gathered from the depositions of persons questioned after his death in 1826: in the case of his schooldays, after a gap of half a century. Many of these reminiscences were never produced in court, sometimes because they were felt to be not relevant, often because there were doubts about the witnesses' reliability. Even the most conscientious had made up their minds which side of the case they were on before pen was set to paper.

None the less, the evidence regarding this part of his life is overwhelming. The one or two witnesses who tried to remember him as a normal schoolboy carried little conviction. 'Silly Marsden' he was from an early age and the name stuck all his life. He often had to be coaxed to go to school, either a servant or a neighbour's child escorting him, his mother bribing him with sweets. At school he was never heard to repeat a lesson with the other boys, but spent most of his day penned in the usher's long pew; or, if he was very restless, two other boys were detailed to sit one on each side and keep him quiet. No one remembered him joining in the playground games. The attitude of the other boys ranged from more or less good-natured teasing to total indifference. There is no doubt that some of his peculiarities livened up lesson time, particularly (everyone remembered this) his bell-ringing. The Lancaster free school was in the priory church yard, almost under the tower. When the bells rang, 'Silly' Marsden went into ecstasies, flinging up his arms to pull imaginary ropes, and ding-donging at the top of his voice. At playtime he sometimes collected a group of little boys and turned them all into bell-ringers, imitating the whole peal, and rewarding them with sweets. When his incarceration in the master's desk had tried him severely, and playtime came at last, he would erupt like a cannon-ball, rushing out and kicking wildly at any boy who got in his way. 'Look out', they would cry, 'here comes the flying Major!'[5]

On the whole, even in that rough age, his contemporaries seem to have treated him as a natural source of amusement rather than with any great malice, which was not true of Lancaster town, where he was often tormented by both children and adults. On one occasion he paraded the streets, announcing himself as Jesus Christ, and got a flogging from Colonel Bailey for his pains. His peculiarities may have been embarrassing, but they threatened no one, for he was in fact an easily frightened, essentially biddable child, 'never sulky or obstinate – he was very timid but if flattered was easily persuaded'. A nicely brought up little girl of his acquaintance recollected that, meeting him in the street, she made him take off his coat and put it on again the wrong way round. Then she buttoned it up the back and sent him on his way. And though if he went on his own he would not arrive at school, a small boy, four or five years younger, could safely escort and deliver him.

He was not unteachable, he was not an idiot, but he certainly had what would now be classed as a mental impairment, mild rather than severe. His sojourn at Slaidburn had been brief and unfortunate. He was flogged and dismissed for buggery. What this amounted to is unclear; any sexual attraction he felt in later life seems to have been to girls. Buggery was a capital offence if proved against an adult, but in this case it cannot have reached the ears of authority. No doubt the good fortune of his escape from prosecution was drummed into John Marsden, and his tenacious memory seized upon the fact, for in later life he was fond of relating the circumstances.[6]

At Kirkby Lonsdale he learnt rather more than he had done at Lancaster. 'A weak, silly fellow', as a schoolfellow said, but somewhere along the line he acquired a nice, tidy round handwriting, though whether he could do more than copy someone else's composition later became a major point of contention. He learnt to read after some fashion, though it is doubtful whether he did much of it for pleasure. It seems certain that as an adult he could make out something of the news in the paper, and he could look up words in the dictionary. His memory was very good for isolated facts; the lack was in the reasoning power to put the facts together, or to draw conclusions from them. Whether he ever learnt to tell the time is uncertain: Mary Denny, his brother's foster sister, who knew him as well as anyone, said she tried many times to teach him from the clock in her father's bar, and also to do simple addition, 'but he muddled before he got to any sum and in two or three hours appeared to have forgotten the little he knew'. One of his brother's servants remembered Henry Marsden taking off his cap and beating his brother with it for going into the kitchen at Wennington Hall, where there was a large clock on the wall, and asking the time. People remarked that as an adult if someone asked him the time he would take out his watch and show them the face. The young usher at Kirkby Lonsdale, a lad of sixteen, also tried patiently to teach his nineteen-year-old pupil to reckon up numbers, using a bundle of quills: 'He was not able to count them after repeated trials ... I requested him to do it repeatedly, and he never could; I told him how much his brother would be gratified if he was able to count half a hundred quills.' [7]

There was some thought that he might be prepared for the army. At Kirkby Lonsdale 'he was attended by a man who had been in the Militia and received drilling lessons from him'. He was seen 'standing opposite his shadow, talking to it and making strange gestures to it, as if he were practising the manoeuvres he had learnt'. Some said he was turned away from Kirkby Lonsdale also for 'unnatural practices'. In any case, he was nineteen and too old for school. He was sent away to Weybridge, in the company of a Mr Croft, a parson, to tutor him, a step which might with advantage have been taken long before, instead of the years of sitting in school, 'out of the way from home, out of harm's way, doing nothing'.

His time with Mr Croft certainly improved him, in manners if not in intellect, though Admiral Tatham attributed this more to his step-father, to whom 'must be attributed that habit of politeness and address observed in both the brothers, for boys do not learn manners at free school'. Mr Croft was heard to remark that 'What the Almighty had denied, it was out of the power of man to supply'. Nevertheless, John Marsden learnt some of the formalities of behaviour in that very formal age, and while he kept quiet, or uttered only common civilities, could pass among strangers. As soon as he opened his mouth further, his disability was as apparent in the parlour as it always was among the servants or in the village street, where the same restraints did not apply.

In the spring of 1778 Henry Marsden's coming of age was celebrated, and John Marsden came home. The occasion was also his own twentieth birthday. There were all the proper festivities: 'the year they roasted the ox' was a landmark in many village memories even fifty years later. Henry Marsden, fifth of the name, was now of age and could take over the running of his own estates. At the same time he assumed responsibility for his defective brother, which Mrs Bailey seems to have been happy to relinquish. She had never been good with him; on the other hand, in the country everyone knew him, made allowances, and on the whole treated him with the respect due to the Squire's brother. There was plenty of space and country amusements, and it was a much better environment for him than a town house squashed into an overcrowded Lancaster street.

Mrs Bailey visited from time to time, but it was the widowed aunt, Sarah Cookson, who took to making longer and longer visits from her house in Clitheroe, acting as housekeeper and chatelaine. Perhaps she had really persuaded herself that his mother was the cause of John's disability, over which she would lament that 'she wished God would take him as he was very unfit for this world'.

One of Henry's interests was the Militia: he would go as far as Leeds to meetings or manoeuvres. John caught the enthusiasm: all his life he preserved a little boy's keenness for dressing up in uniform, for collecting facts about battles and famous generals, for the basic military drill he had been taught as a schoolboy. Sometimes Henry conducted his own war games at home, and John was willing enough to be included, but his temperament could not cope with the rougher aspects of the game. One of the Hall servants remembered one occasion.

Some militia men were on furlough at Wennington. They had a sham fight and had laths for weapons. Mr John Marsden was posted in a small plantation with the militia and had two small brass cannon loaded with powder and also a halberd in his hand. Henry Marsden with the workmen took the hill by storm. He hit his brother on the fingers with the lath but not so as to hurt him, he dropt his halberd, cryed out and wept very much and appeared greatly frightened.[8]

One of the Leeds cousins, Dr Ambrose Cookson, had wide experience of mental problems, spending most of his professional life as physician to the Lincoln Lunatic Asylum, and although he met John only a few times, he had no doubt of the diagnosis. 'We call it connate imbecility', he said. 'Such persons as are connate imbeciles have no power of reasoning or discriminating; they may do little things mechanically; they have no power of mind at all in those cases. I never saw an instance of such a disease being curable; I never saw such a case cured. I rather think it is not to be cured.'

Henry Marsden had a personal servant called George Mashiter, who rode out in attendance upon him, and at home waited at table, cleaned boots and did any personal service that might be required. Curiously, nobody thought that it might be as well for John to have a servant; perhaps it was not the custom for young people under the age of twenty-one. Though all the servants were urged at different times to look out for him, 'no one in particular was engaged to take care of him'. A new young gardener called Robert Humber, a favourite with Henry because they had been boys together at the free school, was appointed when both he and the Squire were about twenty years old. Because he was a thoroughly sensible, reliable young man, Robert was very often called upon to have an eye to the younger brother, for whom he seems to have developed a protective feeling, even escorting him to 'the necessary'. Whether the escort was needed because he would have used some improper place if not taken to the proper one is not recorded, but it is apparent that some of John's personal habits could be embarrassing.

Humber of course had his work to do, so for the most part John wandered about the village, sometimes roistering with Tommy Thompson, the village idiot, hallooing up and down and beating the hedges with sticks, sometimes hovering about the cottages, particularly where there were any girls, snatching at their breasts 'in a very indecent manner'. Mrs Denny told him to behave, and Mary Denny was well able to take care of herself, but many would have been embarrassed to call the Squire's brother to order, whatever his mental state. Henry, who was, said George Mashiter, both 'kind and severe' to his brother, told him to keep out of the poor neighbours' houses, but did nothing more positive, for which one can hardly blame him, since he was no more than a boy himself. For whatever reason, perhaps the weight of the responsibilities he was required to carry, Henry took to drinking heavily.

The manservant George Mashiter had not been in service more than a couple of years when he gave notice; he was about to get married and wanted to rent a farm. House service was a fertile meeting place for young people, but married couples almost always moved out to live, even if they continued to work as indoor servants. Henry Marsden had a farm coming empty; he let it to Mashiter and gave him a farewell present of £50 to help him set up. Then he looked round for a new servant; and so George Wright came to Wennington Hall.

2

George Wright

The key actor in the story, and in many ways its most remarkable character, is George Wright, born in Aughton, christened in Halton in May 1758, two months after John Marsden was christened in Melling. As the crow flies across the River Lune, seven miles separate the two churches.

Wright is a Furness name, but the family were, it seems, settled in Caton, across the river from Halton, by the end of the sixteenth century; neither better nor worse off than their neighbours, which means at a very basic level of subsistence farming. The John Wright who moved across the river about 1720 (George's grandfather), appears to have been an illegitimate son of this family, who, within the strict limitations of the time and place, bettered himself. He probably went over the sands to North Lonsdale to work, as he seems to have married Jane Maychell at Colton in 1719. He married her by licence, which at the time was one of the first signs of conspicuous consumption: anybody who aspired to a modest advance beyond the level of his neighbours showed it by claiming the privacy of a licensed wedding.

Moreover, when John Wright died in 1743, his son George was sufficiently schooled to sign his name to his father's administration bond. This George (father of the George Wright with whom we are concerned) also married by licence, and in 1770, at the age of forty-eight, became a freeman of Lancaster, but in what way, or by exercising what trade, is not known.

Later there was much contradictory evidence about the Wright family background. It was to the second George Wright's advantage to claim for himself the best upbringing that he could, to show that his advancement in life had been a natural progression. It was to his opponents' advantage to claim for him the most miserable upbringing that they could, to show that no honest man could have climbed so far and so fast. The truth seems to be that the family were at the poverty level, but with aspirations towards something better.

George the elder was a labourer with John Heysham of Highfield in Aughton, a wealthy yeoman, farmer and timber dealer; perhaps from this circumstance arose the younger George's claim that his father had been a dealer in timber, which the surviving neighbours were quick to deny. 'Old Wright never was a grower of wood, he had no land to grow it on' ... 'He had a son a clogger and another a wheelwright and he might buy a tree or two for their use but she never knew or heard of his being a woodmonger or buyer or seller of wood' ... 'might grow a few willows at Lune side the same as other farmers did'.[1] He was commonly known as 'Peastick George' and it was not too certain, so the rumour went, that all the peasticks came from land on which George was entitled to cut them. In 1759 John Heysham died and left his workman £40, out of which he was then able to rent a smallholding for £7 or £8 a year, 'a small Cottage House with a Small Barn and a small quantity of land and kept a cow or two'. As he was already married with four children, this relief came none too soon. 'His wife was generly poorly and a helpless sort of a Bodey and they appeared to be hard put to it to get a living and pay their way.' It was even said that from time to time they depended on parish relief; and yet during this impoverishment George the elder was entered as a Lancaster freeman, a privilege which his sons were then entitled to by patrimony.

In 1773 they had a more decisive stroke of good fortune. George's elder brother Henry, who may have been the landlord of the Black Bull in Church Street, Lancaster, died childless, and left his brother some property in Skerton which was said to have brought in about £30 a year.

At this time young George was fifteen. Apprenticeships had been found for his elder brothers Henry and John, who seem to have been steady young men, happy to settle to a decent trade, the one as a wheelwright, the other as a clogger. The younger brother clearly had different ideas for himself. A neighbour said: 'His father used to find fault with his aversion to work and tell him he would be a Gentleman but he wanted tools to set up with ... He went to school because he would not work and used to fish and shoot instead ... He never did anything but go to school, hunt and fish and had the reputation of a poacher.'

All of which was true, but could be interpreted more sympathetically. A younger boy 'was particularly aquainted with the present George Wright when he lived at Afton, has gone a fishing with the shakel net with Wright into Lune on the night time many times, and scoors of times, never got any share of the fish and Wright used to tell witness he used to sell the fish at Kellet for money to pay for his schooling with'.[2]

Young George Wright clearly had ambition, as yet unfocussed. Over Kellet school was not of a high standard, which was probably why he could afford its fees; he learned to read, to write after a fashion (he was still spelling rabbits 'rabets' as a middle-aged man), and to do minimal arithmetic. There is the ring of half-truth in his own story that he found himself a clerk's post with Mr Salisbury, an attorney in Lancaster, but not finding himself suited to the law left it.[3] The truth perhaps was that he got a servant's job to spy out the possibilities but, finding a great discrepancy between his standard of learning and that necessary to work in an attorney's office, abandoned this ambition for the moment. Another of his Aughton friends said, 'George Wright was a desent scholer, he used to shear and work husbandry till he got a little money and then have laid it out in learning and improved himself that way'.[4]

He was about twenty when circumstances changed. He was observed once too often carrying home a Lune salmon. At the same time he had a quarrel with a neighbour, Ellen Millar, the one who said he went to school in order to dodge working. As many people knew afterwards, George's temper was fierce and unpredictable, and although the woman was heavily pregnant he knocked her down (she said) and dragged her through a duck pond. She complained to the local squire and magistrate, but evidently he did not think the case good enough to warrant a prosecution. However, he saw his way to ridding the parish of a nuisance: 'The loard of Halton sent a man over to tell him that if he did not get out of the neighbourhood within a quarter of a year the Loard of Halton would have him pressed for carrying a gun, fishing and being at such a loose end.'[5]

He lay very low for a couple of months, possibly at Hornby, where he was in the habit of helping out on fair days at the Royal Oak where the local doctor lodged. Nobody seemed to know whether it was Ann Walton's house and Dr Geldart was the lodger, or Dr Geldart's house and Ann Walton ran the public side of it for him. They all seemed quite sure that the horse was the Doctor's horse, as the most commonly repeated memory of George Wright in his youth was that he looked after Dr Geldart's horse.

The Doctor took an interest in the young man who was so much sharper, more ambitious and more determined than most of his peers. Moreover, there was a family connection, the elder Wrights having been servants to the Doctor's parents at some time in the past. Thinking it would be a good thing to get him even further away from Halton, and knowing that Henry Marsden of Wennington Hall was asking around for a possible servant, George Mashiter being about to retire on grounds of matrimony, Dr Geldart wrote a letter recommending his protégé.

Another recommendation, later regretted, came from John Denny, landlord of the Wennington alehouse, and an intimate acquaintance of Henry Marsden's because of his wife's relationship to him as foster mother. Henry Marsden himself may also have been impressed by the fact that George Wright followed him all the way to Lancaster (he was staying at the Sun Inn, presumably visiting his mother) to apply for the position. He appointed George then and there, 'engaged him for £20 a year and vittles, lodging etc. Wright's situation was to be errand Boy and Boot and Shoe cleaner' – what the coarser neighbours called 'a lickplate'.

It is necessary again to underline the fact that all these vivid memories were gathered many years later, when the situation at Hornby Castle had become the Lune Valley's own long-running scandal. It is fair to assume that most of the local witnesses were retailing stories which they had repeated a hundred times before, in the bar parlour or at the village pump. A meteoric rise to riches in any circumstances does not engender sympathy, and by the time the anti-Wright party was lobbying for witnesses, notebook in hand, George Wright was for a number of reasons the best-hated man in the Lune Valley.

In his own deposition, Wright insisted that he had been appointed as 'Under Steward', a much more prestigious job, and the first step on a semi-professional ladder; so the opposition went to a great deal of trouble to elicit evidence that downgraded him, hence the emphasis on boots and errands; in particular the question of whether he ever wore livery was constantly raised and never satisfactorily answered. Livery was the badge of the common servant: the privilege of emerging from uniform as one rose in the hierarchy was a real step up, and one much prized.

Life at Wennington Hall was not at a pretentious level. When George Wright first went there, sometime in the summer of 1779, the family consisted of Henry and John Marsden, and Mrs Cookson, whose visits now began to run together until finally she took up residence altogether. Henry, whose tastes as head of the family naturally set the standard for the rest, was not, according to his ex-servant George Mashiter,

an expensive man – he had three horses, the best cost £20 – he seldom went from Home to any distance – once or twice had a drinking party, could not on these occasions expend £20. Went once to Cambridge, the journey ... did not cost more than £100. He was not expensive in his Cloaths, he never gamed or kept expensive Company, his chief associates were Captain Nowell, Mr Jagger and Mr Bailey.[6]

Their main entertainment was to foregather in Bailey's house, at Wennington Bridge End, and drink hard.

According to one memory the staff numbered eight, but this was probably indoor servants, or at least those who gathered for dinner in the servants' hall, for not all of them lived in the house.

James Chorley was the House Steward and overlooker of the works, he paid all the workmen, both them employed about buildings Masons Carpenters work or Laborers and those employed in the management of the land ... a widower and boarded at Richard Armitsteads a shopkeeper at Wennington – he was a man of good property and a good scholar – he was a man of Character and Mr Henry Marsden placed the utmost confidence in him.[7]

He was not the chief steward of the estate, a post held by the family's confidential attorney, George Postlethwaite of Lancaster. One of Chorley's more ceremonial tasks was to carry into the dining-room the main dish of meat for the family: dinner was the formal meal of the day and its organisation flashed very important signals regarding ownership and precedence. At a later stage witnesses were questioned endlessly about dinner-table organisation as throwing light upon the respective positions of people within the household: who sat at the head, who at the foot, who carved, who ordered the servants, who called for a fresh bottle of wine.

Once the dining-room dinner had been served, the carving of the kitchen dinner fell to Mrs Scott, marking her importance as housekeeper. She was also the cook, assisted by a kitchen maid. The only other female servant at this time was a housemaid. Besides Chorley, there was 'Mr Bayley the farming man', who had an indefinite role, probably because he had been a long while in the family and was now more or less retired. He had his own house in the village, ate with the servants but was called 'Mr' by everyone, and had certain responsibilities with regard to the estate; he was also, as has been seen, a drinking companion of Henry Marsden, whom he had known since babyhood. 'Farming man' seems to indicate that he planned the outdoor work, whereas it is only said of Chorley that he paid the workers. Then there was Robert Hartley the coachman, George Wright, the newly appointed personal servant to Henry Marsden, and Robert Humber, the gardener. The latter, who was often in the house waiting at table if there was company, or undertaking other jobs as requested, saw and heard a great deal which for fifty years he kept strictly to himself, and was from time to time the receiver of Henry's confidence.

As far as one can tell, against this domestic background John Marsden was left to drift. His disability was too severe for him to make progress on his own, and not quite severe enough to make it clear that he should be constantly attended. He was mercurial but also ridiculously timid, and this probably kept him out of most trouble. All the village knew his terror of dogs, pigs, turkey-cocks, geese and spiders, and as there was always more or less livestock on the village green, even the small children became accustomed to 'setting him past' whatever was causing alarm. As Mary Denny described him: 'A very weak body and very foolish ideas ... He rambled about from neighbour's house to neighbour's house and talking such stuff as he was master of.' He spent a good deal of time at the Dennys' alehouse and, if the customers were not careful, he would, as Mary Denny said, 'lick up anybody's glasses that were in the house'.

The right minder might have done much with him, perhaps chiefly through his love of music, which was a passion that had started with the priory church bells and could never be satisfied. Apart from the psalms in church on Sunday, and what he could scrape for himself out of a fiddle that he carried everywhere, there was little music to be had in a quiet backwater such as Wennington Hall. Robert Humber said that 'he never saw John Marsden read or write or attempt to learn any thing except making a squeaking noise on his fiddles'. He himself 'was a Singer at Melling Church for thirteen years and had learnt to sing by Notes and he is quite certain that John Marsden never played any regular tune'.

He rode, of course, as every man in his station of life rode if he were to get around at all. He wore a red coat on hunting days, but seems never to have done more than amble out on a quiet horse, with an attendant not far off. He fished a little, but was either frightened of firearms or never trusted with them, as he seems never to have carried a gun. He accompanied Henry on at least one occasion as far as Leeds, and called on the Cookson relations there, who noted that he talked 'wildly and strangely'. Henry had occasionally to go into Yorkshire to consult on business with John Bentley, his attorney and agent for the Bradford estates.

In the autumn and winter of 1779 the village began to talk. Henry Marsden was drinking very heavily and Mrs Denny

> endeavoured to persuade him to desist. It gave her much uneasiness being much attached to him so much as to her own children. She used

to tell him he would soon kill himself if he drank so much Brandy and he replied 'Never mind, Mother. I'll take care of you'.[8]

It was plain that his health was deteriorating rapidly. Mrs Cookson was still living part of the time at Clitheroe, but she soon moved permanently to Wennington. She commented loudly that she was giving up a good home of her own to make a home for her nephews, but no one was in doubt that she had worked to bring this situation about. She was, it was said, a woman 'of intriguing disposition and warm temperament', and to be 'Madam Cookson', lady of Wennington Hall, suited her a great deal better than living a quiet widow's life in Clitheroe.

She was fifty-three years old, and the 'warm temperament' was still active. Village whisperings grew more excited. Henry Marsden never went to church; Mrs Cookson went with her nephew John, attended by George Wright, and people noticed that after a while he no longer took himself to the servants' seats but sat in the family pew beside her. The delicious scandal grew and spread and lost nothing in the telling – a servant lad of twenty-two and a widowed lady almost old enough to be his grandmother. 'They were frequently together', said Robert Humber primly, 'and she admitted him to her presence more freely and took more notice of him than he thought a Lady in her situation should have done towards a servant, and ... George Wright conducted himself with more familiarity than a Man in his situation ought to have done.'

One who heard and relished every detail was Thomas Parker, a tailor's apprentice. Although he and his master, John Selby, lived usually in Melling, a mile down the road, at the beginning of 1780 they were living in at the Hall for a few weeks, as the custom was in the bigger houses. They were making new liveries for the servants, and after fifty years he remembered that the coats were to be stone colour with green collar and cuffs. While they were there, George Wright was suddenly dismissed, no reason given. Henry Marsden was a quiet man and a mild master, not given to taking dislikes or dismissing people in a hurry. But he had taken a violent dislike to George Wright, and all the whisperers said that it was no wonder: he and Mrs Cookson had been 'too kind'.

George Wright's bundle was packed up and ready to go, and his shirt had been washed in the village. Washing days came round only every three months, but it had been noticed that George Wright had so little linen that he had to get a shirt washed in between whiles by a laundress outside the Hall. It was said that Mrs Cookson had also had her marching orders and was ready packed, but the newsmongers were less certain of this; she might have disguised the embarrassing fact by claiming it was merely a routine return to Clitheroe after a winter away.

Then, in March 1780, just before his twenty-third birthday, Henry Marsden was struck by a paralytic attack and, although he lingered for two or three weeks, it was clear to everyone that he was unlikely to recover. He never again 'quitted his room and only removed to an easy chair whilst his bed was made'. Thomas Parker remembered the sequence of events well, for the liveries were set aside as soon as the master was dead and the tailors set to making mourning clothes. He remembered Henry Marsden's death for another reason too. While the body 'lay in state' in the study, he was delegated the unwelcome chore of unlocking the door to neighbours who came to pay their last respects. He noted John Marsden going in and out with them, apparently unmoved by his brother's death but pleased with his new position: sometimes he rubbed his hands and said, 'Now it is all mine'.

Years later, Robert Humber, respectable, retired, living in Kendal, had difficulty making up his mind how far he should unburden himself of the memories of that strange time. He could not discuss the matter with his wife, Ellen, who had been housemaid at Wennington Hall, and one of the women actually in the room when Henry Marsden died, for she too was dead. It had all happened nearly fifty years before, and the husband and wife had no doubt many times gone over together this bizarre episode in their lives before deciding that it was a great deal safer to keep it locked behind their teeth, particularly as Robert had remained in the service of Wennington Hall for a further fourteen years. Silence had not blurred the edges of his memory; the sequence of events and its details remained as clear as yesterday: it was simply a case of whether he should now speak out.

He did not make up his mind easily. His first statement, when he was asked in 1826, was to the effect that in 1778 John Marsden 'was in my opinion at that time perfectly competent to manage his own affairs – could converse freely and sensibly respecting agriculture gardening or other subjects – he very frequently, indeed almost every day had conversation with me in the garden'. And that was almost all he would say.

Eight months later he made a very different statement. Possibly what changed his mind was George Wright's own deposition, in which he painted a picture first of having come to Wennington Hall in the modestly responsible position of Under Steward; of having won Henry Marsden's respect and confidence; of having sat up with him at nights during his illness; of having been with him when he died. Much of what Humber said never came to court because it was not provable, too many key witnesses having died in the meantime, but he showed no further hesitation in speaking out. He described John Marsden's behaviour in the clearest detail, but he also had a circumstantial tale to tell of Henry Marsden's last illness.

During this time, Humber slept in the closet which opened out of his master's room. As he said, Henry always 'showed great partiality for him', owing to their schoolboy friendship. The partition to this little room was only of boards, and he could hear easily enough if he were wanted. He continued to sleep there but, as the situation worsened, someone also sat up in the sick-room. Sometimes he took this duty himself, sometimes it was Thomas Robinson the coachman or William Robinson the groom, sometimes it was 'old Mr Bailey'. On no occasion was it George Wright. When Mrs Cookson suggested him, the patient 'was much agitated when his name was mentioned and said "no, no"'.

It was apparent to everyone, including Henry Marsden, that he had not much longer to live. His illness does not seem to have impaired his thinking or his speech. He called in Robert Humber, told him that 'things were going comically' and that he ought to make his will. He told Humber to say nothing to anybody, but to ride over to Bradford and summon his attorney, John Bentley. Why he would rather send fifty miles than ten is not mentioned; perhaps he suspected that the 'comical' influence had already touched the office of his Lancaster attorney.

Robert Humber rode over at once. He slept the night in Bradford, bringing Bentley back with him early in the morning. Having seen his client, Bentley spent the whole day writing in the library with the door locked. Humber was tired after his double ride and went very early to his bed in the closet. Sometime after nine o'clock that night he was woken by voices in the next room: Bentley's voice he recognised, and that of James Chorley the house steward. Bentley was reading: he droned on for some time, and then said 'Are you satisfied?' Henry Marsden said 'I am, but let me look at it'. Then there was silence, but he heard Bentley say something about it being signed. He heard the heavy inkstand being moved, and next morning noticed that a small round table was out of its usual place by the head of the bed. Meeting Bentley in the garden before the attorney took horse again for Bradford, Humber said to him 'Well, have you made the will?'. Bentley said yes, that the estate was to go to the heirs at law for ever.

Henry Marsden died soon after, being buried in Melling church on 18 March 1780, three days before his twenty-third birthday. Robert

Humber recollected that, about a month later, he was given a brown paper parcel by Mrs Cookson. He was told that it was the will and that he was to take it to Lancaster to be proved before the surrogate. He delivered the parcel as requested to an attorney's office. This seems to have been a ruse to deceive him, for clearly a will would have to be proved by the executors named in it, not just delivered by hand. If the brown paper parcel existed, as no doubt it did, Humber being a very honest witness, it did not contain a will. The one which Bentley had drawn up was never seen again.

On 12 April 1780, before Robert Hodgson surrogate, John Marsden took out administration papers for the estate of his brother Henry Marsden who had died intestate. In his large and childish writing, he appended his name to the oath ('You shall swear that Henry Marsden Esquire, your brother, deceased, made and left at the time of his Death, no last Will and Testament that you know of or believe ...'). The highly respectable sureties were the Reverend John Tatham, Vicar of Melling, and John Postlethwaite, attorney, Steward to the Wennington estates. Their signatures were witnessed by 'George Wright, House Steward'.[9]

3

Sarah Cookson

George Wright, aged twenty-two, with a minimum number of shirts to his back and no wider experience than the village inn and the servants' hall, saw the world opening before him and grabbed at the chance. How far he could foresee or assess the consequences we cannot know, but the boldness of action was worthy of a better man and a better deed.

Sarah Cookson, as yet in every way in the superior position, and familiar with aspects of the law from the suit in Chancery already behind her, must have been the instigator of the plot; but she had found an accomplice who was a manipulator of no ordinary skill. She was greedy enough to be easily tempted by the idea of living out her life as the guardian of her defective nephew and the chatelaine of his estates. The actual crime of concealing or disposing of the will, if it were discovered, would be hers; once she had committed herself, there was no way back without criminal implications. Perhaps she did not take into account, in her infatuation, that she laid herself open to blackmail and that Wright would not hesitate to use this handy weapon.

They must have moved very speedily to neutralise those who might have given the game away, and in this Henry Marsden's own anxiety about the 'comical' goings-on around him had led to a secrecy on his part which in fact assisted the plotters. His own mother, Mrs Bailey, was in the house when he died, but seems to have known nothing about the will, and was very hastily shuffled away. 'The Mother was dismissed,' according to the Admiral's manuscript, 'indeed it is understood, through the Aunt's influence, rudely hurried out.' Then there were three witnesses to be dealt with, that is, two official witnesses in the room and one behind the panelling.

James Chorley perhaps would not have realised what was happening. It is unlikely, when he was called in to sign, that he had any idea of the details of the document, so for all he knew Mrs Cookson's assumption of the position of John Marsden's guardian was what Henry Marsden had intended.

Robert Humber knew there was a will, and may well by some slight remark have shown that he knew; he was put off the scent, successfully or not, by the trick with the brown paper parcel. He knew nothing of the terms of the will, except what Bentley had told him about the 'heirs at law', and we have no way of knowing what that meant to him. In any case he kept his counsel, and his job, for the next fourteen years.

The real stumbling-block should have been John Bentley, who had drawn the will and witnessed it, but Henry Marsden's use of Bentley was in fact a stroke of luck for Cookson and Wright. If Bentley had been more upright and less malleable, he would not have been approachable, but he was in debt to the Marsden estate, probably heavily so; two years later he went bankrupt. How the lever was applied we do not know, but it all happened with unhesitating rapidity. The administration bond was in due and proper form applied for and awarded just three weeks after the funeral by Henry's next of kin, his brother John; and from then on whoever controlled John Marsden controlled the estate of the late Henry.

At a time when it would have been invaluable, there was no possibility of resurrecting this story for use in a court of law. Robert Humber was a reliable witness with a good memory but there had been a wooden partition between him and the actors, and John Bentley was long dead. Bentley's son, not unnaturally, was tight-lipped, but a friend and fellow attorney told, outside the court, what he knew. Bentley had never actually admitted making the will, but in his cups he would admit that a will had been made and suppressed, and that he was privy to the suppression. 'He was much afraid of Wright – no man on earth he was so much afraid of ... When Jack Bentley had got liquor he would tell Mr Lambert what a Villain and rascal Wright was.' He would also tell of a later time when Cookson and Wright quarrelled and he was terrified by letters from Mrs Cookson threatening to disclose everything. He 'used to Damn the Letters and say he did not know how to answer them'.[1]

It is a fair certainty that in the missing will John Marsden was bypassed, suitable provision having been made for him, and the property entailed, as Bentley said, on the heirs at law, the four sons of the Reverend Sandford Tatham in the order of their births. It is also probable that the claim of Sarah Cookson had been ignored. A few months earlier she would have been a natural choice as John Marsden's guardian, but her behaviour with Wright had aroused Henry's anger and disgust to the point of summary dismissal. She probably got nothing at all, which may well have been the trigger for the whole conspiracy.

The choice of the heirs at law was not a new idea of Henry Marsden's, but one imagines that Sarah Cookson would have come in for some intermediate benefit had she not blotted her copybook. Henry had told his intentions to his cousin the younger Sandford Tatham during a visit paid by the latter to Wennington Hall in the spring of 1777. Henry was then still a few days short of his majority, but no doubt his mind was full of the will that he would soon be signing. He said specifically that he would leave his mother's property, worth about £300 a year, to John, which would be quite enough for his needs, while the rest would go to the heirs at law. As an interested party, Sandford Tatham must have remembered the conversation with accuracy, although he was only third of the four brothers. At this time the others were all alive, but all three died childless, and in the end Sandford was the sole survivor.

A few days after the signing of the administration bond, Sarah Cookson set out for London with her nephew John and George Wright. There remains a little account book in which John Marsden, in his round childish hand, set down the expenditure of such money as he was allowed. On 29 April the journey south is marked by a shilling 'to the chambermaid at Loughborough', and thereafter 'at the play', 'to the groom for seeing the King's Horses', at the Exhibition', 'for a map of the London streets', 'at St Paul's', 'at Westminster Abbey', 'at Asliss [Astley's] Riding School', 'at the play', 'at the play', 'at the play', 'at the play' ... until 6 July when the entry 'expenses at Kirkby Lonsdale' shows their return.[2]

The real purpose of the visit is not known. It was suggested at a later date that Mrs Cookson was exploring the possibility of a commission of lunacy. If so, she would have found that to be impossible while Mrs Bailey, John's next of kin, was alive, although her death, which took place a few months later, may already have been anticipated. A commission of lunacy drew the legal line between competency and non-competency. Under a commission of lunacy a person had no civil rights. Without one he had all his civil rights, but might live in a grey area in which his friends and relations exercised their influence to prevent him, for instance, from serving on a jury if he were called. What other influences they might bring, in the case of such a one as John Marsden, to help him look after his wealth and his estates, was then, as it still is, a very grey area indeed, demanding exceptional integrity. As we have seen, Henry Marsden, young though he was, had no intention of leaving his brother in charge of more than a bare competence, too little to attract hyenas.

Inquiries in London would have shown Sarah Cookson that a commission of lunacy would give the heirs at law a legal standing, although after her sister's death she, the aunt, would doubtless have been named as committee. While it is difficult to believe that at this stage George Wright saw his way clearly ahead, the immediate prospect, with the administration bond drawn and Sarah Cookson devoted to his interests, was too rosy a one to make its disturbance desirable; if he were involved in any discussion of the future, he would surely have argued for leaving sleeping dogs alone, which was indeed the result.

The London journey had no particular outcome, although it was said that Mrs Cookson arranged for George to have dancing lessons, and perhaps some other training in gentility. It must have been on this occasion that miniatures were painted of the two young men: John's suggests what later portraits do not, a classic physiognomy of a certain kind of mental defect; George's seems to have been painted entirely through Mrs Cookson's eyes, as a fair, almost fragile, sprig of refinement.

A more significant occurrence may have been the beginning of an acquaintance with the solicitor Giles Bleasdale, an acquaintance which ripened over the next fifty years into the closest partnership between himself and Wright. When it came to a court of law, Bleasdale distanced himself as far as possible from George, claiming that he had known Marsden long before he had known Wright, and that while he had met the former several times in London, and had stayed with him at Wennington, he had never even met Wright until after the move was made to Hornby Castle in 1793 or 1794.[3] This is so palpably untrue, given the total impossibility of visiting Wennington at any time after Henry Marsden's death without making Wright's acquaintance, that it undermines all the rest of his evidence. If he could, and did, lie so plausibly in this regard, there is nothing to make one give credence to anything else Bleasdale said.

Giles Bleasdale's part in the story is crucial. He was a poor boy from Clitheroe, born in 1753, and therefore a little older than Wright and Marsden, but still at this time only in his middle twenties, who had started his legal career in the Lancaster office of Thomas Barrow. While serving his clerkship he had come in contact with John Marsden, then a schoolboy; Barrow conducted the Baileys' defence in the suit in Chancery brought against them by Mrs Cookson. At some time Bleasdale left Lancaster and practised in London, in the end as senior partner in the firm of Bleasdale, Alexander and Holme. This was a respectable and well-reputed firm, which acted for prestigious companies such as the Hudson Bay Company and London Assurance. The junior partner,

1780		£	s	d
25. March	To Cash paid for Expences at Clapham			4
26	To do. paid for do. at Buxton ----			7
	To do. gave to the Landlord ---			6
26	To do. gave at Melling Church ---		1	6
	To do. paid for Expences at Wray ---			5
31	To do. paid for do. at Kirkby Lonsdale ---			8
1. April	To do. paid for Ale ---			
15	To do. paid for Expences at Hornby ---			
11	To do. paid for do. at Wray		2	9
24	To do. paid for Cambrick Handkerchiefs		18	6
	To do. gave to Mrs. Shirrow		10	6
	To do. gave to the Ostler at Bathmill		1	
	To do. gave to Miss Latham at Clitheroe		2	6
26	To do. paid the Hairdresser		1	
29	To do. gave to the Chambermaid at Loughborough.		1	
30	To do. gave to the Chaise Driver			6
1. May	To do. paid at the Play		6	
2	To do. gave to the Groom for seeing the Kings Horses		1	
3	To do. paid at the Exhibiton		2	
	To do. gave to a Lieutenant	1	1	
4	To do. paid for a Memorandum Book		6	
	To do. paid for a Map of London Streets		6	
5	To do. paid at the Play		6	
6	To do. paid at do.		9	
9	To do. paid at St. Pauls		10	6
11	To do. paid at the Play		9	
12	To do. paid at do.		6	
14	To do. gave at the New Church in the Strand.		1	
15	To do. gave at Westminster Abby		2	
18	To do. paid at the Play		9	
19	To do. paid at do.		9	
20	To do. paid at do.		6	
21	To do. gave at Covent Garden Church		1	6
	To do. paid for Cider			6

John Marsden's Account Book. Extract from the first page, showing the visit to London in April–May 1780. (*David Battersby*)

Bryan Holme, a Lune Valley boy, born at Tunstall, educated at Wray school, was one of the founders of the Law Society. During the course of the lawsuit, one of Bleasdale's most valuable characteristics was his apparently total respectability. He made a sizeable fortune from his profession without any known doubts as to the integrity of his methods.

Cookson and Wright, whatever the exact business which took them to London in 1780, apart from having a delightful jaunt backed by more money than either of them had ever had to spend before, must have needed legal advice. To make or remake acquaintance with a clever young lawyer quite unconnected with the Wennington estate was valuable. To find one, without other personal ties, who soon showed an eager desire for Wright's friendship, was a bonus.

What exactly was the basis for this exaggerated regard will not now be discovered. One person who knew both men well in later life said that she found it 'very mysterious'. Bleasdale never married; he had nephews, but abandoned them in favour of Wright's family, on whom he lavished all his affection and generosity, apparently caring more for their advancement than even their father could do. His visits to Wennington began now, in the 1780s, and the intimacy continued and deepened, until he spent every summer within two or three miles of the Wrights. He finally sold up in London and retired to a cottage on the Hornby estate for the last fifteen years of his life.

The intimacy may have been based on shared secrets, but not on an ordinary working relationship. Bleasdale was never solicitor for the Marsden estates, which in the north were in the hands of a Lancaster firm, and in London (there was some Marsden property in Middlesex) in those of Thomas Greene of Gray's Inn. Greene, a member of a local family from Slyne near Lancaster, made a huge legal fortune, was friend and patron to George Romney, and enabled his family to settle as landowners at Whittington Hall. It seems unlikely that Greene would have been approachable on any grey legal matters, whether from absolute honesty or self-protective caution.[4]

When the party returned at the beginning of July 1780 from London to Wennington, it became clear that John Marsden had developed a strong antagonism to his mother. One of the symptoms of his defective intelligence was his acceptance of certain ideas, usually in the words in which they were first suggested to him, and his immovable tenacity thereafter. Robert Humber remembered 'Mr John Marsden, soon after the decease of his brother Henry, kicking his foot thro' his Mother's picture, he punched his foot through, it was afterwards patched up'.

In Mrs Bailey's last illness in December of the same year, Dr Campbell, the family doctor, went to Wennington to try to effect a reconciliation, as he gave evidence later:

> She was extremely low-spirited and dejected, and continually calling out respecting her son: she said she had not known in what she had offended him; but that there would be nothing she would leave undone to be reconciled to him, but that he never came near her ... in consequence of which, I went to Wennington with this message from his mother; I had an interview with him there.
>
> Who was present? – Mrs Cookson, the whole time.
>
> What did you say? – I told him the situation of his mother; and I used every inducement in my power to prevail upon him to come to see her.
>
> Did you tell him what she said? – Yes, I did.
>
> That he had not been to see her, and she had not the least idea how she had offended him, and would do anything to be reconciled to him? – Yes.
>
> And did you mention she was likely to die? – Yes, I did; she died the day afterwards.
>
> And what answer did you get from him? – The only answer I could get was 'My mother has not treated me like a gentleman'; and this was the constant answer he gave me to every entreaty I made to him.
>
> Did he explain how? – No, nothing more than that. I certainly thought the answer deficient in point of sense as well as of affection, but I attributed it more to Mrs Cookson, who appeared to agree with him in sentiment, than as arising from himself. I attributed that kind of answer to her presence.
>
> Did she join you in the propriety of his going to see his mother in her dying moments? – No ...
>
> Did Marsden or Mrs Cookson explain how his mother had used him ill? – No, not at all, but he appeared to be entirely under her control, and I attributed his sentiments more to her than to him.
>
> Then you came away? – Yes.[5]

Mary Denny remembered that, after the first London visit, George Wright came into the alehouse, flung himself into a chair with his feet up on another, and announced that James Chorley was dismissed, and he was promoted to Under Steward. Immediately following Mrs Bailey's death, there was a second London visit, and thereafter George became senior Steward over the whole estate, in place of George Postlethwaite attorney of Lancaster, 'a man in high Estimation, and unfit to be bent to their purposes' ... 'an honourable easy man, and he appears to have been got rid of by degrees'. John Rutherford, servant to John Marsden's ex-tutor Mr Croft who was now incumbent of Gargrave, could speak to the change, since he and his master happened to be staying at Wennington Hall for the shooting:

> Do you remember any person speaking of Wright as Mr George, in the presence of Marsden and Mrs Cookson? – He was formerly called Mr George, before he got to Mr Wright.
>
> Did you hear Mrs Cookson say anything to Marsden, as to Wright being called George? – Yes; he was christened Mr Wright then; the other name was checked. He was not called George after that.
>
> Who checked any person calling him by that name? – Mrs Cookson. Whom did she check? – Some of the labourers.
>
> Was Mr Marsden there? – Yes.
>
> Did she tell Marsden to go and tell them not to call him any more Mr George, but Mr Wright? – Yes.
>
> What did Mr Marsden do after that; did he go and tell them this? – He ran fit to break his neck to get to them.[6]

The same witness succinctly summed up the developing relationship between master and man.

> How did Mr Wright treat Mr Marsden? – Sometimes roughish.
>
> How did Marsden behave to Wright? – Very civilly.[6]

'Sometimes roughish' was not a bad description of the new Steward's treatment of everybody. Setting aside the rights and wrongs of the situation, a barely educated young man, admittedly with the support of the lady of the house, but with no other natural resource on his side, had to impose his personality on everyone he met, and particularly on the servants, labourers, workmen and tenants of the estate, with whom he had been an equal or an inferior a few short months before. It is a tribute to an extraordinary personality that he did it, and no surprise that he did it by developing a character as 'a very stern and passionate man'. Through Mrs Cookson, he had of course the power of the purse strings, but the total dominance he was able to exercise seems to need more explanation than that. He had a bad temper and a very rough tongue, and he used them freely, losing no chance of imposing himself. 'From this time', said Mary Denny, 'Wright became very insolent and overbearing ... He took the liberty of being master.' But there seems to have been an attraction, possibly owing as much to fear as to liking, which secured him allies. Even Robert Humber, being the better educated of the two, helped him to do his accounts for the next fourteen years.

His dominance over Sarah Cookson seems to have been absolute. Within a few weeks of Henry Marsden's death he was 'in the parlour', seated in Henry Marsden's armchair at the head of the table, Mrs Cookson at the foot, John Marsden relegated to the side. 'She [Mary Denny again] has seen Mrs Cookson walking arm in arm with Wright, like Man and Wife – they were much talked about.' His bedroom was moved from among the menservants in the garret to one on the first floor, immediately next door to Mrs Cookson. Even John Marsden was aware. 'There will be a yong babey coming by and by', he confided to one of the servants.

Robert Humber was early in the garden one day when visitors came, a Mr Sagar and his son who ran the Marsden mills at Colne and needed to see Wright on some problem about the business:

> I was coming out of the garden, and he wanted somebody to go and acquaint Mr Wright.
>
> Nobody went? – No, everyone was laughing at another. I said if they would not, I would do so.
>
> Did you so? Yes? – I knocked three or four times, and nobody answered, then I opened it and looked; I stopped and looked, and then he came out of Mrs Cookson's room, with his clothes upon his arm; I told him who wanted him, and I went away; he had his clothes over his arm; I saw nothing but his shirt that he had on.
>
> You were standing at the three steps, when he came out did he do anything when he saw you there? – He rather gave back, but we never mentioned it to each other afterwards.'[7]

And Robert Humber, the least garrulous of servants, never spoke of the incident to anyone except his wife for over forty years. Although he was not officially an indoor servant, Humber noticed other things as well, and also, doubtless, kept them to himself. At Wennington the deer in the park used to come up to the parlour windows, and it was the custom for Humber to come in after dinner with a basket of cabbage leaves and vegetable peelings so that the family could amuse themselves by feeding the animals.

> Do you recollect on any of those occasions when you went into the room with leaves, did you see anything? – I recollect when I opened the door to get a basket with leaves, I saw Wright draw his arm out of her bosom.[7]

Everybody remembered the pair walking arm in arm 'like man and wife'. Indeed after the second London visit a strong rumour went round that they were secretly married. A search of the marriage registers provides no foundation for this, but it was a convenient rumour for Wright, as it must have done much to cement his position.

It is clear that, having taken on this large professional job of running a big estate, with ramifications into various counties, for which neither he nor Mrs Cookson had experience or training, George Wright did it not merely adequately, but extremely well. He seems to have had an inbuilt flair for land management. Although he never managed his own accounts, first relying on Robert Humber and later a clerk, and his grammar and spelling were always shaky; and although he never bothered to refine his thick accent and appeared to despise the social skills, the estates under his hand improved in every way. It was said, in grudging praise, that he suffered no one to cheat John Marsden except himself.

Moreover, he trained Marsden as he undoubtedly needed training. The lad whose mother could never control him, who had capered and pranced through the streets of Lancaster behind her sedan chair and, when she vexed him, announced that he was going to drown himself, and stood under the cistern spout until he was sopped through; who had to be restrained in school with a boy sitting on either side; who rampaged through the fields with Tommy Thompson, and charged in and out of the neighbours' cottages without a by your leave; who had two schoolboy episodes of 'unnatural practice' behind him, and showed every sign of wanting to get at the girls; this irresponsible character was now steadily brought under control, partly by Mrs Cookson, but even more by another a year older than himself.

It was a harsh control, which in the end had to depend on fear. It was noticed that after they came back from London John Marsden no longer came to the cottages. He ceased even to visit Mrs Denny. Servants who talked to him too much were threatened with losing their jobs: 'What have you to do with Mr Marsden? Damn you, I'll turn you away, you have no business to interfere with him.' So reported Elizabeth Sedgwick, kitchen maid in 1780, to whom Marsden seemed to take a liking. He used to come to her for paper when he wanted to go to the 'necessary', which she tore for him out of a big old Bible kept for the purpose. Her fellows teased her: 'they all used to laugh ... and say she had gotten a famous place to be Mr M.'s bum-fotherer'. He used to appeal to her to get the turkey-cock out of the way before he could get to the privy, and sometimes was trapped inside because the bird was strutting and gobbling outside, seeming to know which human being it could challenge.

It was not only the turkey who had the mastery. George Wright, who loved every kind of country sport and now could indulge himself legally, which must have been one of the sweetest rewards of his new position, used to ride to the hunting field with John Marsden. Thomas Parker, the tailor's apprentice, following the hounds on foot, saw the two of them many times, Marsden on the best horse, according to his station, Wright on the inferior beast. Then, like a playground bully, Wright would call on Marsden to swap horses, and being a natural rider, would gallop away after the hounds on a hot scent. 'People used to remark on it', said Thomas Parker, 'a servant taking away his master's horse.'

4

Sandford Tatham

The history of the Tatham family is mainly drawn from Admiral Sandford Tatham's narrative, which he wrote as an old man to prove that he was indeed John Marsden's heir at law. By that time he was the last survivor of the six first cousins who were the only descendants of the third Henry Marsden of Wennington, who had died in 1743. Although written from memory by a man aged eighty, every checkable detail is found to be minutely accurate, and the whole carries conviction.

Elizabeth, or Betty, Marsden, sister of Henry Marsden the fourth of Wennington and therefore also of Sarah Cookson, had married her cousin, the Reverend Sandford Tatham, against the wishes of her family, or of her mother at least, her father being already dead. Tatham was very poor, while she had been left £1000 by her father's will. Whether that was the root of the family's objection or not, future events showed that they were right to mistrust the alliance. The couple were married in 1751, but four children later, in 1759, the Reverend Sandford Tatham, Vicar of St Laurence, Appleby, applied to the consistory court of Carlisle for a legal separation from his wife Elizabeth *a mensa et thoro* (from bed and board), on the grounds of adultery. Unfortunately no details have survived but, after a long drawn out case, the divorce was granted in October 1760 – a divorce which we might call a legal separation, since it did not allow for remarriage on either side.[1]

The Admiral's sympathies were evidently with his father, 'as honourable a man as ever lived, who by birth, education, station, habit and conduct through life maintained the character of a gentleman'. In spite of examination of all likely and some unlikely parish registers, the evidence for this marriage has never been found. The Admiral swore by the family tradition that it had taken place in the Ellel Chapel of Cockerham, near Lancaster, but the entry is missing. He maintained that certain pages had been removed from the register, but a close examination of the register in question shows that there is no possibility of this. This was before the Hardwicke Act of 1753: clandestine marriages were common, and an unscrupulous parson could augment his living by marrying couples without asking questions. No Lancaster marriage licence is in existence for such a marriage, but at the time there was no rumour of anything wrong, and an absolute assumption that the couple were regularly married. There might have been two grounds for calling the Admiral's legitimacy in question: first, that his father and mother were never married; secondly, that his mother had foisted another man's bastard onto the Reverend Sandford, who responded by divorcing her.

Old Madam Marsden, Betty's mother, was living in Lancaster at the time of her daughter's marriage, and presumably became reconciled to her, as the young couple seem to have lived with her for some months of their early married life. The children were: William (born at Hutton-in-the-Forest in 1752); Henry (born at his grandmother's in Lancaster in 1754); Sandford (born at Hutton in 1755); and Charles (born in Lancaster in 1759 after his parents had separated). A daughter born between Sandford and Charles survived only a few months, but the boys flourished, except Henry, who from an accident in childhood grew up as something of a cripple.

No doubt to alleviate the family's poverty, William from the age of three was taken to live with his grandmother in Lancaster. She died in 1759 and William spent the rest of his boyhood in the care of his aunt, Sarah Cookson. In spite of these years spent effectively as his mother, when the time came Sarah seems to have had no compunction about cutting him out of his position as his cousin Henry Marsden's heir at law. To do her justice there was, by the time it became an issue, the complication of his being classed as an enemy alien. He was educated at the Lancaster free school, then in 1768 at the age of sixteen went to America, having been offered a place with 'a highly respectable Merchant and Planter at Richmond in Virginia', although he later worked as a civil engineer. In the War of Independence he declared himself, and may have fought as, a Republican.

When their parents separated, Henry and Sandford remained with their father until, at the ages of ten and nine, they were sent to school at Bampton. Being intended for the Navy, Sandford left the Reverend William Langhorn's school in 1769 and on the 7 Sepember, four days before his fourteenth birthday, 'was entered on Board the Stag Frigate of thirty-two guns, commanded by Captain Joseph Deane, and bearing the Broad Pendant of Commodore Sir John Lindsay K.B., appointed Commander in Chief of His Majesty's Ships in the East Indies'.

Henry's career is less well documented. He went to London in 1775 aged about twenty, and seems to have lived there for the next six years, his occupation uncertain, although no doubt some occupation he must have had. His brother repudiated the idea that it could possibly have been 'in trade', though his fierceness seems unnecessary since both the American brothers spent some time of their lives in merchant houses.

> Mr John Taylor Wilson, the Attorney who gave evidence at the Assizes for the Establishment of the Will, asserted (for what purpose he best knows) that Henry Tatham had *been a Tea Dealer in London*, though it is not of much importance to contradict him, yet the assertion is without the least foundation. The fact is that he never was a Tea Dealer, or *had any concern with Tea Dealing*. He never was engaged *in that or any other Trade* in the whole course of his life.[2]

(The attorney had confused him with some other Tatham cousins, of Southampton Row, who were tea dealers.)

Charles the youngest, born at Lancaster after his parents separated, was abandoned by his mother through choice or necessity, sent to nurse in a village near Kendal for his first thirteen years, and then despatched to join his brother in Virginia. Elizabeth Tatham seems to have gone to London soon after his birth, presumably in the company of the other man, though the Admiral was discreetly silent on this point. Her portrait remained hanging with those of her brother and sisters in the dining-room at Wennington Hall, where Henry Marsden used to point it out to visitors, as Robert Humber often heard when he was waiting at table. Mary Denny 'has frequently heard Mr Henry Marsden mention his Aunt Mrs Tatham and lament the situation she was in'. The Admiral's memoir offers no more details about her life other than that she lived in Westminster, died in lodgings in Chelsea and was buried there in August 1778.

Her will welcomed her sufferings from 'a complication of maladies' as payment for her sins, which seems to acknowledge that the divorce was justified. She was by no means penniless, having still £600 of her patrimony to be distributed. This she left to three of her sons but not to Sandford who had been the chief beneficiary under his father's will the year before. There was no intention to treat him less generously than the others – if any of them died childless, he was to be included in the share out.[3]

The situation in 1780, at the time of Henry Marsden's death, was that William and Charles were in America, officially classed as enemy aliens, Henry Tatham was in London, and Lieutenant Sandford Tatham was several thousand miles from home. The last named had, however, made or renewed acquaintance with members of the north country family in 1777, when, having recently passed his Lieutenant's examination and been commissioned as Fourth Lieutenant to a ship of the line, the *Bellisle* of sixty-four guns, he had to apply for leave to deal with business after his father's death. It is not stated why Henry, the elder of the two, did not undertake these duties, but perhaps his health precluded it. In any case Sandford was the one most involved; the other three were left £50 apiece, as though they had already had their main share, but the residue was to be in trust to buy Sandford a 'commission in the army or in other promotion or advancement', a curious phrase to use of a son who had already been in the Navy for five years. The will offers no hint that Sandford senior doubted the legitimacy of any of his four sons.[4]

On this leave in 1777, for the first time in his life Sandford Tatham junior visited Lancashire. He spent some time with his aunt Sarah Cookson, at her house in Clitheroe, and together they went to Wennington to stay with Henry Marsden. John was in Weybridge with the Reverend Henry Croft, so Sandford missed meeting him. He got on very well with Henry, who was pleased to take him round and introduce his cousin, the naval Lieutenant. Between other more prestigious visits, he did not fail to take him into the Wennington alehouse to meet the Denny family.

It was on this occasion, their only meeting, that Henry spoke of how he intended to make his will. Sandford continued his round of visits by going to the Baileys in Lancaster, and then went further north to Appleby, where he stayed with the Reverend Henry Lowther, his uncle by marriage, husband of his father's sister.

He does not relate what he did with the rest of his time, whether he visited his mother in London, or stayed with his brother Henry, but in September his leave ended and he was appointed to a new ship, this time as First Lieutenant to a frigate, HMS *Boston*. Finding that this ship was stationed in the Irish Channel, and preferring a more exciting life, he managed to exchange into HMS *Oiseau*, and was therefore off the Newfoundland coast when Henry Marsden died in 1780.

He preserved an affection for his misguided aunt, Sarah Cookson, and his ingrained sense of hierarchy, fostered by naval discipline, prevented him from ever quite believing that she did what she did out of infatuation for George Wright. There is a suggestion in his narrative that criminality was preferable to the degradation of falling under the influence of a servant. 'There is little doubt', he said, that in appointing Wright as Steward:

Mrs Cookson chiefly consulted her own views, and thought Wright would be subservient to her, but she went too far and committed herself when Wright made use of her to further his own Interest, Established himself, and ultimately ruled her altogether, *she not him.* It cannot well be believed that Mrs Cookson intended the disinheriting of her own sister's children, though she desired to be Mistress of the property and Establishment during life ... How she became placed in this degraded situation will probably never be known, we cannot peep into the *Dark Closet* and discover by what secret transaction she had committed herself and instead of ruling him, being subservient to all his designs, but hints have been given, that about the time of Henry Marsden's Death there were other Transactions besides those of an amorous complexion which will not bear the light.[5]

The next year, 1781, Lieutenant Sandford Tatham was on sick leave in London. The *Oiseau* had returned from the West Indies with a very sick crew, whether from malnourishment or, as they believed, because the French crew had left behind the seeds of disease in their captured vessel: 'many men died, and of those that escaped, many suffered from eruptions and ulcerations bearing the character of inveterate Sea Scurvy'. As the sickness was incurable at sea, Tatham and others were ordered on shore.

He found his friends and relations in London that spring of 1781 overflowing with gossip about the Wennington situation 'with somewhat severe remarks on the conduct of his Aunt Mrs Cookson, with regard to George Wright, the footman, whom she had made her associate in the management of the Estates, and seated at her table'. Some of them had probably seen the menage at first hand quite recently, because the second visit to London had just taken place. Sandford had some very interesting conversations with legal acquaintance on the subject of commissions for lunacy, and found out that the only person who could bring an action for one was the next of kin. Interesting, but not very relevant, as ahead of him in the line were Mrs Cookson herself, getting older but still in good health, and his two brothers, William and Henry.

Mrs Cookson, hearing on the family grapevine that Sandford was in England, now wrote to him, 'complaining of the reflections which had been cast upon her, the scandalous reports which had been circulated, and the ill usage she had received, particularly from Colonel Bayley'. As Tatham had just been invited north to spend his convalescence with his Aunt Lowther,

in his way to Cumberland he took the opportunity of complying with his Aunt Cookson's request, and went to Wennington, the carriage meeting him at Lancaster. He arrived at Wennington in the Evening, the next morning went to visit his nurse and returned to Dinner. After Dinner being left alone with his aunt, she opened the business which had been the subject of her letter, and particularly complained of the ill usage she had received from Colonel Bayley. She said that the measures she had recourse to were absolutely necessary from her *Nephew Marsden's Incapacity*, that she had left her quiet Home, and undertaken for the sake of her Sister's Children viz., him [Sandford] and his Brothers, a very disagreeable and harassing Task, and that Mr Wright's assistance was necessary to her, as no other person could so well manage him. He [Sandford] differed in opinion and suggested that many young Clergymen of Talent and well acquainted with rural affairs would be very glad of such a situation, and at the same time act both as Steward, companion to Mr Marsden, and visit with him the Gentry round him, and by such instruction as his understanding was capable of receiving, give him a chance of improving, but that by placing Mr Wright as she had done *on a footing with herself and his Master* and endeavouring as she was then doing to force a person so recently in a low menial capacity into the houses of the Neighbouring Gentlemen with whom her family had always associated, she must not wonder if the Public made reflections on her conduct (as was the case) and that it would be useless for any one to attempt to put an end to the reports while the cause remained, that she might continue Wright if she found him necessary as Steward, he might have his Office in the House and a separate Table or for the present lodge and board out of the House.[6]

Battle was joined. The aunt lost her temper, forgot entirely her argument that she was only acting in the interests of the Tatham brothers, and reverted unforgivably to Sandford's peculiar family history. The Admiral's narrative draws a veil of filial decency, but it seems that Mrs Cookson, in round terms, pointed out that the son of divorced parents had no right at all to be denigrating the respectability of a poor but honest man. The nephew replied that respectability had nothing to do with it, but that an ex-footman was no fit companion for an officer and a gentleman and that, while to walk out of the house at midnight would fuel further rumours, he would leave after breakfast and would she please order a chaise.

So Sandford Tatham left Wennington Hall after a scant thirty-six hours, and never went back. His aunt sent him on his way in the Wennington Hall carriage, since a hired post-chaise would have excited comment, but one imagines that there was comment anyway. He found, then or later, that his name had been added to the list of undesirables, and that John Marsden's mind had been programmed to dislike and fear him. This, he believed, was done by instilling into Marsden the fixed idea that his cousin Sandford had plotted to make him subject to a commission for lunacy, a phrase which he may not have understood but which was easy to turn into a looming terror.

Two other of the Tatham brothers had brief contacts which were no more fruitful. In 1784 Charles, 'as volatile and inconsiderate a young man as could well be imagined' in Sandford's phrase, came over to England in charge of a shipload of tobacco for his employers. It is not to be wondered at that he lacked the Navy's idea of education and manners, having spent his first thirteen years parked with a village foster-family and the next twelve in the colonies.

Sandford, who was back on the active list but still based on shore, went north to Lancaster again in 1784 to visit old acquaintances (but not Wennington Hall) and to take up the freedom which he could claim by patrimony. Henry and Charles went with him for the same purpose, and although there was some slight difficulty owing to Charles's domicile, all three were enrolled as freemen of Lancaster. This gave them each a vote, and all three cast it in the ensuing parliamentary election for Lowther and Reynolds, the Tory candidates. Charles, 'a most determined zealous republican', according to his brother, engaged himself busily during the days of the election canvassing for the Tory interest. He doubtless regarded the whole affair as a lark. He was partial to larks, and in that humour went over to Wennington with a friend, although there was also the more serious business of claiming his small inheritance under his mother's will from Mrs Cookson, the executrix.

The two young men came back chortling over the situation at Wennington, which they described in ludicrous detail, but Sandford, although amused, did not feel that his younger brother's report added anything of use to him in his self-imposed duty of keeping a watching brief on his cousin Marsden's affairs. Charles returned to America and seems never to have revisited England. Somewhere along the line he married, no one seemed quite sure where or to whom, but died childless in 1798.

Four years after the youngest brother's visit, the eldest, William, also visited, for the first time in twenty years. In 1788, he also made his duty call to Wennington. Having assessed the situation, he spoke his mind, but his opinion was no more welcome than Sandford's had been, perhaps less so, since some years had elapsed and the menage was irreversibly established. 'However judicious his advice might be, it was of no avail and instead of doing good, he did harm; his Aunt became his enemy … and her hostility and Wright's insolence drove him out of the House, without effecting anything.'

A story was later told which suggests that some of William's 'advice' may have been more practical than judicious.

> James Robinson says he has heard his brother Thomas Robinson of London say when Mr J.M. lived at Wennington Hall at one time there was an appointment to go to dine at Mr Stephen Smith's at Wray. Thomas Robinson was the coachman at the time and said he took the coach to the front of the Hall when Mr M. and G. Wright came and got into it. One of the Mr Tathams was going along with Mr M. to Mr Smith's. Mr Tatham stop't a little behind Wright and Mr M. and the coach was waiting, at last Mr Tatham went and looked into the carriage and saw Wright in the inside, with that he got hould of Wright by his hare which was tied up in a club and puld him out and tould him if he would go he might get up behind the same as other servants do.[7]

There is no date to this memorandum which, being second-hand, never reached the witness stand, but it must feature William: Charles never stayed in the house, it can hardly refer to the crippled Henry, and Sandford would have related it of himself with relish.

Henry, the 'little deformed man' who 'used to play whist very well', was better tolerated by Mrs Cookson, and over several years paid long visits to Wennington, becoming in the end a permanent inmate of the house. Because of his disability he was practically a pauper; and, as several witnesses said, he was of a very amiable and uncritical temperament. He was also very fond of his aunt for all her kindness to him, and no doubt all these elements combined to make him careful to guard his tongue.

> When Mrs Cookson first invited him to take up his residence with her it was understood, and is believed to have been the fact, that she was desirous to associate him with herelf in the management of Mr Marsden's affairs. Henry, the second son of her sister, Elizabeth Tatham, was the oldest of her Nephews in England, and well qualified for her purpose, being a sensible man, a good Accountant, and of an easy, mild, conciliating disposition. That he did take a part in the management is clear, being the person who is said to have purchased for Mr Marsden the place afterwards occupied by Giles Bleasdale.[8]

(This was Wenning Cottage, in Wennington village.)

By 1787 Mrs Cookson was over sixty and the last survivor of her siblings by ten years. We may presume a slow crescendo of muttering among the rest of Marsden's family as they waited for her inevitable decline, a reckoning of cousinships. Who stood next in line? Who could or should intervene in support of the Tatham brothers? Who might benefit after John Marsden's death? In the end they came to a decision to do nothing, which of course was all they could do. At least, they may have said, Henry Tatham had his feet under the Wennington table as an outpost of the establishment, albeit a doubtfully effective one.

5

Wennington Hall

In the years after 1780, while Mrs Cookson was still alive, life seems to have settled down for the inhabitants at Wennington Hall into a sufficiently contented pattern within narrow boundaries. The lady of the house was not entirely without female companionship. Miss Elizabeth Tatham, having no home of her own, had been offered one by Mrs Cookson, and lived in the family for the rest of her life. Elizabeth was first cousin to the four brothers, one of the two daughters of their father's elder brother, John, a Lancaster attorney who had died young. Elizabeth, it seems from some slight evidence, was herself not the brightest child. As a girl, living in Penny Street, Lancaster, where her mother kept a little school, she was often used to look after her second cousin and near neighbour, John Marsden, but could not do much to protect him from the hootings and miseries of the rougher citizens of Lancaster.

Elizabeth and her sister should not have been as poor as they were. They had expectations as heirs at law to their uncle William Tatham of Askham. On his death in 1775 the estate, which was heavily in debt, was sold. The trustee then went bankrupt, and the attempts to claw back some of the proceeds dragged on for years, during which time Mrs Tatham had difficulty in supporting herself and the children. The younger sister 'married imprudently' and went to Jamaica where she died childless, so all the expectations settled on Elizabeth. After Mrs Tatham's death she first lived with some relations at Slaidburn, but then went to Wennington Hall as companion to Mrs Cookson. Shadowy and self-effacing, ('a sensible conversable woman ... she was fond of talking of the Lancaster people'), few witnesses mention her, but she has a small place in the story none the less, and George Wright turned her to account.[1]

In these years local society kept away from Wennington, shocked and angered by the double scandal. It is difficult to judge whether the strong rumours of illicit relations or the advancement of a servant into the parlour had the greater effect, but the result was the same. Dorothy Butler, a very near neighbour and a girl of fifteen in 1780, remembered well the time after Henry Marsden's death.

Were you acquainted with the family of Henry Marsden at Wennington? – Yes, my father and mother were intimate with his father and mother.

Do you remember Henry Marsden taking possession of his property? – Yes ...

Do you remember about that time a person named Wright coming there? – I do not recollect when he came, but I remember George Wright's being there as a servant.

Have you ever been there when he waited? – I remember perfectly his waiting once at tea when we were there.

Do you remember the death of Henry Marsden? – Yes.

Do you know whether he was long ill? – No, a short illness; my father and my uncle, the Rector of Bentham, were both sent for when he died.

Bentham is not far from Wennington? – About three miles.

After Henry Marsden died, do you remember John Marsden riding over to Ridding? – Yes.

Was any person with him? – George Wright.

Did Mr Marsden come in? – Yes.

Do you remember Mr Marsden saying anything about Wright? – He said several times to my mother 'Mr Wright is now my steward; Mr Wright is at the door' ... I think my father said 'Would Mr Wright like a glass of ale?'; he sat at the door and held his master's horse.

He was not invited into the house at that time? – No ... There was a long interval without any intercourse during the change ...

What was the nature of the change that occasioned that long interval without any intercourse; tell us what alteration took place, and other people will be able to think about it? – Mr Wright being taken into the parlour, Mr John Marsden not being considered by my father as companionable, and Mr Wright being taken into the parlour, the intercourse was unpleasant, and particularly as there were unpleasant reports.[2]

Other acquaintance, old and new, were not so choosy: the doctors, the lawyers, the clergymen, the middle class of men who had professional reasons and were not averse to dining at the gentry's table, whatever the circumstances; they came, but they did not bring their wives.

Since there were few visitors to the house, memories of John Marsden in these years, when they do not emanate from the servants' hall, arise from the hunting field. Not that Marsden was ever a great sportsman – very much the opposite – but it was almost the only public place where he was seen. The same stories are repeated so often that one might be inclined to think that witnesses were stretching their memories to include second-hand anecdotes: at least ten witnesses, for instance, tell the 'crop-eared mare' story as personally heard. In fact, it is likely that they were telling the truth; one has to remember John Marsden's habit of endless reiteration. This tale bears all the marks of an idea introduced to him by someone as a joke, which then became his standby remark whenever he was riding the old horse. It matches with the Reverend Robert Procter's evidence that almost every day Marsden used to say to him that they must go fishing together, but at the end of fifteen years the expedition was as far off as ever.

In his younger days Marsden had one or two quite good horses, probably the remains of his brother's stable, as witness the occasions when George Wright was seen to force an exchange and gallop off to enjoy the action, but for a long time he rode an old quiet brown mare called Daphne, which happened to have had her ears cropped. The joke was to hear Marsden say – and from the frequency of the repetition one guesses that people encouraged him to say – that he was looking for a crop-eared stallion for Daphne, because a breed of quiet, crop-eared foals would result, and that would be very desirable.

The local hunt was a sort of cooperative. The Gibsons of Quernmore Park kept a few couple of harriers; Thomas Townley, the hunting parson of Heysham, kept a few more; so did the Bradshaw brothers of Halton Park, so did Wennington Hall, and others. Probably these dogs were never all brought together at once, but two or three lots would meet and hunt somewhere in the area. Marsden, a very poor and nervous rider, enjoyed putting on his red coat and going to the meet, but seems to have enjoyed little else, usually managing to fall behind when the pace got warm. The servant who went with him for the occasion would frequently leave his charge with someone else ('Look after master, for he can't look after himself') and take the chance of a gallop.

There were many stories current of how he would get into a field and then be unable to find his way out. This was partly due to very poor sight, and partly to a kind of panic which overtook him when he could not find his bearings. There are many tales of his being set on his way by casual passers-by, either on foot or on horseback, when he had evidently become quite disoriented, though to better eyes within sight of home.

Did you ever speak to him in your life? – Yes [said John Hayes, a labourer living near Wennington Hall].

When? – When he was hunting.

I believe that was the only time? – Yes; I believe it was.

What did he say to you? – He asked me what way he must go; I said 'I cannot say. You are going a-hunting are you'.

Was that all? – 'Which way shall I go?' said he. I said 'I do not know where you want to go'.

Tell us all. – I will. I said go through that gap, and you will meet with the dogs that are coming towards us. He said 'How can I go among all those brambles where there is no road?' Said I 'It is very good land, you cannot take any harm'. 'Oh', says he, 'I shall be hurt and lost altogether: I shall be bogged.' I said, 'There is none, it is a meadow'. He said 'Oh, it is all very right, I will go'.

What said you? – 'I will lead you', and I accordingly led him.

Did he say anything more? – Yes, he said 'I will not go as there is no road'. I said 'Which way will you go?' 'Oh no,' he said, 'he would not go at all for he would be lost.'

What more did you say? – I said 'I will open the gate and shew you to the high road' and he answered 'Do so', and I opened the gate and turned him out upon the road, and his own man Clemenson was coming, and I led him into conversation when he passed, and he said 'Oh', says he, 'do not take any notice of what that man says'. I came here to tell my story and I shall tell it.[3]

Thomas Bleazard was less long-winded, but his evidence was much the same.

Have you seen him out hunting? – Yes.

Have you seen him in a field? – Yes, I have.

Have you ever observed how he got out of a field? – Yes, I have; I have seen him sometimes riding up and down the field, and could not get out when the gate was quite open.

Have you seen any one go in to help him out? – I have gone in myself.

How have you helped him out? – I led him into the road through the gate by taking the bridle of the horse.

Where were the hounds in the mean time? – They were got out of sight.[4]

If Mrs Cookson was cut off from her social equals by her behaviour, and John Marsden by his defects, George Wright seems to have voluntarily cut himself off. No doubt he visited his family, and it was said that Mrs Cookson gave him £200 to establish his parents in a small farm in Bentham, but there is no suggestion that any of his relations came to Wennington. Whether under persuasion or not his brother, the clogger, who had set up business in Hornby, moved further away.

1   John Marsden (1758–1826). Painting, *c.* 1816, by James Lonsdale
(1777–1839) (*G. P. Bowring*)

2 John Marsden (1758–1826).
Miniature, *c.* 1780, by unknown artist
(*Hugh van Asch*)

3 George Wright (1756–1846).
Miniature, *c.* 1780, by unknown artist
(*Hugh van Asch*)

4 William Sharp (1774–1861).
Painting, 1861, by unknown artist
(*Peter Sharp*)

5 Giles Bleasdale (1753–1831).
Painting, *c.* 1816, by James Lonsdale
(1777–1839) (*G. P. Bowring*)

14 The Reverend Dr John Lingard
(1771–1851)
(*National Portrait Gallery*)

15 Pudsey Dawson (1778–1859).
Painting by an unknown artist
(*Robert Bell*)

16 The eight boxes containing the material concerning *Tatham* v. *Wright*
(*David Battersby*)

17   Rear-Admiral Sandford Tatham (1755–1840). Engraving, 1836–37, by
Richard Dighton (1795–1880) (*Olivia Ley*)

It was during these years that an intimacy began to grow between Wennington and the nearest Marsden relations, the Listers of Giggleswick. Anthony Lister was John Marsden's second cousin but, as Admiral Tatham once said, if the inheritance of the Marsden property were to go by primogeniture, there were half a hundred others in front of him. A family tree drawn according to the accepted rules shows John Marsden on the extreme left of the chart, and the Listers on the extreme right. As was said earlier, Henry Marsden, John's grandfather, had had two sisters. The elder of the two, Elizabeth, married William Dawson of Langcliffe Hall, and the result of that union was a sprawling web of Dawsons and Cooksons. The younger sister, Jane, married Charles Nowell of Cappleside, Rathmell, and their daughter, Elizabeth, married Anthony Lister of an old Giggleswick family. He was vicar of that ancient parish from 1741 to his death in 1756. His son, another Anthony, is the one of whom we speak, and he was therefore the youngest of the youngest family line where John Marsden was the eldest of the eldest.

Henry Marsden spoke slightingly of Anthony Lister, his second cousin, and would not visit, because he was nothing more than a grazier and lived in a converted inn, the Bell. But though not quite at the level of Wennington Hall, the family were respectable enough and, after Henry's death, a friendship grew up. Sarah Cookson, with her nephew and George Wright, paid visits which were returned. Anthony had an only child, young Anthony, born in 1778, and John Marsden loved the boy. It would not take extraordinary foresight on the part of the father to see that this was a relationship well worth fostering. In theory there was nothing to prevent John Marsden marrying and having a family but, to those who knew him and his aunt better, it was clearly not in her mind that this should happen. When he talked of girls, as he sometimes did, she strongly discouraged the idea, pooh-poohing it as an impossibility.

It has already been suggested that the whole cousinship, after the manner of families, was extremely interested in the ultimate destination of the Marsden fortune. That interest must have been sharpened when Henry died apparently intestate. There may also have been speculation as to whether all the Tatham brothers were legitimate or not. There must have been even keener speculation as to whether John Marsden would marry and get children, whether he were able to make a will, and if not what would happen. At this stage George Wright's position, scandalous in regard to his connection with Sarah Cookson, was not as prominent to outside eyes as it became after her death. Those family members, Cooksons mostly, who out of curiosity called at Wennington, were affronted that their elderly relative should have acquired a toy boy whom she had elevated to the parlour, but all business was still in her name. She was next-of-kin, but she was getting older. There was no commission of lunacy. What provision should, or would, be made to safeguard her nephew's wealth? (By 'safeguard' the family would certainly have meant 'keep within the family'.)

We cannot now find out exactly how the Listers got their feet under the table. Money is a powerful magnet, and no doubt they were edging towards greater intimacy at the same time as George Wright, who knew very well that when Mrs Cookson died he would need strong allies from some part of the family to prevent interference from all the others, was edging towards them in his turn. The Wennington estate was not vast, but it was a very desirable property, and there were other interests in London, in Bradford and elsewhere. No estate accounts survive, but John Marsden was probably worth £3000 or £4000 a year, which was certainly not being spent on high living. Well-managed, the estate could only increase in value.

John Marsden himself was very susceptible to friendliness, and naturally drawn to relatives, at least until his mind was poisoned. The one time in his life that he met Sandford Tatham, by accident and unchaperoned, in the King's Arms in Lancaster, within a quarter of an hour he was prepared to be a warm and lifelong friend. But the budding friendship, reported at home, was fiercely forbidden by Wright, who probably then used the mysterious 'commission of lunacy' to turn the cousin into an ogre. Marsden took with equal warmth to the Listers, and this was not forbidden. The habit was established by which the Listers took their share in looking after their cousin by having him in their house at Bell Hill in Giggleswick for three or four weeks in the summer and again over Christmas. Though the older Anthony found entertaining his backward cousin a chore ('Let's go without the idiot', he was heard to exclaim when Marsden was late for an outing), he was mindful of his son's expectations. The idea began to float on the family breeze that young Anthony would be the ultimate heir.

The family had no doubt given up all hope of disentangling the Wright-Cookson liaison, though at this stage no one, so far as is known, had any suspicion of the affair of the will which kept the two so powerfully interlocked. Their relationship, though, was not just a consortium of thieves: there is a genuinely cosy domesticity in some of the glimpses provided by the evidence of various servants. Robert Humber remembered them 'in a little parlour, just by the kitchen' occupied in 'copying over George Barnewell for the farmers' sons to act'. Indeed they were often so pleased with each other's company that they neglected poor John Marsden.

They used to go out walking, or sometimes fishing, together. Though John pleaded to come too, his aunt would say 'Stay at home and mind your servants', whereupon he would work off his frustration by jumping violently on and off the parlour chairs.

> John Marsden had very thick and long hair and wore it clubbed up behind with a great quantity of powder, and after Henry Marsden's death [Robert Humber] frequently saw him scratching his head apparently much annoyed by lice, and he asked him to let him comb his hair which he did upon a Newspaper, and brought out an uncommon number, which [Humber] destroyed by putting them into the Kitchen Fire. He did this several times and once when he was bringing them down from John Marsden's room to the Kitchen he met George Wright and showed them to him, and told him it was a shame for Mrs Cookson and him to let John Marsden be in such a state.[5]

Perhaps this rebuke had the good effect of getting a personal servant for Marsden, although his first one, Thomas Waller, was only a parish apprentice when he started at Wennington.

A more attractive domestic view is given by William Humber, son of Robert and his wife Ellen Huggonson. As both the parents were servants at the Hall, the boy spent much of his childhood in Lancaster, probably with his grandparents, but frequently visited his parents and also Mrs Cookson, who was his godmother:

> Remembered when he was about seven years of age [in fact he was younger, not more than five] going to Wennington Hall to see his godmother. She and George Wright were together on the bowling green. Mrs Cookson was very glad to see him. Mrs Cookson threw a Bowl and had [him] do the same. George Wright threw one and all three played together. After they had played awhile Mrs Cookson and Wright went into the Alcove or Shed where the Bowls were kept and which had seats round it. They sat down on each other's knees and played with each other and were very kind. [William] kept trundling the Bowls about. Sometimes he was in view of them and at other times out of sight and frequently within two or three yards of them. They appeared quite comfortable with each other.[6]

And 'quite comfortable' they might have stayed, in this very eccentric household: Mrs Cookson, the elderly mistress and manager, signing the letters, holding the purse-strings; John Marsden the nominal master, whom she ordered about, but also to some extent propped up in his place as figurehead (it was said, for instance, that sometimes he used to read family prayers to the household); Miss Tatham, the timid companion; from time to time Henry Tatham, the amiable cripple, who led an ordinary social life outside among his equals and behaved as though there were nothing strange about Wennington at all; and George Wright, who threw his weight about in the role of steward by day, and came home at night to sit in the master's place at the dining table, and to share the mistress's fireside and bed.

So things went until in 1786 a new wild card turned up on the table: the neighbouring and much more important estate of Hornby Castle came on the market.

6

Hornby Castle

Hornby Castle is, both by history and position, by far the most prestigious building in the Lune Valley. Built to command a great sweep of the Lune as well as the Wenning river and the road into Yorkshire, its ancient pele tower is visible from all angles. To George Wright, brought up on its distant view from the heights of Aughton across the river, this fine house must in his youth have represented the pinnacle of aristocratic grandeur. Early impressions are hard to shift, and it is likely that Hornby Castle remained to him a powerful symbol of absolute ambition. When the unattainable suddenly offered itself as a possible prize, he did not hesitate.

The Hornby estate was neglected, but it was potentially profitable. It was also a place whose romantic appearance was justified by a full and colourful history. A survey of the 1580s gives a picture of its heyday, very much a grand country house rather than a castle with any serious military pretensions:

> First: the Castle is very faire built standing stately upon the Topp of a great Hill having from severall Gates and Wards before ye shall enter into the said Castle and at the Lowest foot of the Hill standeth the first Gate and the Town of Hornby being a Markett Town which Markett is kept on the Monday doth adjoin unto the said first Gate of the said Castle.
>
> Item: on the North East side of the said Castle is the Orchard adjoining unto the Castle Wall which orchard as it goeth by the Old Parke Pale and round about against the River Wenning against the South unto the Castle Wall the same orchard containeth five Acres and a half.
>
> Item: on the South West side of the said Castle standeth the Garden which Garden and the rest of the ground within it doth contain an Acre and a half.
>
> Item: next unto that Garden is a Yard where is built a House to keep Turfe in and one other House which is a Slaughter House and that Yard containeth half an acre.

Item: on the North East side of the said Castle of the second Gate
is another Yard invironed with a Stone Wall wherein is built a faire
Dairye house and adjoining unto that is another Yard invironed with a
stone wall which serveth to be a wood yard.

Item: next beneath that is another Yard paled where is built faire
Barns Stables Garretts to put corn in a Malt house and containeth two
Acres.[1]

It was then in the hands of the Stanleys, Lords Monteagle, later
Morley and Monteagle, who took seriously their position within striking
distance of the Scottish border. The first Lord Monteagle was ennobled
for his part at Flodden in 1513, and built the tower of Hornby Church
in thanksgiving for his safe return. A later lord received the letter of
warning (some say, as he sat at dinner in the Castle itself, but this seems
unlikely) about the Gunpowder Plot in 1604: 'For though there be no
appearance of any stir, yet, I say, they shall receive a terrible blow, this
Parliament; and yet they shall not see who hurts them.'

James I was entertained at Hornby on a royal progress from Scotland
to London in 1617. In the Civil Wars, the Monteagles being both
Catholic and Royalist, the Castle was held for the King, besieged by
Colonel Assheton, and taken by means of a deserter who showed the
attackers how to get in at a window. Prince Rupert on his way to
Liverpool, after his defeat at Marston Moor in 1644, stopped at the
Castle. In 1648 it was occupied again, by the Duke of Hamilton and
his Scottish army. Under the Commonwealth the then Lord Morley
and Monteagle was gaoled for his 'recusancy and delinquency' and the
estates sequestered. Although he got them back again after the Resto-
ration the family was effectively ruined. Hornby was sold at the end of
the seventeenth century to the Earl of Cardigan, whose family sold it
again, in 1713, to the notorious Colonel Charteris.

Francis Charteris, born in 1675, was drummed out of an English
regiment at an early age for cheating at cards, and out of a Dutch one
for stealing, so it is said, a piece of beef, and out of another English
one for making false enlistments (at a price) for people who could thus
escape arrest for debt. 'His career in the army', says the *Dictionary of
National Biography*, 'not being a remarkable success, Charteris ceased
at last to persevere in it, and devoted all his serious attention to
gambling', at which he was very successful indeed. 'By a combination
of skill, trickery, and effrontery he managed to acquire large sums of
money from nearly every one whom he selected to be his victim.' He
very rapidly made a vast fortune, Hornby being one of the estates he
bought with it. It was he who built the country-house front to the castle,

leaving the ruinous old building behind, but dismantling most of the system of interlocking courtyards described in the 1580s. There is no proof that he spent much of his time living at Hornby, although a spate of christenings of his illegitimate children, born to local girls in the 1720s, show that he at least passed through from time to time.

In 1730 he was convicted of rape on his maidservant, a capital offence, but managed to get away with a royal pardon after a short spell in Newgate. He died at his Scottish seat of Stoneyhill, near Musselburgh, in 1732. At his funeral a revengeful mob rioted, almost succeeding in tearing the body out of the coffin. The newly-established *Gentleman's Magazine* celebrated his death with 'An Epigram', which began:

> Here lieth the Body of a Colonel
> DON FRANCISCO
> Who with an inflexible Constancy.
> And inimitable Uniformity of Life,
> Persisted, in Spight of Age and Infirmity,
> In the Practice of every human Vice
> Excepting Prodigality and Hypocrisy;
> His insatiable Avarice
> Exempting him from the first,
> And his matchless Impudence
> From the latter.[2]

Somewhere along the way Charteris contracted a legal marriage and begot a lawful daughter, who married the Earl of Wemyss. Their elder son, having been involved in the 1745 Rising, spent most of his life abroad. The second son, another Francis, inherited Hornby from his wicked grandfather, but it is not clear how much he resided there, or why he put it on the market in 1786.

The poet Thomas Gray, passing on a north country tour in 1765, had visited the most romantic bit, the old tower:

> It is now only a shell, the rafters are laid within it as for flooring. I went up a winding stone staircase in one corner to the leads, and at the angle is a stone single hexagon watch-tower, rising seven feet higher, fitted up in the taste of a modern summer-house, with sash windows in gilt frames, a stucco cupola, and on the top a rich gilt eagle; built by Mr Charteris, the present proprietor.[3]

An article in the *Lonsdale Magazine* of 1822 gives more detail.

> The old part, which is very ancient, is in a neglected state. The walls are strongly cemented and of amazing thickness, well calculated for

sustaining a siege, which has undoubtedly often been their fate. That part, which has originally been the keep, is the only part that remains entire; and may be seen towering over the more recent erections, in its ancient grandeur. A spiral staircase, in the north-west angle, leads to the different apartments of this tower; but the extensive court yards, which once afforded protection to the numerous dependents, in time of civil commotion, have been long since dismantled, by the hand of time and the ravages of war.[4]

By the time this article was written, the house itself had been further altered in various ways, but in the main it must have appeared in 1822 very much as it had in 1786.

It is still an important place; and the structure itself is very much improved [since the 1580s]. All the South and South West parts have been erected since that period; and fit up in a superior style. On the ground floor, there is, in one of the wings, an elegant Breakfast Room, and in the other a spacious Library. The centre is divided into an Entrance Hall and a Dining Room, noble, lofty and spacious. The Dining Room, in particular, is a magnificent Room. On the second floor is a very large and splendid Drawing Room. All these apartments command most delightful views down the vale, which is one of the finest in the north. These views are, however, all reduced to one grand whole, by ascending to the battlements on the tower, to the summer house over the spiral staircase.[4]

This then was the Castle, on sale with almost 3000 acres of land sadly neglected by absentee landlords. It is astonishing to consider the spectacle of George Wright, twenty-eight years old, a brief six years after achieving what he anticipated with pleasure as 'a good place' – cleaning boots, running errands, foddering horses, waiting at table – reading, we must presume, that circular, and conceiving a plan to become the effective master of Hornby Castle. Such effrontery has its own magnificence. The implementation of the vision, over the ensuing forty years, involved of necessity much petty and sordid chicanery, and the steady erosion, so it would seem, of all the softer human traits which might get in its way; but at this moment in the story of George Wright, when for the second time he saw the flash of a brilliant future and grabbed at it unhestitatingly, the vigour and daring characteristic of the man stand out.

If it is reasonable to suppose that Sarah Cookson had been the moving spirit behind the suppression of the will, common sense suggests that in 1786 the first idea was Wright's. Mrs Cookson was over sixty – an

A

P A R T I C U L A R

OF THE

E S T A T E S

OF

The Honourable FRANCIS CHARTERIS;

CONSISTING OF

The Honor, Manor, and Lordſhip of *Hornby*, and the Manor of *Tatham*,
in the County Palatine of *Lancaſter*, with the Cuſtomary, Fee, and Free-
farm Rents, Boons, and Fines thereto belonging; together with divers
Farms and Woods, compriſing near 2800 Acres (Statute Meaſure) of
Arable, Meadow, Paſture, and Wood Land, chiefly Tithe free, and
having Right of Common on ſeveral very extenſive Moors, Commons, and
Fells; the Corn Tithes ariſing within the Townſhips of *Arkholme* with
Caywood, Melling with *Wrayton, Wennington, Hornby, Farlton,* and
Wray; the ſmall Tithes of the ſame Townſhips with thoſe of the Diviſions
of *Botton* and *Roberindale*; the Right of Nomination to the Curacy of
Hornby, reputed to be of the yearly Value of 46*l.* (the Incumbent is about
Thirty Years of Age), and the perpetual Advowſon of the Rectory of
Tatham, reputed to be of the yearly Value of 90*l.* (the Incumbent is
about Thirty-ſix Years of Age), with a Right of Preſentation in the ſaid
Rector to the Chapelry of *Tatham Fell*, reputed to be of the yearly Value
of 80*l.* the Incumbent is about Sixty-one Years of Age.

THE Honor, Manor, and Lordſhip of *Hornby* extend over the ſeveral Townſhips of
Greſſingham, Hornby with *Roberindale, Arkholme* with *Caywood, Tunſtal, Melling* with
Wrayton, and *Wennington; Farlton,* and *Wray* with *Botton;* ſuppoſed to be ten Miles in Length;
including large Tracts of Waſtes and Fells.

The cuſtomary Rents and Boons, and other Rents, due and payable
to the ſaid Manor, out of which no Taxes are paid, viz.

	£. s. d.	£. s. d.	£. s. d.
		9 0 0¼	
Cuſtomary Rents	0 8 10½		
Boons,	13 15 6½		
Fee Farm Rents,	11 9 7½		
Antient Freehold Rents,		25 14 0½	
			32 14 1½

The Fines due and payable to the ſaid Manor from the cuſtomary Tenants are eight Times the
reſerved Rent upon the Change of every Tenant by Death, and a general Fine of eight
Times the whole of the reſerved Rent upon the Death of the laſt general admitting Lord,
and upon all Alienations the cuſtomary Tenants pay reaſonable arbitrary Fines.

Carried over   32 14 1½

Sale Document of Hornby Castle Estate (1786). (*Lancashire Record Office*) old woman, by the standards of the time. In 1780 she had acted to gain the enjoyment of a large country house and a commensurate income. Even though she had thrown away on Wright's behalf the public recognition that should have gone with her position as lady of Wennington Hall, she had looked to spend her declining years in the home of her youth, as rightful representative of an important local family. It is very hard to believe that now she would hanker for a fairy-tale castle, or summon up the energies needed to manoeuvre John Marsden into the figurehead position of purchaser, or indeed face with equanimity the necessity of selling all her family's original estate to buy this castellated pig in a poke. If there had been money available, the addition of the Hornby Castle estate to Wennington Hall, with which it marched, was a reasonable idea: the two together would have made a large but compact and balanced whole. But there was not money available. Selling off the outlying estates, Bradford, Gisburn, the Middlesex interests, made good sense, but would not come anywhere near providing the £53,000 that was being asked.

There is evidence for friction at some time between the partners, but we do not know when: the anecdote of John Bentley, the manipulated Bradford lawyer, who told of a time when Wright and Cookson quarrelled and he received letters from her threatening to blow the whistle, letters which terrified him, is undated and second-hand. There is one other story, emanating from a maid at Wennington, but it cannot be earlier than 1789. It may also be connected with the fact that Wright was by then courting a more suitable partner, in terms of age, behind Mrs Cookson's back. According to the written note, she found out and was 'jelis'.

There was only one usable staircase in Wennington Hall, so servants and masters alike used it ('The old hall stairs were filled up with lumber, and there was no going up'), thus seeing more of each other day-to-day than might otherwise have been the case. Jane Hill, dairy- and kitchen-maid, gave evidence.

Do you remember Mrs Cookson getting a fall one day? – Yes; she fell down stairs; I remember it very well.

And do you remember Wright talking to her about it afterwards? – Yes.

What did he say? – He told her she was drunk or else she would not fall.

What did she say? – She told him she was not drunk at the time, and if she were it was nothing to him; that he had the most daring impudence to say so, but she was not drunk. She said he had taken advantage of her and her nephew, and that he knew her nephew never had proper understanding since his cradle; that she had advanced him, and that he had the most daring impudence to insult her.

(One imagines that not only Jane, but by this time the entire household, was agog.)

What did Mr Wright say to that? – He said several things, but I could not understand it; he kept saying that she was drunk.
Was she drunk? – No, my lord, she was perfectly sober.[5]

If relations are good between two people, and one falls down the stairs, it is usual to help them to their feet, or at least inquire whether they have hurt themselves. This sounds like a brief and noisy interlude out of a more prolonged difference, but whether it had any connection with Wright's ambitions for Hornby, and the subsequent long delays in their fulfilment, we can only conjecture.

It was later said that it was ridiculous to conceive of a man planning in 1786 for an end which did not arrive until 1826. 'A more strange romance never emanated from the most fertile brain of any poet or novelist.' But in fact the story is not comprehensible on any other terms. 'It is said that the object of Mr Wright, throughout a great portion of this long period of sixty-eight years (for that was the time during which Mr Marsden lived) was finally to get a will established in his, Wright's, own favour.'[6] It was not, of course, sixty-eight years; nor do we need to suppose that Wright saw all of the future clearly ahead; but unless we assume that he moved deliberately, we underrate the man and make a nonsense of the story. Wennington first, Hornby second, inheritance third: these were the three acts in the play. Whether he felt moved by destiny, or merely thanked his stars for endowing him with intelligence and determination of a much higher order than most of the people round him, we do not know. The big gap in this reconstruction is the total lack of evidence which might give some view of Wright from the inside. There is no autobiographical narrative written to explain his actions, no self-revealing correspondence, and most of his depositions have vanished. And his descendants, happy enough to benefit from the fortune he made, joined in a conspiracy of silence, which must have been intentional to begin with, though it was afterwards unconscious. They simply wiped the slate and began their family history with his son. George Wright, having against all the odds established a moneyed and successful family, was forgotten.

When the reckoning was done, it was clear that, to acquire Hornby Castle, every last acre of the ancestral Marsden estates would have to be sold, and there would still be need for sizeable borrowings. It was a daunting scheme, and one would give much for hard evidence to show the thinking behind it.

Wright's ambition has to be the vital key. Was Mrs Cookson's complaisance merely a sign that she was as devoted to his advancement, and as malleable to his persuasions, in 1786 as she had been in 1780? Wennington Hall would have to go, and Wennington Hall was the home where she had been born and to which she had belonged all her life apart from her brief marriage. Did she try to fight the decision? Was she blackmailed into agreement? Or was she a more equal partner than that, sharing, even at her age, in the excitement of new worlds to conquer? It could not be ordinary social ambition, but perhaps some feeling of revenge was working – she might be ignored by old acquaintance, but she would be chatelaine of Hornby Castle for all that.

A further suggestion may be relevant, though it credits Wright with an even more remarkable long-sightedness. If the final disposition of the Marsden fortune were to be diverted from Marsden's own family, it would be far easier on the basis of Hornby rather than Wennington. One set of blood ties would have been broken with the sale of the patrimonial acres; it would be the less surprising if another set were also to go with the alienation of the new estates from Marsden's own family.

John Marsden himself was no obstacle. It would not have been at all difficult to inspire his weak mind with the fairy-tale vision of Hornby Castle. Although he had not the sense to know where his own land began and ended, he knew quite enough to have greeted his brother's death with surprising equanimity and repetitions of 'Now it is all mine'. He got satisfaction from the phrase 'Lord of the Manor' which he repeated with relish, though sometimes inappropriately when standing on a neighbour's land.

The advertisement was published in July 1786, and negotiations must have started very quickly. Mrs Cookson and Wright had as their legal adviser at the northern end a Lancaster barrister called Fitzgerald, a crony who spent much time at Wennington Hall while the business was going on, and was, we may presume, author of some of the more important letters that survive, since in style and spelling they are much more educated than any of the principals could have managed on their own. Not many letters are extant, but there are a few exchanged with Thomas Greene, the Marsdens' London attorney.

Later argument was endless on the crucial question of whether or not John Marsden composed his own letters. The evidence overwhelmingly persuades that he could not; that he might be able without much assistance to write a brief formal invitation or most of a rather childish effusion about a man falling out of a window, but that everything else was composed for him, perhaps not word for word, that he wrote it out on paper which had been carefully ruled in pencil, and then brought it to be checked, and if it did not pass muster went back to try again until the final result was good enough to send.

The first of the letters sent to Greene in the summer of 1787 seems to reflect George Wright's style, the second a more educated hand, probably Fitzgerald's.

> Dear Sir, My Aunt is so poorly she has desired me to answer the Letter she received last night. I wish you had concluded the Bargen with Mr Dunn [Lord Wemyss' agent] – when you saw him you had full powers from my Aunts last letters given you which I saw & approve on. If the consequences were of so little concern to me that I would trust to the mere toss up of a die, I would never have bid at it at all, but I look upon it as so necessary to my interest that I beg and intreat you to make no delay to purchase it if even I give a thousand or two advance – as soon as you have concluded the Bargain I beg to hear from you, if you think it not improper please to propose them to keep it a secret awhile.
>
> My Aunt joines with me in Compliments
> and am, Dear Sir,
> Your obedient humble Servant
> J. Marsden.[7]

This letter makes quite plain Mrs Cookson's role in her nephew's business affairs but also ('which I saw & approve on') highlights the insoluble ambiguity of the situation. Marsden was officially in control of himself and his possessions; everybody who had more than a passing acquaintance with him understood that he was not, but there was no legal definition of his position. He was not imbecilic enough to merit the commission of lunacy which would remove his legal status. He simply needed support – honest and totally disinterested support in an ideal world.

A parallel case which had not yet burst upon the newspaper reading public was that of the third Earl of Portsmouth, who was probably more defective than John Marsden, and certainly much wilder in his personal behaviour. His tastes were morbid: an obsession with funerals and slaughterhouses was tolerable as eccentricity; his servants were paid highly enough to put up with his random violence; more difficult to cope with was his habit of carrying a set of surgeon's knives in his pocket and demanding of even casual acquaintance that they would let his blood or allow him to let theirs. To the public eye, however, he lived an almost normal life because he was married to a good, rather elderly, wife, who managed him with skill and kindness. The case only turned to scandal when she died in 1813, and Lord Portsmouth fell into the hands of his attorney, who very rapidly arranged a second marriage with his own daughter. She and her lover terrorised him into submission, until the Portsmouth family, alarmed by the prospect of losing the succession and the fortune, intervened legally to have the second marriage declared void. They won a slow and expensive legal case in 1828. There is interesting similarity between the cases, but John Marsden had no wife devoted to his interests; he had an elderly aunt, who served him well according to her lights, and George Wright.

Ordinary people, who deal in common-sense shades of grey, can readily understand how everyone may collude in pretending that a person is normal while knowing very well that he is not, and shaping their behaviour accordingly. Lord Portsmouth for many years carried on a social life suited to his status; people ignored an extremely bizarre private life until it was brought into black and white notoriety by the courts. In the case of John Marsden, it was the purchase of Hornby Castle which for the first time brought his anomalous situation very near the surface. Thomas Greene, a respectable and intelligent attorney, did not much like his involvement in such a very large transaction. He obviously wrote to Fitzgerald, asking for a letter to cover himself, and got the following.

Wennington Hall, September 7, 1787

Dear Sir, Mr Fitzgerald having communicated a Letter from you to him dated the 3d instant in which you express a wish that I should give my sanction to the treaty of the Hornby purchase. I write this fully to authorise it. I observe you say that Mr D. says we must give £53,000. If that largeness of the sum be the only objection, I request you will on my behalf offer for the estate £53,000 and close with them as soon as possible. And I shall be very glad to hear that it is obtained at that price. If more we must give it rather than let it slip. I refer you to former Letters and leave it to you to settle the terms of purchase as well as circumstances will on the principles in these Letters enable you to do. I am sorry it will be the means of detaining you in Town longer than you intended but I rely upon your attention to it for which I shall always think myself obliged to you.

I am, Dear Sir,

Your most obedient humble Servant

J. Marsden.

My Aunt & the Gentlemen present their Compliments.[8]

It is clear that Thomas Greene had serious doubts about the transaction. The Hornby Castle estate was to cost £53,000 and the agreement he sketched out suggested that £10,000 or £15,000 of that should be paid in cash within six months, and the rest raised by mortgages. 'It is rather a bold undertaking (tho' it may answer very well), provided you can steer clear of Inconveniences which often arrive very unexpectedly', he wrote in answer to the letter above.

A week later a war scare in London brought his doubts to the surface. 'I am just now told 1300 Sailors were pressed last night on the River. I dare not proceed further in your Business without your positive Orders. If a war ensues, which looks daily more and more probable, if you go on with this Bargain your own Ruin may likewise ensue.' He does not elaborate, but a war would make money scarce and the raising of mortgages difficult, and perhaps also delay the sale of the estates. Greene also advised that the agreement to buy Hornby should be kept very quiet. It would not do for prospective buyers of the Wennington estates to know how urgently the owner needed to sell. 'It will be time to get such of your Estates as you mean to sell advertised & would not have you disclose this Agreement on any consideration till after I have had the Pleasure of seeing you in the Country. It may injure the sale of your Estates if it be known & for other reasons keep the secret.'[9]

The secret was kept. It was kept from William Tatham on his first and only visit to Wennington Hall, which ended in acrimony. He particularly resented the fact, as he told a friend, that 'if any papers were on the Table if he went into the room all was huddled up and kept secret from him which gave him offence as he was Mr Marsden's heir'.[10] (We must presume that at this stage Sarah Cookson was representing herself as in temporary charge of things but that the next heir would be the heir at law, which matches with Sandford Tatham's expressed conviction that he could not believe that she ever really intended to disinherit her sister's sons.) But it seems she was playing her cards very close and, in view of the quotation above, it is doubtful whether any of Marsden's wider family knew anything of the Hornby purchase until it was an accomplished fact. Henry Tatham, the only one on a comfortable footing with his aunt, was not yet a permanent resident at Wennington.

The negotiations dragged on until 1791 at least, probably later, as the move to Hornby was not made until 1793, seven years after the conception of the plan. A much later letter from Captain Barrie, Sandford Tatham's colleague and friend, suggests that the delay may have been partly at least due to the fact that Greene withdrew his services as solicitor. He wrote on 1 December 1826:

> When in Town I received the following item from Mr Thomas Gorst ... Mr Green (the father of the present member for Lancaster) was in treaty for the purchase of the Hornby estate, but before the bargain was concluded he thought it advisable to have a legal opinion whether Mr Marsden was fit to conclude the bargain &c. Either Mr Green Bradley or Mr Justice Littledale were consulted and the purchase was broken off on the grounds of the opinion that Mr Marsden was not sound of mind and consequently incapable of concluding the sale of his property. This Mr Gorst says is known to many persons now living in Lancaster.[11]

There is also a lively account of the dismay of a group of solicitors when they were actually faced with their principal in the affair. John Hartley of Settle related how, on 25 April 1788, several of them met at Wennington Hall, where they had been invited to dinner and to spend the night, in order to complete the purchases for their various clients of parts of the Wennington estate. The solicitor representing Marsden was James Barrow and he was also present.

> Had you ever before that time seen Mr Marsden? – Never.
> As far as you could observe of the gentlemen who accompanied you, or met you, were they almost strangers to him? – I believe nearly so.
> Were you introduced to him before dinner? – I think not.
> You all sat down to dinner? – Yes.
> Mrs Cookson sat at the head of the table, did she? – Yes.
> Where did Mr Marsden sit? – On the right hand of Mrs Cookson, and Wright at the bottom of the table.
> How did Marsden conduct himself during dinner? – Very gentlemanly.
> You observed nothing particular? – Not in the least then.
> When the dinner was removed, you had wine, no doubt? – Yes.
> Did Mrs Cookson quit the room? – Yes; Mrs Cookson first, and then Barrow and Wright said they had some business to attend to, and they left the room together.
> Where was Marsden then? – He had taken Mrs Cookson's chair.
> When they left the room do you remember any thing particular in his behaviour? – He began pushing the bottle round, and gave us some toasts.[12]

It is referred to many times in the evidence that John Marsden had acquired very competently the behaviour of a host after dinner: the formal requests across the table to drink wine with one person or another whom it was desired to compliment, and the giving of toasts to be drunk by the company at large. Indeed, the evidence of many witnesses who swore, perhaps honestly, that he was perfectly competent, was based upon the fact that they had really only seen him at the dinner-table, 'pushing the bottle round', calling for more wine from the cellar, and indulging in these formalities.

On this occasion, left alone with the guests, whom he would not have engaged in personal conversation (his 'very gentlemanly' previous conduct was almost certainly a combination of good table manners and total silence), he proceeded to show off his party trick. He asked all the gentlemen to fill bumpers, and to stand up and toast 'Mr Wright and Mrs Cookson'. They had hardly sat down when, in precisely the same words, he called upon them again to fill bumpers, to stand up, to drink a toast to 'Mr Wright and Mrs Cookson – and may they live a thousand years'. A frisson went through the company – the realisation that things were not right. One version of the story says that they had been previously alarmed by Marsden during dinner suddenly becoming talkative, and going on about Miss Butler whom he wanted to marry, 'that they perceived that it was a subject very disagreeable to Mrs Cookson and Mr Wright, that Mrs Cookson said to Mr Marsden "Jack! what can thou do with a wife when thou can't take care of thyself"', but another version puts this conversation at breakfast next morning. In either case, they were sufficiently alarmed after dinner to meet in a huddle in the garden, and come to the conclusion that it would be dangerous to the interests of their clients to go on with the sales.

Next morning they communicated their decision to James Barrow and Wright. Barrow did not try to relieve their fears about Marsden's competence. He merely pointed out that their money would be safe, because it was going to be immediately invested in the purchase of Hornby Castle, that Mr Wright and Mrs Cookson were just going up to London to finalise that deal, and that therefore if the purchases were to be 'questionable', they would have a lien on the Hornby estate to recover their clients' money. They decided in the end to go ahead, but required that Mrs Cookson, Wright and Barrow should all witness Marsden's signature, 'and that each of us should also be a witness, the one for the other'. The bags of gold changed hands, and the solicitors rode off in their different directions; if for their own reasons they preserved a discreet silence then, it was incidents such as this which added to the groundswell of rumour about the strange situation at Hornby Castle. 'From the observation you made of Marsden's conduct on that day,' John Hartley was asked, 'did you think him a person competent to manage his own affairs?' 'I did not, indeed.' [12]

One of the papers signed on 16 April 1788 was not a sale but a mortgage for £10,000 on the newly-purchased Hornby estate. The money was provided by John and Alexander Anderson, London bankers. It was never proved that these were in fact clients of Giles Bleasdale, but it is a possibility well worth consideration. The very close friendship between Wright and Bleasdale was a matter of puzzlement to many people, but it is more easily explained if it had its roots here. It has already been established that, in spite of Bleasdale's denials, he and Wright were by this time well-acquainted and that he had several times visited Wennington.

Negotiations went on very slowly. Gisburn Hall was sold in 1788 to the neighbouring landowner of Gisburn Park, Thomas Lister, afterwards Lord Ribblesdale (no relation to the Listers of Giggleswick), but there was great difficulty in disposing of some of the other assets. A small estate in Whittington went in 1790; the manor of Allerton with Wilsden, near Bradford, was not sold until 1794; the old Bradford manor house not until 1797. Most part of the Wennington land, as has been related, went in various lots in 1788, but nobody offered to take the Hall itself and its demesne of 350 acres. It was not even easy to rent it: there were a good many inquirers, including Alexander Worswick, the Lancaster banker, but his attorney was John Taylor Wilson, who had known John Marsden since schooldays at Kirkby Lonsdale. Although in public Wilson maintained a conviction of Marsden's competence ('From what you knew of him would you at all have had any reluctance or objection in attesting his will? – Not in the least.'), he recommended that Worswick should not rent Wennington Hall without consulting counsel who 'advised Worswick not to touch it'. Worswick bought Leighton Hall instead.

Meanwhile large amounts of money had to be raised by mortgage, and this also, judging by the very large number of different mortgagors referred to, was not without its difficulties. William Housman of Lancaster lent £6000. No date is given to the transaction, and it may have been later, but this does not invalidate the story. He became alarmed and 'called it in, in consequence of an apprehension that he might be involved in some difficulty on the death of Mr Marsden arising from the doubts prevailing as to his capacity'. His alarm was fuelled, as well it might have been, by the fact that Marsden himself brought the annual interest to him on one occasion, 'and having some silver to count, he made the attempt, but never could get beyond a certain amount (very limited), and that after several ineffectual endeavours Mr Housman became quite distressed at the poor man's situation, and begged that he might be allowed to count the coin – to which Mr Marsden immediately consented'.[13]

In 1789 no less than £27,000 had to be raised, which was done from a John Lefevre. It is not difficult to suppose that Mrs Cookson sickened of the constant work and worry, and that the difference with Wright in 1789 was connected with this. The family continued to live at Wennington, while Hornby Castle and its land was rented to a farmer. Then a brilliant solution presented itself. The Lister family, in return for the understanding that they would inherit, should stump up the difference by buying Wennington Hall.

7

Wright in the Ascendant

Sarah Cookson's health had been declining through the year of 1791. In the summer she tried a visit to Buxton, taking John Marsden with her. They stayed for several weeks at a hotel, and ate at the public table with other guests come to drink the waters. Various letters went back and forth between Wright and Marsden, letters which were later produced as evidence of the normal relationship between master and man. It may equally be remarked that they show no permissions sought and granted, no sign of any kind of consultation. Marsden's side of the correspondence (the only one remaining) consisted of agreement after the event: 'I am glad that the Hay is all got in for the Weather at present is very unsettled. I am likewise glad that you are going to sell the Burton Estate: I hope to have a good price for it' … 'I am very well Satisfid to hear that you have let the Farm and the Melling and Wrayton Tithes so well' … 'I am glad that you have lett Beckett's Farm'. Such letters may sound like the natural responses of a gentleman who chose to leave all business in the hands of a trusted steward. One comment was, 'I take it for granted that he had given an order for the sale [of the Burton estate], and Wright was to get a buyer'.[1] If one does not wish to 'take it for granted' they may be read in quite another way.

The Buxton letters are not models of the formal epistolary style of the period but then Mrs Cookson was not a well-educated woman. John Smith, the servant who was with them, described the normal method of composition.

Now, have you ever seen Mrs Cookson give him any letter to copy? – Yes, I have.
   Have you seen him bring it back to her? – Yes.
   More than once? – Yes, or twice either.
   On his bringing it back, did he bring what he had written himself? – Yes, I suppose so.
   What did Mrs Cookson do with it? – She corrected it.

And when corrected, what did he do with it? – He took it to his room, and came back again.

Did she look over it again? – Yes.

How often was this sometimes done, before any one would do? – Half a dozen times, or five or six times.

When it would do, what would Mrs Cookson say to him? – I cannot say.

What became of these pieces of paper? – He used to tear them into bits, and I have taken them up off the carpet in his room.[2]

One letter seems to bear the stamp of John Marsden's own composition. Normally he hated letter-writing, as well he might if it consisted of copying and recopying like a schoolboy in detention, but this one sounds original, a piece of news so exciting to a simple mind that he really wanted to tell someone:

A disagreeable incident happened last Monday to a poor man employed by the Duke of Devonshire in pointing the back part of the Cresent, the Man fell from above the highest Window which was occationed by the Ballastraide giving way, the man & Skaffold & three rows of the Ballustraide with part of the Cornice fell down to the ground the Skaffold was fixed by a Rope & the noize in the fall was like that of Thunder. I thought he had been killed but it is a happy circumstance the person is in no dainger the Gentlemen here advized him to get blooded as soon as he could he is rather obstinate about it.[3]

That was perhaps a composition of Marsden with assistance from Elizabeth Tatham, who was also of the party.

The visit to Buxton ended in some disarray. According to John Smith, Marsden became embroiled with a couple of Irish gentlemen, on what pretext we do not know, but there is other evidence of his getting hold of inaccurate religious statements, and maintaining them with all the obstinacy of the weak-minded; references to Catholicism aroused him particularly. On this occasion, there was actually a challenge and, although Mrs Cookson apologised on her nephew's behalf, evidently the Irish gentlemen were not appeased. What revenge they wanted is not clear, but Marsden retreated to his room and locked himself in, refusing to come out until the danger was past, as he had often hidden in the privy from the turkey-cock. John Smith was dispatched post-haste the eighty-odd miles to Wennington to fetch George Wright, who came, probably in no very good mood, to sort things out.

Sarah Cookson died a few weeks later and was buried at Melling on 5 October 1791. She left instructions that her funeral was to cost no more than £20; and that apart from Mr Bickersteth and Mr Barrow, the doctor and the lawyer, people from the two villages of Melling and Wennington were the only ones to be bidden – an arrangement which may have saved the embarrassment of guests invited but refusing to come. Her nephew Henry Tatham was to have her shares in the Leeds and Liverpool Canal, and her other nephew, John Marsden, 'my watch, and all my rings, jewellery, trinketts, china ware, pictures, and handsome bound books'. Her maid, Rebecca Dodin, 'my olave silk gown, with suitable linnen for the same'; Elizabeth Tatham 'all my other silk gowns, with the best of my body linnen', the rest of her clothes to the women servants, but no mourning, and £5 to the poor of the two villages. All the rest, money and securities, and 'my New Testament with Mr Dodd's notes' to George Wright, who was sole executor. The witnesses were Henry Bickersteth, James Barrow and Robert Humber, the confidential gardener.[4]

Trying to interpret someone else's will is not easy work, but it does seem strange that after their eleven years' close association not a single personal item, bar one of doubtful relevance, came to George Wright. It would not, I think, be out of character had he made it brutally clear to her in her last days (she signed the will about four weeks before her death) that money would be far more welcome than tokens of sentimental value. He was no great church-goer: the New Testament may have been her own idea entirely.

After Mrs Cookson's death, and in spite of his affection for his cousin, Henry Tatham left. Even this 'man of most amiable disposition and universally beloved', who had lived happily with his aunt as a poor relation, could not swallow dependency on George Wright's charity. Fortunately for him, in July 1792 he was appointed Clerk of the Peace for Westmorland by Lord Lonsdale, no doubt through his Lowther connections. This, although the appointment referred to him as 'an able and sufficient Person, instructed and learned in the Laws of England', was a pure sinecure, which enabled him to appoint a deputy to do the work, and still enjoy a modest competence through 'the Fees, Profits and Perquisites thereof'.[5] His needs were not expensive: he lodged with a slater and plasterer near Hornby Castle gates, and ate his dinner each day across the road at the King's Head.

The move may have been voluntary, but George Wright seems also to have been determined to get rid of him. While the household remained at Wennington, Henry used occasionally to visit; but once they removed to Hornby the break was complete, and John Marsden never spoke to him again. 'If Mr Marsden who had been much attached to him, saw him, he would turn back to avoid him, it was believed and understood ... from fear of the resentment of Mr Wright.'[6] The last man to take umbrage, Henry used to watch him pass the window, and shake his head: 'Poor silly Jack ... poor fellow'. He lived until 1797 and, like many of his family, died suddenly of a stroke in his early forties.

After Henry's departure, the strange menage at Wennington consisted of George Wright, John Marsden and Elizabeth Tatham. From time to time, they were visited, said Jane Hill the maid, by 'Mr Lister who came out of Yorkshire, and a Mr Fitzgerald a lawyer from London ... but they had not much company'.

Deprived of his aunt and his cousin, kept from other companionship by the harsh tutelage of Wright, it seems to have been now that John Marsden developed his odd fetish for checked aprons – the working aprons that the servant girls and village women wore. William Thompson, who came to Wennington as a boy of twelve just after Mrs Cookson's death, and did a little of everything – sometimes drove the plough, sometimes attended Marsden, sometimes waited at table – remembered:

> He hath seen a checked apron in Mr Marsden's Bed – has also seen one in his Drawers. The lasses (that is, the Servant Maids) when they missed a Checked Apron knew where to look for it. They used to say Mr Marsden had got it. I uphold it, it was known to all the servants that he would take their checked aprons and take them to Bed with him. Sometimes it would be found in his Bed, sometimes in his Desk. I never knew him meddle with any other sort of Apron, or any other Women's apparel.[7]

> Mr Marsden [according to Jane Hill] very frequently came into the Servants' Hall where they were ironing the clothes and when the servants were not looking would take away as many chequered Aprons as he could conveniently take from the Horse, or stand, on which they were hanging, he took them into his bedroom and would then sit for hours counting the Stripes in the print with a pin and burst out into most violent bursts of laughter. When he could not succeed in getting them in the Servants' Hall he would take from the servants' rooms or any other place in the House into his own room. He has even taken them from Witness' Clothes Bag. Witness lived about three months at Wennington before she went to Wennington Hall. She recollects frequently seeing Mr Marsden stop children who had chequered aprons and examine them very minutely, he would seem quite delighted and would laugh very heartily.[8]

This habit, judging by the number of people who remembered it, seems to have lasted all his life, though whether continuously or recurrently it is not possible to say; perhaps it was a comforter in times of stress. Agnes Hogarth went as a maid to Hornby Castle in 1799:

The Maid servants had a Wardrobe in their Bed Chamber in which they kept their Cloaths. She hath missed her checked apron from her Shelf in the Wardrobe and found it in Mr Marsden's room. She hath heard him go along the passage, sometimes run and she hath heard his watch chain rattle as he went along, she suspected what he was about and would have kept out of the Way that he might not know she noticed him. He would keep it all Night and in the Morning that is in the Course of the forenoon she hath found it neatly folded up but different from what she did it, in the Lobby Window near her Bedroom when he took her apron away in the manner described she always fancied he was tipsy. When the drawing room was locked up so that he could not pass that way to get to the Maidroom, she hath known him come down into the Hall and run up again as if he was uneasy, and she hath taken her Checked apron and flung it over the Cloaths press which stood at the foot of the back stairs, as if it had been carelessly thrown there while she went into the room, and she hath found it gone and then he would have ceased from going up and down stairs and remained quiet. This was at a time when they had Company and she thought he was tipsy.[9]

Anthony Lister's servants at Bell Hill developed a theory that he had once been in love with a servant maid in a checked apron, and they too were in the habit of leaving one handy so that he could take it to bed.

If John Marsden's life was closing in, George Wright's continued to expand. He had begun to court Margaret Robinson, the 'cobbler's daughter' of Melling as John Lingard called her, before Mrs Cookson died. Although she was later sneered at for 'the awkwardness of her manners and the vulgarity of her language', it would seem that she should rather be admired for her willingness to marry into such a strange situation and, once there, to see herself as the housekeeper refusing, as far as possible, to move out of that sphere. 'Mrs Wright was accustomed to rise the first in the family and make up the kitchen and other fires, to cook the dinner, and when the general wash came round, to stand at the washing-tub and labour like any other woman servant.'[10] She sat at the bottom of the dinner table opposite her husband, it is true, but if there was company she dined elsewhere. The glimpses caught of her in the evidence show her doing the ironing, or refusing to have fires lit in spring once the chimneys had been swept and the paint washed, or getting angry with John Marsden because he hated the smell of his flannels when they had been washed in the old-fashioned way with 'chamber lye' (stale urine).

She seems to have been a kindly, unimaginative soul, good to Marsden within her very limited powers, contented that her husband should, as she no doubt believed he did, shine in society and mix with the great and the good, but not wishing to join him, and finding her satisfaction in modest housekeeping and the raising of her family.

The courting, carried on in secrecy until Mrs Cookson's death, resulted in many private walks through the woods to a rendezvous at old Mrs Robinson's in Melling. When he was a free agent, Wright used to go off to Hall Barns, Margaret's brother's farm, and stay the night. His absence was a ready signal for the Wennington servants 'to sit up and have a lark and enjoy themselves', having got rid of Marsden by telling him, when he came into the kitchen and asked the time (in spite of the 'very large clock with a large face and figures') that it was already ten o'clock and they were all just on their way to bed.[11]

The wedding, however, was delayed until the move to Hornby had been made. The move took place in the autumn of 1793, and on 4 March 1794, at Hornby Chapel, George Wright 'gentleman' was married to Margaret Robinson. Their first child was probably William, who died young. Then followed Eliza (1796), John Marsden (1798), Margaret (1800), Jane (1802), Dorothy (1804), Henry (1807) and William (1808). By 1797 it was very apparent that the Castle was not suitable for a lot of children, and in that year a new wing was built, consisting of kitchen, housekeeper's room and other offices, with rooms over them; there were three bedrooms over the kitchens, and two nurseries over the brewhouse. Gillows of Lancaster were appointed to do the fittings, and one of their joiners said that George Wright 'directed everything and seemed entirely Master of the House. He used frequently this expression "I say, I'll have it so" and was very peremptory in his orders'.[12]

It does not seem that this new building was a sign that money had become easier. Among the extant scatter of letters emanating from Thomas Greene's office in London, there are several indicating that 1796 and 1797 were particularly tight years, owing to the Mr Lefevre who had lent £27,000 wanting it back again. He said he needed it because he was buying himself an estate in Hampshire: perhaps, like William Housman, he also had cold feet.

Various plans to raise the sum, or raise enough of it to keep the creditor happy, were outlined to Greene, whose feet were also cold, as he kept denying that he could raise any money in London and insisting that it must be raised in Lancashire. Banks and bankers were still few and far between, and it was one of an attorney's normal business interests to put borrowers and lenders in touch with each other.

It was suggested that £8000 might be raised by selling off the corn tithes of the estate; a bill was to go through Parliament to enfranchise the customary tenants which might raise between £2000 and £3000; £7000 was ultimately borrowed from a Mr Bell, a lawyer; if they could sell a house in the Strand it would bring in £500. It is not possible to follow all that was happening from the few letters available, but their atmosphere is tense, although the civilities are kept up by postscripts concerning barrels of oysters and presents of game exchanged between London and the country.

The letters between Lefevre and Hornby Castle over the period show increasing anxiety and diminishing expectations on the one side and smooth delaying tactics on the other:

From Lefevre:

It is impossible for me to describe the very unpleasant situation to which I am reduced by not receiving the small part of the Mortgage money which I requested ... oblige me so far as to supply me with £7000.
(27 August 1797)

Mr Carter has given me notice of an immediate Action upon my Bond unless it is satisfied without delay, this I promised him should be done relying on your Assistance ... oblige me with a draft for £5500.
(25 October 1798)

This circumstance gives me real uneasiness and exposes me to a variety of applications ill suited to my present concerns, or to the impaired state of my Health ... at least remit me £3000.
(14 March 1799)

I most particularly entreat you to send me up any sum you may have to spare £1200 or £1500 before the 1st of June.[13]
(25 May 1799)

Over Marsden's signature:

Nothing ever hurt me so much as not having it in my power the last January to comply with your request, the times being so that it was impossible to dispose of property on any terms ... I am in treaty for some tithes which I hope to conclude very soon but the money will not

be paid for those till the 13th January, as all money transactions in this
part is at that time of year.

(30 August 1797)

am using every means in my power ... I am now offering tithes for Sale
to each landowner by which means I hope and trust I shall be enabled
to accommodate you.

(25 October 1798)

my disappointment the week before of £8000 which I expected to have
received on the 16th instant and to have remitted to you the Sum you
mentioned.

(25 February 1799)

I have sent this day to a friend of mine to desire he will accommodate
me and offered him as a security for £3000 property worth £11,000 ...
nothing ever gave me such uneasiness and anxiety of mind by dis-
appointing you after I had every reason to expect the money in February.

(17 March 1799)

I shall still persist in using every means I am possessed of to procure
the Sum you want ... my mind has been so much agitated by disap-
pointments that I have not had an easy hour.

(9 April 1799)

Money has been so exceedingly scarce here that property was not to
be sold at any price.[13]

(28 May 1799)

No more letters have been preserved, and how the unfortunate Mr
Lefevre's affair ended does not appear, but we may be sure he wished
he had never embroiled himself. It would seem to be at this juncture
that the idea arose of selling Wennington Hall to the Listers for the
necessary £27,000. It must have seemed to Wright and to his crony
Giles Bleasdale a solution beautiful in its simplicity. It is much more
difficult to see why the Listers fell for it, but they did.

The elder Anthony must, it seems, have regarded the transaction as
more of an investment than a gamble. At some time before this,
probably before they left Wennington, John Marsden, never a good
rider, had had a serious accident out hunting. He had fallen on the
pommel of his saddle. The injury kept him in bed for several weeks,
and the result it seems was effective castration. His aunt Cookson and
George Wright had never intended to let him marry, and now there
was much less reason for a woman to entice or entrap him, since there
could be no children. So the inheritance would go by will, or if there

were no will, to the heir at law – at this time William Tatham; 'American' Tatham, as he was often called.

There was already a will in existence. Sarah Cookson had made sure of that very soon after Henry Marsden's death. The first one, it is said on rather shaky but quite plausible evidence, had named her as the chief beneficiary. Whether in that one, or another after her death, the Tatham brothers were prominently named. But the Tatham brothers had been successively alienated from John Marsden's affections: it was no surprise, after just one brief meeting, that Sandford's name was blackened, but the case of Henry Tatham, the kindly, affectionate, intimately known cousin, shows how easily Wright could engineer Marsden's responses.

Young Anthony Lister was the most obvious next choice. Marsden loved the family, with whom he spent a couple of months each year, and was devoted to the boy, who spent much of his school and university vacations shooting and fishing and enjoying himself at Hornby. It would be quite within Marsden's understanding to make choice of him as his heir. 'Who would you like, when you are dead, to have your lands and your castle?' Nobody ever doubted, on either side of the case, that such a simple question, disinterestedly put to him, could be satisfactorily answered. How early it was answered in Anthony Lister's favour it is not possible to say. The only evidence for a whole series of wills is from Giles Bleasdale, which is tainted, but we may I think believe him when he said that Marsden rather liked making wills, and changing them, and that he had taken pleasure in throwing one into the fire, saying 'There go the Tathams'. This simple level of understanding his own position of power matches with Miss Dorothy Butler's succinct phrase on another occasion: 'He was dressed in scarlet and told me he was Lord of Hornby Castle, and seemed extremely happy.'[14]

The Listers, therefore, only had to believe that Wright would stay on their side or, if push came to shove, that their influence over Cousin Jack would be the more powerful of the two. Where a good deal of money is involved, it is easy to be optimistic. There were warning voices. As young Anthony Lister used to ride between Bell Hill, Giggleswick, and Hornby Castle, he often dropped in to the Ridding in Bentham, where Thomas Butler lived, who in 1780 had refused to invite the newly-elevated George Wright into his house. His son, another Thomas Butler, and a near contemporary of Lister's, 'cautioned him as to the Arts of George Wright', and warned him that Wright would use him. Lister was confident that, though he hated Wright and Wright hated him, he visited Hornby for his cousin's sake and could manage the situation. It is probable that a number of people, faced with George Wright's thick accent and lack of spelling, mistakenly presumed him to be no match for a gentleman.[15]

Friends and Neighbours

John Marsden lived at Hornby Castle for thirty-two years, under the direction of George Wright. Wright ran the estate and managed its owner, controlled all input and output, comings and goings. He did not try to soften the edges of his dominating personality and everyone, it would seem, trod very carefully in his presence. Even Giles Bleasdale, who was perhaps most nearly his equal, was seen to suffer in silence the rough edge of his tongue, and others on whom he had to rely to compensate for his educational weaknesses never showed any sign of taking advantage of their position. William Sharp, the confidential attorney, showed in every word he spoke how in Hornby Castle he hovered on the edge of subserviency. George Smith, the confidential clerk, who must have written Wright's letters and known almost all there was to know, never took advantage. Mrs Wright kept in the background and the children were dutiful. Poor little Miss Tatham suffered herself to be put to bed among the maidservants and lived in such poverty that Sandford Tatham, speaking to her when he passed through Hornby on a rare occasion, sent her money to buy linen for underclothes; when she died in 1809, her long delayed inheritance having either arrived or being on the brink of arrival, she left almost every penny to George Wright's family.

As soon as they moved to the most prestigious estate in the Lune Valley, Wright set about building up his social position. It was accepted that no local ladies would visit, Mrs Wright's society consisting of farmers' wives coming for tea and cards and to admire the children, but he in his position as Steward, a very knowledgeable, very efficient steward, was constantly out in the world mixing with professional men and gentlemen. He had something to offer. He had the traditional old-fashioned hospitality of a country house, where a good dinner was set on the table every afternoon at a table big enough to take guests without embarrassment; and he had the control of a sporting estate – hounds in the kennels, deer in the park, moorcock on the moors, salmon and trout in the Lune and Wenning, young rooks in the spring elms, hares, rabbits, partridges, the occasional black game. Sport is a wonderful leveller and Wright himself was a keen and competent sports-man. People found themselves on terms which they might not have expected, and mixing with others whom they might not have chosen. Even people like Charles Gibson of Quernmore Park kept up a courtesy visit once a year because he also had hounds, while less choice neigh-bours, like the Bradshaw brothers of Halton Park, did not mind who provided them with sport and a good round of beef afterwards.

There was always a preponderance of professionals over gentry, the professionals consisting mainly of solicitors and clergymen, though Alexander Worswick the banker, John Stout, the well-to-do draper of Lancaster, Richard Gillow the furniture-maker, Anthony Eidsforth the West Indian trader, all just climbing into gentrydom, were pleased with this intermediate step. There were at that time a lot of people on the make; in another twenty or thirty years, when they had attained their goal, they would not have dreamt of patronising, or being patronised by, George Wright. But the same twenty or thirty years would alter his status too. He was climbing along with them, and it is noticeable that some of his most respectable acquaintance, including, it must be said, one or two ladies, date from the 1820s.

As both Marsden and Wright had a vote, and could, moreover, process into Lancaster at election time with the Hornby estate voters behind them, canvassing politicians could not be less than polite, and one in particular was happy to pay for years of political backing by supporting Wright with inventive enthusiasm. John Fenton Cawthorne was popular in the area for certain gestures, such as his generous support of the Lancaster schools, but loathed by his tenants in Wyresdale for his meanness. He was court-martialled in 1796, being cashiered for fraud-ulent misapplication of the funds of the militia regiment he commanded, and expelled from the House of Commons as a result. However, he bounced back to win a Lancaster seat in the Tory interest several times between 1812 and his death in 1831. He was constantly in debt: he is said on one occasion to have asked his dinner guests to slip the silver into their pockets, because the bailiffs had arrived.

It is perhaps understandable that a slight air of seediness pervaded the guest list of the Castle. Many of the local gentry refused steadfastly to be on terms of dining at Marsden's table. The list of genuine 'broadcloth', in the current idiom, was thin and relied heavily on the legal profession. There was Thomas Greene of London and his brother-in-law Thomas Greene Bradley, and Messrs Baldwin, Dowbiggin and

Sharp, members of the Lancaster firm who represented the Castle interest. William Sharp, in particular, a young attorney whose senior partner handed over the Hornby Castle work entirely to his junior, grew grey in its service, but never lost his starry-eyed satisfaction at being on such special terms with such a special place.

> Did you see Mr Marsden occasionally, or at all, or frequently, or how? – Frequently. I was in the habit of staying all night, for two or three nights in a week, for a long period, and saw a great deal of him ... I used frequently to go and stop all night and take breakfast for the sake of the ride out.
>
> Was Mr Marsden in the habit of calling upon you in Lancaster? – He did. I should think he hardly ever came to Lancaster that he did not call, or if he were going to dine out he would call and ask me to go with him. He would take me in his carriage ...
>
> Have you dined there occasionally? – Very often. A great deal in parties, but generally in their own family way. I never omitted, if I was in the neighbourhood, to go there to dine, without invitation ...
>
> Now at Mr Marsden's table did you meet many persons or few? – Almost all the gentlemen of the neighbourhood visited him; all the respectable gentlemen in the neighbourhood visited him.[1]

And he proceeded to detail the 'respectable gentlemen' with a relish which shines through the shorthand-writer's notes.

The Reverend Thomas Clarkson of Heysham and his brother Townley were two of the most frequent parsonical visitors. Thomas was a sporting parson with a doubtful reputation. ('Was he a gentleman?' 'Yes, for anything I knew.' 'Is that the way you speak of your master, with whom you were seven years?' 'Yes; he was a gentleman; he was a clergyman.' 'And a man of weakly habits?' 'Yes he was.')[2] He kept hounds which may have begun the acquaintance, but it ripened into a closer association. George Wright began to take a particular interest in Heysham, an outlying parish on the River Lune, quite hard to reach from Lancaster because of the mosses in between, but which suddenly, for its pure sea air and spectacular sunset views over Morecambe Bay, began to be popular for rich men's summer residences. George Wright looked ahead to his well-earned retirement and began to negotiate for land.

One of the most useful perquisites of a big estate was the advowsons it included: the rights of presentation to church livings. When the Hornby estate was advertised by the Wemyss family, the advertisement included the ages of its sitting parsons at Melling, Hornby, Tatham and Tatham Fell, so that prospective buyers could estimate how long it might be before they could use this patronage.[3] John Marsden also had in his gift the lucrative vicarage of Gargrave near Skipton, part of the old Marsden estate. The sitting incumbent was Mr Croft who had been his tutor. In 1806 the advowson was sold by Wright in a shady deal to old Anthony Lister, so that young Anthony could move in as vicar.[4] This promotion, and his expectations regarding Hornby Castle, allowed young Anthony to marry Mary Yorke of Wetherby, a very well-connected and, it was said, very ambitious woman. Young Anthony moved into the best circles of Craven and York gentry, leaving behind his father, a man, it was said, 'whose Manners and Appearance were not superior to Wright's'.

This was not achieved without friction, and the Listers also came to feel that they had been cheated over Wennington Hall. It is not known whether they paid the full £27,000 that Wright wanted, but in a situation in which there was no competition at all, almost any sum could be reckoned as above the market value. It would be easier to sympathise with young Anthony Lister had he been in a different profession. While clergymen may be supposed to be above trading their moral standards for gain, that is perhaps a sentimental attitude, especially in days when the church was a profession for aspiring gentry, on the same footing as the army and the law. If he deserves any sympathy, it is because he was outclassed and outgunned from start to finish. Wright chose well, or worked well with Mrs Cookson's choice, and was never in less than total command of the situation. More than one person who inquired whether it was true that Lister would inherit from Marsden heard Wright answer that 'it depended on how the Chap behaved whether he got anything'.

Twice, over the years, a convenient way of keeping the Listers in line turned up, and was as readily exploited. Much correspondence was produced in court by Wright's counsel as proof of John Marsden's normality, but these two series can also be read as deliberate ploys to tease Anthony Lister with the suggestion that he must not regard his inheritance as necessarily safe.

The first series was from William Dawson of London and St Leonards, a second cousin with a large family and a greedy wife. They were rich merchants, with a country house near Windsor and a town house in Manchester Square, but they were also probably living beyond their means, having three sons to educate and five daughters to settle in life. The first letter came out of the blue, instigated, it was always said, by Mrs Dawson. William Dawson and John Marsden had met at least once at Hornby, probably only once. Wright, therefore, may have had an

opportunity to assess the visitor. The letter, read from one angle, was
a piece of family courtesy, innocuous enough, referring to family news
and to plans, then in the air, for extensive modernisation of Hornby
Castle.

You will be surprized at receiving a line from me but I cannot resist
communicating to you as well as to my other friends an event that is
soon likely to take place in my family. My second daughter Harriot is
going to be married to Mr Charles Shand the only Son of a Gentleman
of the first respectability in this neighbourhood and of considerable
fortune. This union affords every prospect of happiness and is every
way satisfactory to all the connections ... Should any occurrence bring
you to London I should be happy to shew you the improvements I have
been making at my residence here under the directions of Mr James
Wyatt who has planned me a Hall that is universally admired in the
Gothic Style and quite adapted to your beautiful situation.[5]

The response from Marsden, after the proper civilities and congrat-
ulations, ended with what could be read as an enticement to anyone
whose mind was moving that way: 'Should you favour me with another
letter, you will oblige me by informing me how many children you
have and their names'. The required list was not long in coming, and
many years afterwards Mrs Dawson admitted that her mind had indeed
been moving that way, though she denied that they were fishing for
anything other than possible small bequests. The correspondence continued in a desultory fashion until John Marsden's death, or rather it
continued on William Dawson's part, telling of his sons' professional
advancement, his wife and daughters being invited to 'Mrs Egerton's
on Castle Hill to meet her Majesty', house improvements and marble
fireplaces, and a good deal about his own health. Two of the sons paid
brief visits to Hornby, but it would seem that the correspondence, as
far as Wright was concerned, had served its purpose and was allowed
to lapse.

In the same year as the first Dawson letter, 1811, another letter
arrived from an Alexander Marsden of Ireland, giving details of his
family history and his own career – he was the Chief Commissioner of
Revenue for Ireland.

In such a situation I need not add that my income is ample, and my
circumstances altogether independent. Having married happily several
years ago, I have Three Daughters; and I regret to add they are the
only persons of the Family which was settled here, who carry the name
to the next generation, neither of my Brothers having Children, tho'

married; and my Sister being Maiden ... my Girls are, one with another, about fifteen years old, well looking and very well educated.[6]

Marsden's answer to this undisguised opening of negotiations was more welcoming than it had any need to be unless the correspondence was to be used in skirmishing with the Listers. It is clear that Wright had no intention of allowing Marsden to marry, but the answer appeared to leave all avenues open. Marsden gave details of his own family history (later quoted as evidence of his intelligence, but which was in fact, apart from those names and dates which could be gleaned from the inscriptions in Melling church, all wrong). He issued a general invitation to Alexander Marsden, 'and should it be in the Shooting Season, I think I can promise as much diversion in that way as most private Country Gentlemen can Command'.

Soon afterwards the invitation was taken up. Passing through Hornby with one of his daughters, as he said, Alexander Marsden sent up a note from the inn, and they dined with their supposed relative. One wonders what they thought of the meeting, and whether there was any significance in the fact that the letter of thanks from Dublin said 'I am sorry to tell you that my Daughter who was with me at Hornby Castle has been very much indisposed since her return'. The correspondence continued, borne mainly by Alexander Marsden, giving family news, commenting on the political events of the day. It faded out in 1820.

From 1806 onwards an important place in Castle affairs was held by the Reverend Robert Procter of Hornby. He was a local man, born at Long Preston in 1761, and had attended Kirkby Lonsdale school for a while with John Marsden; he was about three years Marsden's junior in age, but a long way ahead of him in attainment. His first appointment, in 1784, was as Curate to the old Vicar of Tunstall, whom he then followed as Vicar, until 1800. While he was at Tunstall he married Jane Tatham of Cantsfield and raised a family. He held two other curacies in the Lune Valley, Claughton and Gressingham, but resigned them in 1806 to become Perpetual Curate of Hornby. This benefice he retained to his death, for many years making ends meet with a small preparatory school – perhaps a dozen boys living in his house, his wife looking after them and he teaching them. He had two daughters and one rather unsatisfactory son, Edmund, who was sent off to the East Indies to make his fortune.

Never a strong man, either in health or character, Procter had an important role as John Marsden's intimate and best friend in the village, a role he may have acquired because of their shared schooldays, and perhaps played the better because he too suffered under Wright's heavy hand. In his early days at Hornby, when money was very short at the Castle, great pressure was put on him to lend Marsden £500, which Wright knew that he had, and he gave in. At a later time, far from having any cash to spare, he himself was in debt to Wright, by dribs and drabs, until the sum added up alarmingly (one suspects the unsatisfactory Edmund), and then indeed he was open to pressure, which was duly applied.

His brother-in-law, Edmund Tatham of Cantsfield House, also came within the Castle orbit. This family had the most tenuous connection with the Admiral, but had been long established in the village of Cantsfield. It had always been prolific in parsons, and a first cousin, the Reverend John Tatham, was Vicar of Melling, the next village to Hornby and its mother church.

The Reverend Robert Procter spent a good deal of time at the Castle, and as Wright's daughters grew up there was some intimacy between them and the Misses Procter, leading to tea-drinkings and card-playings in one house or the other. John Marsden frequented the Vicarage; he would talk to Procter as he would talk to no one else. Although the young ladies found his company extremely irksome at times, they tolerated him with good humour.

Jane Procter, the elder daughter, could speak to more than twenty years acquaintance during which time, she said, she saw John Marsden almost every day, either at the Castle or at her father's house. 'He seemed to have no employment but playing the same Tune on his Violin.' Often he was very silent, but when he talked it would be on the same subject as yesterday and the day before: 'He used daily for months together to talk of his new seat in the chapel, and of the new pulpit and organ for some years.' He used to talk to himself aloud. Sitting by the window, she often heard him in the street outside saying 'Shall I call on Mr Procter?' and then answer himself 'No' or 'Yes'. 'He seemed to possess no authority in his own house and was as submissive as a child to Mr Wright. If Mr Marsden was sitting in the arm-chair when Mr Wright entered the room, he generally rose and left the chair for Mr Wright, in whose presence Mr Marsden was more reserved and more on his guard than at other times. He was afraid of Mr Wright hearing him talk to other persons.'[7]

She heard him scolded like a child for dropping cake crumbs or spilling on the tablecloth. She quoted Jane Wright as saying that her father always picked a quarrel with Marsden the evening before company was expected, and found occasion to give him a good scolding 'that he might not expose himself by an excess of spirits the ensuing day, for after a quarrel of that sort, Mr Marsden was in low spirits until they were reconciled'. She saw the family start dinner without him, serve him last with what was left on the dish, leave him out when the cake was handed round, hand him a plate and then pull it away, jog his elbow as he was going to drink his tea, 'not only while they were children but after they were grown up. He bore all patiently. Mr and Mrs Wright did not check them, but laughed'. It was mean, it was petty, and given the claustrophobic conditions of life at the time, lamentably understandable.

Mary Procter, the younger daughter, may have been less soft-hearted than her sister. She had no hesitation in acknowledging that Mr Marsden's 'sayings and doings afforded (on account of the imbecility which they manifested), a constant source of amusement'. For years he spent about two hours a day in her father's house, she said, and always had something private to say to Mr Procter, and was very suspicious that Mary would listen 'which she frequently threatened to do'. 'Mr Marsden was sometimes troublesome.' He would try to pat and kiss the girls, and Mary kept him in order by threatening to prick him with a pin, or taking her yard measure and laying it conspicuously on the table, when 'he would laugh and seem afraid and do as he was bid'. And on other occasions, at the Castle, she would say 'I hear Mr Wright coming', which had a magical effect. Mary sometimes tried him on his multiplication table: 'He could never tell how much 3 times 7 made unless he were allowed to begin 3 times 3 and continue. But if he were asked how much 7 times 3 made he was puzzled, grew angry, and would answer no more'.

Even Mr Procter was not guiltless in the matter of a little teasing. Once friends were present who had been regaled with the saga of the checked aprons. 'The bell was rung, and the servant maid having put on a narrow check (the narrower they were the more lovely in his eyes) came in with a box of cards. Mr Marsden was talking but instantly became silent, knit his brows, fixed his eyes upon the checked apron, and with a smile of delight followed the motions of the girl until she left the room.' Then her father said 'Squire, what do you mean? I will not suffer you to take liberties with my servants'.

Whatever the rest of the small Hornby society thought of him, George Wright had one great friend, Giles Bleasdale. In 1810 Bleasdale rented Wenning Cottage as a holiday home, and in 1816 retired from his London office to the north. He said it was to be near some poor relations, but the poor relations were thirty miles away in Yorkshire, and his visits to them were not remarkable for their frequency. The house was done up for him very pleasantly by his landlords, using of course the materials and the workmen from the Castle. The garden being small, he enclosed a piece of the Common, apparently with Wright's approval, and lived very comfortably, with a housekeeper and a manservant.

Hardly a day passed without traffic between the cottage and the Castle – a footpath was cleared through the woods by the Castle wood-men to facilitate it. Bleasdale walked over to dine, or some of the family walked over to him. The Wright girls took turns to stay at his house. He and Wright could be seen at times walking arm-in-arm in the Park, endlessly conversing. At other times they spent many hours in the study together. Nobody could quite fathom why they were such friends, least of all, Mary Procter:

> Mr Bleasdale on all occasions seemed more alive to the interest of Mr Wright and the advancement of his Family than Wright himself. Bleasdale omitted no occasion of speaking of Wright in terms of the highest praise in his absence, and before Mr Marsden he loaded the Family with benefits, he made the Ladies presents of Piano Fortes, Trinkets, Gold Watches, Silks, Linen, Boots, Gloves and Stockings etc. etc., to the family a constant supply of Tea, Furniture, Brussels Carpets, Table Linen, Crockery etc. and to John Wright large presents of money as often as he left home, and yet when seen together and observed, the manner in which Wright treated Bleasdale, it would have been thought that the latter owed a debt of gratitude to Wright and his Family. Wright and Bleasdale were often closeted together for hours. Wright seemed to possess an extraordinary influence over him, he often contradicted Bleas-dale so rudely that the latter could not conceal his feelings, but though his lips quivered with vexation he never retorted, but bore it patiently.[8]

There appeared, she concluded, and said that others had noticed it too, 'something very mysterious in their friendship'.

A

HISTORY

OF

ENGLAND

FROM THE

FIRST INVASION BY THE ROMANS

TO

THE ACCESSION OF HENRY VIII.

BY THE REV. JOHN LINGARD.

IN THREE VOLUMES.

VOL. I.

LONDON:

PRINTED FOR J. MAWMAN 39 LUDGATE STREET.

1819.

Title page of John Lingard's *History of England*.

9

Dr Lingard

The Reverend Robert Procter was not the only cleric in Hornby. Unusually for the time, across the road from the parish church, there was a Catholic chapel. And while this remote village housed in the Castle the makings of a legal cause célèbre, in the small, neat house in the village street below, there dwelt a nationally and internationally renowned churchman. This was the Catholic priest, Dr John Lingard. As his own flock of souls numbered under a hundred, his church duties were light, and Dr Lingard had time enough to pursue his studies, which were directed to the task of writing a complete history of England. Even more remarkable, this great work was not to be a polemic for his own church but a work in which the truthful picture, modestly and moderately drawn, could not fail to make friends, he hoped, among all just men:

> It has been my constant endeavour to separate myself as much as possible from every party: to stand as it were aloof, the unconcerned spectator of the passing events; and to record them fairly in these pages as they come in review before my eyes. That they should always appear so to others, in the same light in which they appeared to me, I cannot expect, but before the reader accuse me of prejudice, let him be assured that he is free from prejudice himself.[1]

After 1826, Sandford Tatham had no more vigorous or useful ally than John Lingard. He was a late comer on the scene, arriving in 1811 and staying until his death in 1851. He had been born in Winchester in 1771, of a Catholic mother and a father who was probably a nominal Protestant. John Lingard the elder was a prosperous house carpenter; John Lingard the younger was an only child, a bright, cheerful and attractive boy. A Catholic education in those days meant education abroad. Sixty-five years later, he wrote to a friend: '30 September 1782, a boy called John Lingard entered the portals of Douai College. Deo Gratias. I have always kept this day with a bottle of my best wine. I wish you were here to partake with me.'[2]

Things were becoming easier for Catholics. In 1778 the Catholic Relief Act had been passed, partially repealing the Penal Laws, and by another coincidence, one of the chief immediate causes of this Act, which Edmund Burke and Charles Fox supported with all their powerful eloquence, was also found in Hornby village. Thomas Benison, a wealthy lawyer, was the second, or perhaps third, of a family which had made its money by conducting the legal business of Hornby Castle. About 1730 he built himself a handsome house in the village, married a local Catholic woman, and had one daughter, also brought up a Catholic, who became his very considerable heiress. Anne Benison married in 1752 John Fenwick, a rich local landowner of Burrow Hall, but when he died in 1757 in a hunting accident, without children, all his estates, which included hers, went to his brother, a lawyer of Gray's Inn, and this brother invoked the rusty Penal Laws to claim all of Anne Fenwick's inheritance as well as her husband's.

Fortunately for her, Mrs Fenwick was a woman with a good education and a great deal of determination. Even better, she knew some important people in London. It took her fifteen years, but in 1772 Lord Camden took a private Bill through the House of Lords to defeat her brother-in-law and return her inheritance to her. Out of this result, which was generally welcomed by the public, came the Relief Act of 1778. By that time Mrs Fenwick herself was dead, but she had left her chaplain, Thomas Butler, enough money to build a comfortable house next door to her own, with a chapel under the same roof and a handsome garden, and a farm whose rent would endow the chapel. She also left him furniture and plate to live like a gentleman of modest means, and, having no children, her family portraits. These still hang on the stairs in the Hornby Presbytery.[3]

The Relief Act for which her case had been the trigger was not universally welcomed. Hostility broke out in the Gordon Riots of 1780, a week of wild anti-Catholic terrorism. In London the chapels of Catholic embassies and more than fifty houses of known Catholics, as well as public buildings, were burnt and looted by frenzied mobs. The government, although inert in face of the violence, was at least not blackmailed into repealing the Act, and the long, slow advance towards the Catholic Emancipation Act of 1829 proceeded, an advance in which Lingard's influence, though it cannot be measured exactly, was not insignificant.

John Lingard spent twelve years at Douai, the English College near Lille, setting out a boy of ten and returning at the age of twenty-two. Like other clever boys he learnt, as well as Latin, Greek and Hebrew, to speak and write French as fluently as English. Almost all of those who attended the College were destined to return as priests to a country which still had some draconian laws against them on its statute books. All the same, in no way did they lose their Englishness, and Douai College was a centre of fervent expatriate loyalty. On more than one occasion, the local magistrates sent round to request that the young gentlemen should not disturb the peace quite so noisily when there was news of a British victory. 'The salutary and incontrovertible truth', wrote another of the College's alumni, 'that one Englishman can any day beat two Frenchmen was as firmly believed and as ably demonstrated at Douay and St Omer as it could be at Eton or Winchester.'

Lingard's passion was for history. He read as much English history as he could, and in particular, since these were probably the books most readily available, the history of the Reformation and the Catholic Church in England, from which he derived a standpoint not wholly orthodox. For instance, in view of the machinations of the early Jesuits, he found the reactions of Elizabeth's government understandable. 'For certainly the conduct of Fathers Campion and Persons furnished a very plausible pretext for the first *murderous* laws against us, and the gunpowder plot for the second batch under James I.'[4] Later he found that reconciling the honesty of a good historian with the loyalty of a good Catholic, and in particular with the anxiety not to rock the boat which was sailing towards Catholic Emancipation, was a difficult and delicate task.

After his return to England, the English College at Douai, broken up by the new regime in France, was reconstituted at Ushaw in Durham. There Lingard was ordained a priest, and there he worked until 1810, when after the death of the first President, he was pressured to succeed him. At forty he was an impressive figure, a fine teacher, a first-class scholar, a thinker who could argue cogently and moderately, and a maker of many friends. He also had a few enemies, mainly in the conservative wing of his own church.

He had already had a literary success with *The Antiquities of the Anglo-Saxon Church*, published in 1806, which had gone through two editions and had reached a wide audience. 'My object is truth', he said, 'and in the pursuit of truth I have made it a religious duty to consult the original historians',[5] which was not at all the obvious statement then that we might consider it now. Historical writers, even serious ones, were often content to cobble up the opinions of other writers. In contrast, Lingard had taught himself Anglo-Saxon as part of his 'religious duty'. ('The knowledge of that language', he said in a typical throwaway line, 'though an easy is not a common acquirement.')

He refused the Presidency of Ushaw, and of St Edmund's College, Ware, which he was also offered, on the grounds that he would not do the job well. 'I have not sufficient nerve. Of a timid and indulgent disposition, always eager to please and abhorring the very idea of giving pain, I am not the person to preserve discipline or to struggle against difficulty ... It is a lesson which I have learned from experience.'[6]

In 1811 a sensible hierarchy appointed him to Hornby. There he had a widely scattered cure of about thirty families, from Aughton, Arkholme, Hornby, Wray, Gressingham, Bentham, a nice little house, and enough money, between Mrs Fenwick's endowment and what he could earn by his pen, to live in very modest comfort and indulge his great gift for making friends in every walk of life. When the Lancaster Assizes were on, Henry Brougham, afterwards Lord Chancellor, Frederick Pollock, an uncompromising Tory, and James Scarlett, an uncompromising Whig, the three legal stars of the northern circuit, never failed to hire a chaise and come out to Hornby to dine and enjoy an evening of excellent conversation. Robert Procter across the way, ten years the senior but a much weaker as well as a less intelligent man, found him a tower of strength when times got rough.

The peace and quiet of Hornby made an attractive background for a scholar, but the logistics were not easy. Acquiring books was expensive, borrowing them almost impossible. Even if Lingard travelled to London, as he did from time to time, there was as yet no British Museum Reading Room, no London Library, and it was extremely difficult to get access to the State Paper Office in the Tower of London. He corresponded voluminously with anyone who could provide him with original copies. His immediate neighbours could not help much. To them he was less the scholar than an invariably cheerful and humorous companion, a keen gardener, and in the winter a skater, whose ability to 'cut his name in the ice' was long remembered. As a matter of course, when he arrived he was invited to dine at Hornby Castle; but he disliked what he found there so much that he cut his visits to a minimum, and after about six years gave them up altogether, which Procter could not afford to do.

Lingard valued the customs and manners of good society very highly – perhaps he was a bit of a snob. He once wrote to a friend at Ushaw: 'I think it would be well if you were to instruct the divines not only how to behave at the altar but also at table. I mean as to drinking wine etc. when asked. I have observed some of them holding their knives very oddly'. It appalled him to find John Marsden, however mentally incompetent, seated at the side of a table of which George Wright took the head and Mrs Wright the foot. Although there was nothing in common, courtesy drove him at first to call on Mr Marsden every five or six weeks, and dine at the Castle when asked, eight or ten times a year. Marsden sometimes called on him, and dined with him once or twice. If they met in the village, they would stop to talk.

It was very difficult, Lingard said, to maintain any conversation with him alone. 'You were obliged to talk with him as with a child, to ask him questions which you would be ashamed to put to any sensible person.' In company with others Marsden appeared to more advantage; Lingard noticed that he would repeat remarks which he had heard, particularly if they contained a pun, surprising those who thought them spontaneous:

> I have heard Mr Wright make a remark, which Mr Marsden has after-
> wards repeated to different persons ... Sometimes Mr Wright would
> check him, calling out, what do you know about that? Mr Marsden used
> to talk about politics, but had only confused notions such as a child
> would pick up from the discourse of others. I asked him about the
> Jacobins. He told me they were Men that sought to pull down Kings
> and Lords of Manors. Why sir, they would pull down Hornby Castle if
> they could. All the friends of Mr Fox were Jacobins – all Dissenters. If
> you mentioned a Dissenter he would say 'He is a Dissenter sir, he is a
> Jacobin'.[7]

On one occasion, Lingard and two or three other gentlemen being present in the Hornby Castle dining-room, John Marsden rose from his seat and went towards the door, upon which George Wright said to him in a stern manner 'Where are you going?' and John Marsden muttered some answer which was not distinctly understood. Wright then called out to him in the same manner 'Where are you going I say?' and Marsden said that he was going to give a letter to a servant. George Wright then said, 'Where is it?' and Marsden answered that it was in his pocket. George Wright said 'Put it on the sideboard and come and sit down', upon which John Marsden took a letter from his waistcoat pocket, laid it upon the sideboard and resumed his seat. Lingard could not be certain whether he smiled or was in tears, but he appeared to be in distress and to be endeavouring to conceal his feelings under a smile.

The incident decided Lingard that neighbourliness could only go so far, and it had gone far enough. He did not choose to seem to under-write by his presence a regime in which 'George Wright spoke of John Marsden as the Owner of Hornby Castle but acted as if he were the Master of it himself'. At the time, in 1817, he was just about to join some friends in a visit to Italy and Rome. When he came back, he never accepted another invitation to the Castle. For his pains, he found that Marsden was schooled to refer to him as a Jesuit, and to say that he was no longer invited because he repeated elswehere whatever he heard at the Castle.

In 1819 the first three volumes of *A History of England from the First Invasion by the Romans to the Accession of William and Mary* were published, in 1820 the fourth. They had an immediate and resounding success, and made John Lingard famous, although some members of his own church took bitter exception to the moderate tone of his writing. He was offered a bishopric, which he refused. He used some of the profits to build a new chapel (the old one became the kitchen of the priest's house). He did not ever wish to leave the quiet backwater where he felt his pen made him of more use than he could be in a more prominent position. All he wanted to do was say his prayers, read his books, write his letters, play a hand of whist with one friend and drink a glass of wine with another, walk his dog, tend his garden, and plough on slowly with the remaining volumes of *A History of England*.

Throughout these years, the Hornby Castle estate flourished under George Wright's stewardship, although it did not flourish nearly as much as he said it did. Many people thought, on his authority, that the mortgages had been gradually paid off. Nothing of the kind: in 1826 they stood at the same level, some £27,000, as they had when the purchase was completed thirty years before. George Wright, however, was now the owner of considerable property in his own right. The first of his estates was The Snab, in Gressingham, across the river from Hornby, but the one which gave him most pleasure was the land he acquired in Heysham, where in about 1816 he built a handsome little gentleman's house for himself, called Heysham Lodge or, later, Heysham Head.[8] When this was finished he spent several months a year there with his family, always taking John Marsden with him. Marsden was not fond of this annual migration and, since he dared not ask Wright direct, would ask the servants repeatedly when they were going back to Hornby. He could spend hours scraping his fiddle through the tune of 'Dainty Davie' in either house (in this respect at least the Wright family seem to have been remarkably tolerant) but he missed the park and gardens which, as he grew older, were the limit of his rambles.

He was more subdued but no less eccentric as he grew older, and the stories circulated and multiplied and lost nothing in the telling. One that was frequently repeated, because the cause of it could be pointed out in clear view on the old pele tower of the Castle, was that of Marsden asking in puzzlement why the gilded eagle did not sing like the caged thrush in the village street.

Many of the stories featured the topsy-turviness of the master being in subjection to his man, the situation which Lingard found so distasteful, and which the village found worthy of gossip to the very end. Did Wright really threaten Marsden with a whip when he was recalcitrant? Did he really threaten to lock him in the cellar? There was no doubt that he ordered him about like a dog, but then he ordered everyone about like dogs, including his own children. The servants were confused. Roger Chester, Marsden's servant from 1819, seems to have been an odd, emotional man, who vacillated in his attitude: sometimes treating 'the damned old fool' in as cavalier a fashion as Wright did, but sometimes giving way to bursts of tearful fury in the servants' hall at the unfairness of his master being so miserably used. They were all used to ignoring Marsden's bell, but then Marsden might ring five times in as many minutes, and not know what he wanted if anyone answered.[9]

The workmen knew that they must not respond if he asked them for any service, but it was not easy to turn him out of the workshops if he hung about, pestering them, as he often did. He was, after all, Squire Marsden, owner of Hornby Castle, and they must often have heaved a sigh of relief when Wright's approach sent Marsden scampering through a back door, out of sight.

Joseph Hetherington, a plumber, was examined on his experience in 1811 or 1812, when two water-closets were being installed at Hornby Castle.

Were you at work for some time there? – Perhaps ten days or a fortnight; I cannot say.

Did you see Marsden? – Yes.

Did he come to look on when you were at work? – Yes; he came to speak to the man who was assisting me, and he asked if he had got finished.

Who was that that did so? – Wright.

But I mean, did Marsden come to talk to you? – No; he never came near enough to pass a word.

Did he ever give you any directions? – No, never.

Did Wright come to give directions as to the work? – Yes.

Were there two water-closets, one above and one below? – Yes.

Some of the water, I suppose, came from the one above to the one below? – Yes.

In what state was the work then? – Not in a finished state.

Was the seat and pan put down? – Yes, that was completed.

Was the stucco part of it complete, or the plastering? – No, some parts of it only were complete; there was no door.

Did Wright come to view it? – Yes.

Did the water come in? – Yes.

It seemed to answer, did it? – Yes.

When Wright was there, did you see Marsden? – Yes; he was standing near, and he spoke to the men; Wright said, 'we will go and look at the other above'; and he and the man accordingly went above.

When they went above, what did Marsden do? – He took hold of the handle of the water-closet, and pulled it, the same as the others had done, and the water rushed in; and as soon as he had let go the handle and looked at it he went out, and returned with a piece of paper in his hand, which he tore into pieces; and then he pulled the handle up again and put some pieces of paper into it; and when he saw it turn round again, and the paper also, he smiled at it; and when it had done running he drew it up again, and put some pieces of paper into it, and laughed again.

Did he appear to be amused with it? – Yes.

How many times did he do this? – Two or three times.

What happened then? – Wright came down after he had done that, and said to him, 'What are you doing there?' and he took him by the back of the collar of his coat, and pushed him out before him.

He had asked him first 'What are you doing there?' – Yes; and added, 'if he caught him there again, he would take a horse whip to him'.

What did Marsden do? – He went away, and we saw no more of him then.

What did Wright say then? – He said that the door was to be fastened up, so that Marsden could not get in. He called to one of the men to make the door-way up, so that Marsden could not get in again.

When Wright went away, did Marsden come back again? – Yes, in a short time after that he came back again.

Did Wright give any reason, why it should be fastened up; what did he say ... state it all? – He said, that if it were not made up, he was sure that Marsden would come and spoil the closet, or let the whole of the water out of the cistern.[10]

The Will

Whether there was any advance notice of a deterioration in John Marsden's health, or whether the organisers of his life had remarkably good fortune, he signed the codicil to his will on 23 February 1825. Six weeks later, on 6 April, George Smith, Wright's confidential clerk, noted in his diary that 'Mr Marsden suffered a slight attack of apoplexy'.[1] The codicil was an update, dealing with all acquisitions to the property made since the main will in 1822:

> that is to say, I give and devise unto Mr George Wright, in my said will named, his heirs and assigns, as well all that my freehold messuage, with the appurtenances, situate in Hornby, lately purchased by me of Mr Giles; as also, all other hereditaments whatsoever, now vested in me, or of which I have now the power to devise and not already devised by my will. Upon the like trusts, and for the like intents and purposes in all respects as are in and by my said will expressed and declared of and concerning the hereditaments thereby devised to him. And I hereby ratify and confirm my said will, with this addition thereto.[2]

The details of how the transaction was carried out were told much later by the Reverend Robert Procter, one of the witnesses, to John Lingard, and Dr Lingard wrote them down for Sandford Tatham. George Wright was not involved. George Wright was so uninvolved that this in itself becomes a suspicious circumstance, since all other evidence points to the cavalier way in which Wright normally summoned Marsden to his study, said 'Sign here', and then dismissed him.

The codicil was dictated verbatim without notes by Giles Bleasdale to George Smith, no other person being present. The signing took place at Edmund Tatham's house: Marsden asked Procter to meet him there, and himself went with Bleasdale in the carriage. Procter drove his wife in their gig, but on arrival she left the gentlemen alone. Bleasdale took the paper out of his pocket and said to Marsden, 'This is your will, and a codicil to it'. Marsden said 'Yes' and the signatures were appended. Bleasdale took up the papers and folded them, and was just tying them up with tape when Marsden said: 'Stop, let me see what that is about'. Bleasdale handed him the paper, he took it to the window while the other three stood by the fire, and brought it back again without a word. Bleasdale took it up and put it in his pocket. Nothing more was said on the subject, but Procter said to his brother-in-law, as soon as they were alone, 'Now, what do you think of that?' Tatham could say nothing but 'It is very odd'.[3]

The unease of the two witnesses was the greater since they had also witnessed the main will, three years before, and had been very uneasy then, but somehow they had got into the situation and could not get out of it. Edmund Tatham, a shy, quiet man, said afterwards to his brother-in-law Procter, 'I was drawn in to sign that will. I could not refuse without breaking with them and that I did not dare to do on account of you and your family. Had it not been for that, I would have had no acquaintance with them'.[4]

Robert Procter had much to lose. He was in debt to Wright, and could not afford to have the debt called in. He held his vicarage from Marsden and could hardly now maintain his patron's incompetence. Later, Procter produced two different rationalisations of why he witnessed a will which he did not believe the testator was competent to understand. One version was that he thought that Bleasdale for his own reputation's sake would not be associated with a doubtfully honest transaction, and so he concluded that the will must be within Marsden's comprehension, and that the numerous sheets on which it was engrossed were just lawyer's verbiage. The other version was that he thought he was just witnessing a signature, and this he did, and what the signature was appended to was legally nothing to do with him.

Neither version carries much conviction, and would have rung very hollow had Procter ever been required to explain himself in a court of law; but as things turned out, Wright's counsel were too wary of his possible revelations to bring him near a witness stand. Why Sandford Tatham's counsel did not call him is less easy to explain, but there are suggestions in some of Lingard's letters that they had serious doubts about his mental health. Under the anxiety of the preparation for the 1830 trial at York he seemed on the edge of a nervous collapse. He was constantly having to be reassured that he would not be called on Wright's side, so the Admiral's party, out of kindness to the old man (he was then seventy), or more likely from fear as to how he would stand up to Pollock's cross-questioning, also forwent his evidence.

In spite of the careful stage-management, and long before he had any cognisance of the complexity of the will, Procter must have known very well, if he had stopped to think about it, that Bleasdale and Wright were in the business together. Bleasdale's smooth presentation of himself as Marsden's attorney, under Marsden's direction, could not be made to fit. But Procter evidently did not stop to think about it: from the letters of his clear-sighted friend, Doctor Lingard, he emerges as a weak, bumbling, well-meaning, fuzzy-minded individual, who would dodge drawing an awkward conclusion until, like a rake-handle, it sprang up and rapped him on the nose.

He simply witnessed Marsden's will because he did not see how to get out of it. He may have been used before, but the important one, that is the last, was signed on 14 June 1822. As with the codicil, the stage-management was excellent. The witnesses were apparently chosen, and certainly invited, by Marsden himself and no one else. He asked Procter to dinner at the Castle, to transact some business for him, and asked him to bring Edmund Tatham. Before dinner, Wright keeping well out of the way, Bleasdale burnt the old will, sheet by sheet, and brought out the new one, which was duly signed and witnessed. To indicate how much Marsden understood of the property he was dealing with, a story may be quoted which was current in the locality, told a hundred times by John Bradshaw of Halton. It was probably true, or at least people had no difficulty in accepting it to be true, and Procter must have heard it. Bradshaw met Marsden one day, who said to him, 'Jack, I have been making my will'. 'Then I hope you've left me something', said Bradshaw facetiously. 'No', said Marsden, 'but I've left Mr Wright twenty thousand pounds a year.'[5]

On the occasion of that signing, business over, they joined the family for dinner, and after dinner, as had been done before on similar occasions, Marsden's health was drunk: 'Mr Marsden, and may he live forty years to come.' Wright growled from his place, 'If you do, you'll be in somebody's way, I say'.[6]

What ill effect Marsden suffered from his first stroke in 1825 is not related. He was mobile, since he went to Heysham in the summer and to Gargrave in the New Year of 1826, but George Smith's diary no longer records his going out to dinner with the neighbours he used to frequent: Bleasdale or Procter; or Edmondson at Grassyard; or Greene at Whittington; or Stout, the prosperous draper of Lancaster; or William Sharp. It cannot be certain whether these are significant omissions, but there was probably limited damage: one who had always been slow and clumsy was now slower and clumsier – stories of his being scolded for untidy eating seem to belong to this period of his life.

Fifteen months later, on 25 June 1826, George Wright and his son John, Giles Bleasdale and Thomas Brancker, Wright's son-in-law, had all gone together ('in Mr Marsden's carriage', according to George Smith's deadpan diary entry) to the election at Appleby, where George Wright was a freeholder probably by right of Elizabeth Tatham's estate. On that day Marsden was late for dinner, but this was nothing new, and nobody waited for him, in spite of later insistence that of course, since he was the master of the house, dinner was always delayed until he was ready. Mrs Wright and her family sat down to the meal. The dishes were cold on the table before anyone thought of going as far as the library to find out why Marsden had not appeared.

When they found that he was not in the library nor in his room, there was alarm. His man, Roger Chester, was sent for, presumably from his own dinner, and George Smith, and a search ensued. He was found in the outdoor privy. (It is not beyond the bounds of possibility, given the plumber's evidence, that he had never actually been allowed to use the indoor water-closets.) 'I burst open the door', said Smith, 'and found him laying on the floor with his small-clothes down and his watch on the seat. He had dropt in Apoplexy but still breathed. Roger Chester and I carried him upstairs and put him upon his own bed.'

It was clear enough that he had suffered a massive and probably fatal stroke. Mr Procter was sent for from the village, and said they must get a surgeon to bleed him. The two boys at home, Henry and William, and at least one servant, were sent off in different directions. 'Henry Wright took horse and rode to Kirkby Lonsdale for Mr Batty. The groom (Thomas Parker) rode to Wray for Mr Wildman, and William Wright ran to Hornby for Altham.' All of them came, but their ministrations had no effect. It seems unlikely that Marsden ever regained consciousness.

The Appleby party returned in the evening. Their next step was to send the groom at top speed to apprise Anthony Lister at Gargrave. So much for later protestations that no one knew the contents of the will or who were the heirs. It might be suggested that Anthony Lister, as a near and dear relation, would naturally be sent for to his cousin's deathbed, but it was noticeable that none of the rest of the family was notified, and it was reported that Giles Bleasdale was furious at the stupidity of thus linking Anthony Lister with the will. The Dawsons heard a few days later by letter from Sandford Tatham, but the Cooksons of Leeds, to their indignation, found out only after a delay of several weeks, when they saw the news reported in a Yorkshire newspaper.[7]

Sandford Tatham was certainly not notified, although he happened to be no further away than visiting relations in the Lake District. As luck would have it, he had met William Sharp the attorney for the first time a few days before and, on being told who he was, approached him with a kindly message for his cousin Marsden. Sharp would not have kept this information to himself, so the Castle was well aware of the Admiral's whereabouts – 'watching in the neighbourhood' it was afterwards said.

There is no reason to think that John Marsden, in his bare little bedroom (he had never slept in the master bedroom, which was appropriated to Mr and Mrs Wright), was not conscientiously nursed. Mrs Wright, at least, was reported to be in great distress. He died six days later, on 1 July 1826, so that there was time for the main actors in the drama to be on cue, and they seem not to have wasted that time.

When Wright notified Sharp, 'I have the melancholy task to inform you that our friend Mr Marsden departed this life at half-past three o'clock this afternoon', Sharp replied immediately with an effusion which he must surely have been polishing for days:

> However we may regret the death of our most worthy and much-valued Friend, and I do most sincerely regret him, yet it is a great consolation to know that he has possessed all the comforts and attentions this world can afford and is gone hence with a lively hope of the blessings of a future state.
>
>   The rich have lost a Friend the poor a Benefactor. His Heart and his Purse were always open to Kindness and Charity. He is now no more. Let us imitate his good example. We cannot help regretting but let us not repine at the inscrutable ways of Providence. It is our duty to believe that he orders all for the best and we must submit ...[8]

Marsden's death was at half-past three and Hornby is ten miles from Lancaster. Before he sent off the above, Sharp had, as requested, seen the undertaker and despatched him to Hornby by chaise. Others had been busy too. Sandford Tatham, having heard of his cousin's approaching death, was staying at Moor Platt in Caton, half way between Hornby and Lancaster. He did not need, as Sharp said, to have a 'person waiting at Hornby to give him immediate intelligence of Mr Marsden's death' – Dr Lingard's ear was as close to the ground as ever, and Mr Procter, as the local clergyman, was inside the Castle itself.

Admiral Tatham got hold of John Higgin, his attorney. Then Higgin's clerk smartly delivered a caveat to Sharp, not in his capacity as the Hornby Castle solicitor but because he was also Deputy Registrar of the Probate Registry in Lancaster.

To William Sharp Esq. Deputy Registrar

Sir, I Sandford Tatham of the Close of the Cathedral Church of Lichfield
in the County of Stafford but now resident of Lancaster in the County
of Lancaster, a Rear Admiral of his Majesty's Fleet as heir at law and
next of kin of John Marsden late of Hornby Castle in the said County
of Lancaster Esquire deceased, request and authorize you to enter a
Caveat against the granting Probate of the Will of the said John Marsden
deceased or Letters of Administration to his personal effects in the
Consistory Court kept at Lancaster aforesaid.

I am, Sir, Yours very Respectfully,
    Sandford Tatham
        Rear Admiral
Lancaster 1 July 1826 [9]

And although all this had happened since poor John Marsden took
his last breath at 3.30 in the afternoon, there was still time for two
letters to catch the evening mail and arrive simultaneously on the
desk of James Scarlett, the leading counsel on the northern circuit,
offering him retainers to represent on the one hand Admiral Tatham,
and on the other Anthony Lister (so much again for the polite fiction
that the contents of the will were a secret between the testator and his
attorney) in whatever trial of strength was going to take place between
them.

John Marsden was buried not in Melling Church, with his forefathers,
but in a vault in Hornby Chapel, where a neat brass plaque can be
seen below the altar steps. The bearers were various gentry and near-
gentry of the neighbourhood: apart from William Sharp and Giles
Bleasdale, most of the others had probably not seen him in years. The
chief mourners were 'Mr Wright, Mr J.M. Wright and Mr Lister arm-
in-arm, and Henry and William Wright arm-in-arm, habited in
mourning cloaks. Roger Chester and I [George Smith] walked next.
Hills (Mr Lister's groom) next, and Thomas Parker groom and Richard
Dobson gamekeeper next. I dined with the tenants at the Castle Inn ...
the number that dined was fifty-four'. The conversation no doubt was
animated and interesting.

It was soon over. John Marsden as a person had never mattered
much, and now mattered not at all. He was safely and respectably
buried, and the small group of interested persons could go back to the
Castle and read the will. At least Bleasdale said in his evidence that
the will was read after the funeral. Sharp thought it had been read
immediately after Marsden's death. As the only person who was

genuinely astonished by the terms, Anthony Lister probably remembered very clearly when it was read, but his evidence has not survived.

The will and its codicil had been kept in a box to which John Marsden had the key, a key which he always kept in his breeches pocket, as everyone knew. Later, some scorn was poured on the likelihood of a man keeping a key in his pocket for years and years, and it still being found there after his death. In fact, given the circumstances, it was very likely. Bleasdale said that he had suggested the box, or found it, or had it made, and once Marsden was persuaded that his breeches pocket was the proper place for such a valuable item, there the key would have stayed, and would have been shifted from one pair of breeches to the next, for as long as he lived. His habits died harder than most.[10]

Bleasdale had always played soft man to George Wright's hard man – the one frightened Marsden, the other flattered him. Unlike Wright, he never teased or bullied him or made him the butt of jokes, spoke to him with all the courtesy of two gentlemen, took time to talk to him, invited him to his house with or without Wright. He had been drawing up wills for Marsden, who evidently enjoyed the process, since James Barrow, Mrs Cookson's attorney, was drowned at Carlisle in 1798. William Sharp, let it be remembered, was Castle attorney for all ordinary and estate business, but he had no hand in any of the wills.

The 1822 will, as has been said before, was only the last of a long series. How many, no one knew. There were some early ones, Anthony Lister supplanting the Tathams along the way. In 1816, the year Bleasdale retired to Wenning Cottage, Wright appeared as trustee. In 1819 or 1820 Anthony Lister was squeezed out of first place in favour of his son. Later, he was reinstated. In 1822 the conspirators, for so one must call them, had, as they thought, got things arranged just as they wanted. Even if Marsden had lived much longer, this would have been the last version, supported by codicils. In it Lister's share had been pared down as much as was safe. As it stood, it might just be credible – they could not get away with more.

The will was contained in thirteen sheets of paper, and it went directly to its point, mentioning only two legacies before the main dispositions were unfolded. Not a servant, a friend, a charity got a penny. There was no provision of mourning for the household, of topped-up wages, or of pensions for old retainers. The two legacies were of £6000 for Marsden's godson, John Marsden Wright, and £5000 for Margaret Wright, his goddaughter. The gift of the Upper Salter estate in Roeburndale, which he had previously made to John Marsden Wright, was ratified, and the same beneficiary was to have the advowson of the vicarage of Gargrave.

'All my ready-money, securities for money, and all other my personal estate and effects, whatsoever and wheresoever', were to go to George Wright as trustee, to be disposed of in liquidating debts and paying the legacies.

> And whereas, for some time past, a system of management hath been carried on under the superintendence of my confidential friend the said George Wright, with a view to the improvement [of the estate], and the gradual liquidation of the incumbrances affecting the same: and I am particularly anxious that a similar system shall be acted upon after my decease, under his superintendence, and whom I therefore intend to invest with the most ample powers in that behalf.[11]

To summarise, for the period of twenty-one years, George Wright was to have total control over every part of the estate except the actual Castle premises, able, in the interests of good management, to do exactly as he pleased: to pull down and put up buildings, to use all the resources of mills, coal mines and quarries. He could grant tenancies to whomsoever he pleased, and the tenancies so granted at any time up to the last day of the twenty-one years could themselves be for twenty-one years. The timber on the estate was at his absolute discretion to cut and sell. Everything was at his disposal, in the way of 'buildings, repairs, fencing, draining, or planting or other improvements; and to make, or consent to, any inclosure of commons, or waste lands, in all of any of the townships or parishes in which my said manors and real estates are situate'. He was to hold back £2000 a year out of the estate to liquidate debts (or to make sure that the legacies were paid). He could raise mortgages on any part of the estate, and could invest any sums so raised in his own name as he pleased. And for his labours he was to be paid £1000 a year, not merely for twenty-one years but for life if he lived longer. And he had the right to employ another person at a salary of £400 a year to help him in his task. But if he died, or wished to retire, he could nominate someone to take on his £1000 a year post to work out the rest of the twenty-one years.

What, in the meanwhile, of Anthony Lister, who, we may imagine, was hearing the sound of many chickens coming home to roost? Anthony Lister, who was to change his name to Marsden, was to enjoy the Castle and its premises, strictly upon a repairing lease, and knowing that George Wright was in possession of the land almost up to his door and could moreover, 'erect any new messuages or other buildings'

I John Marsden of Hornby Castle in the County of Lancaster Esquire do make publish and declare this Codicil to my last Will and Testament in manner following that is to say I give and devise unto Mr George Wright in my said Will named his heirs and assigns as well all that my freehold messuage with the appurtenances situate in Hornby lately purchased by me of Mr Giles as also all other hereditaments whatsoever now vested in me or of which I have now the power to devise and not already devised by my Will Upon the like trusts and for the like intents and purposes in all respects as are in and by my said Will expressed and declared of and concerning the hereditaments thereby devised to him And I hereby ratify and confirm my said Will with this addition thereto In Witness whereof I have hereunto set my hand and seal this twenty third day of February in the year of our Lord one thousand eight hundred and twenty five. —

Signed sealed published and declared by the said John Marsden the Testator as and for a Codicil to his Last Will and Testament in the presence of us who in his presence and at his request and in the presence of each other have hereunto subscribed our names as Witnesses thereto — — —

Edm. Tatham
R. Procter
Giles Bleasdale

John Marsden

Codicil to John Marsden's Will, 23 February 1825. (*Lancashire Record Office*) 'including any new lodges or other offices to be annexed to the said capital messuage'.

> Provided also, and I hereby further declare my will to be, that the said Anthony Lister shall and do, within three calendar months next after my decease, or within three calendar months next after my said godson John Marsden Wright shall have taken holy orders as a Priest of the Church of England, resign the vicarage of Gargrave aforesaid, of which he the said Anthony Lister is at present incumbent, to the intent that the said John Marsden Wright shall and may be duly presented and inducted thereto.[11]

And that if the said Anthony Lister objected, he would get nothing at all, the estate going on to the next heir. The next heir was Charles John Lister, aged eleven, and his sons after him, but if he died without male issue (he was, it seemed, a frail little boy), then, his younger brother not being mentioned at all, everything would devolve upon John Marsden Wright, who would also change his name to Marsden, and inherit every last pebble and penny.

It was commonly said, among those who knew or thought they knew, that this marginalisation of the Listers was due to a quarrel between Anthony Lister and Wright. Bleasdale's evidence supports this. Dr Lingard, that assiduous collector of information, believed that the temporary break, when Lister was excluded in favour of his son, followed a snub to the Wright family.

George Wright himself, who had been made welcome enough by old Anthony Lister at Bell Hill, never visited Gargrave, home of young Anthony and his well-connected wife, and evidently accepted this piece of class distinction. But he, or perhaps his wife, about 1819 proposed that their daughter Margaret should go with Marsden on his visits. The idea may have been born innocently enough, quite possibly simply with the intention of her looking after him. But it was not welcome at Gargrave, and Robert Procter once, when he was angry, let out what he had heard. 'At that time', said Lingard,

> while under the influence of passion, he told Wright what Lister had most certainly said ... that he could not assent to it: if she was there he must introduce her to his friends as Miss Wright. Who was Miss Wright? they would ask. He must answer the daughter of Mr M.'s steward; and they would then ask if he thought such a woman fit company for them. When Wright heard this story, he also flew into a passion, and Mr P. is of opinion, from what happened afterwards, that it had great influence in determining him to exclude Lister from the will in that year.[12]

Marsden, of course, reflected Wright like a mirror, and it may be significant that in 1820 his usual summer visit to Gargrave, according to George Smith's diary, was cut to three days. There is good reason to lay the blame for the coolness on Mrs Anthony Lister rather than her husband. She was often referred to as 'the grey mare' who is always the better horse, and much of Lister's obstinacy in sticking with Wright and the will is also referred to her determination to live in a castle, a determination from which she gained little satisfaction, as she died in 1834.

The quarrel had been patched up, in that there are in fact references to the Misses Wright going to Gargrave, but Wright did not have a forgiving nature. After the will-reading, the Lister household must have been in turmoil, not only outwitted but deprived in such a peculiarly insulting manner by the demand that Lister should immediately resign his living.

It was not an easy dilemma: to settle for the bird in hand, the comfortable but unexciting vicarage, or to go on with the gamble which might in the future establish his son as Lord of the Manor of Hornby, but which meanwhile involved the humiliating necessity of playing Wright's game, and might in the end deliver no goods at all. All summer the reports of his heart-searchings echoed round Craven and further afield. William Dawson, as might be expected, had no sympathy at all with the Lister bid, which his family regarded as 'illicit subversion of the estate to go to a distant relative'. He wrote with some satisfaction: 'Mr Lister appears to be in an extraordinary position'.[13] Sandford Tatham picked up the vibrations: 'Anthony Lister certainly had an inclination to abandon the will and told Lord Ribblesdale so and Lord Ribblesdale cannot account for his conduct.'[14] John Higgin, Tatham's solicitor, reported less politely from London: 'I find there's a rumour afloat that Mr Lister is disposed to bolt'.[15]

Whatever his neighbours thought, Anthony Lister made up his mind, before the three months was up, to line up with Wright and the will in the hope of greater things hereafter. George Smith's dry entry for 30 September 1826 read: 'Mr Sharp came from Lancaster this morning to Hornby Castle when the business was settled and Mr Lister signed a Resignation of Gargrave which was witnessed by myself and Roger Chester. Mr Sharp and the Reverend A. Lister left the Castle after dinner.'

11

Legal Manoeuvres

Admiral Tatham always maintained that his presence in the area when John Marsden died was pure chance, but it was chance at least given a helping hand. He was fond of presenting himself as the traditional bluff sailor, but in fact he had spent the last thirty years on shore, in society a good deal more sophisticated than that provided by the wardroom. The Navy took great pride in the development of its officers into characters of openness, integrity and courageous vigour – of 'heartiness' in fact, a word which has since been debased into mere mannerism. In Sandford Tatham's case there was also a native shrewdness, trained to action.[1]

It was chance that there was a Lancaster borough election in that June of 1826: as a freeman he came north to use his vote. So far as the election went, he might have saved his trouble: John Fenton Cawthorne, who in spite of his doubtful activities elsewhere had bought his way into the town's affections by his generosity, and Thomas Greene, son of the rich London attorney who had with some nervousness acted on behalf of Marsden in the purchase of Hornby Castle, were elected unopposed, but Tatham made other good use of his time. He had plenty of contacts from whom to collect information on affairs at the Castle, and it may well have been now that he first properly made the acquaintance of Dr John Lingard, who was to prove one of his strongest supporters ('I have an indefatigable Assistant of no Common Powers there').

The election was on 9 June, but a week later Tatham was still in Lancaster. On 16 June he left a letter with solicitor John Higgin, making provision for the future, no doubt the outcome of a great deal of legal discussion. In the case of his cousin's death occurring during his own lifetime, 'I desire you will act as my attorney and whenever it shall be necessary you will in my name commence such process at Law or in Equity as you will deem expedient'.[2]

John Higgin was a member of an important Lancaster family. His father at this time was Keeper of Lancaster Castle, a post held previously by his grandfather and subsequently by his brother, in an unbroken run of service covering a hundred years. Higgin was Town Clerk as well as a lawyer. He was not very successful in his personal affairs: he went bankrupt in 1829 through unlucky investment, and later lost his job as Town Clerk because the Corporation complained 'they could not get on comfortably with him'. The real problem was that, though energetic and industrious in his profession, he simply could not handle money, a serious disadvantage at any time, but particularly so in the case of a protracted lawsuit.

When Sandford Tatham concocted his letter, and then went north to see his relations in the Lake District, John Marsden was apparently in his normal health. As the Admiral returned through Lancaster, he was greeted at the King's Arms with news of his cousin's serious illness, and delayed his journey south. At this time he and his wife were based in the midlands. They had a house in Spa Place, Leicester, which was currently let, and were living with her sister in Lichfield. Headquarters were promptly moved to a house in Dalton Square, Lancaster, next door to that of Dr George Brown, a Catholic priest, and a friendship developed here as well. At times during the campaign when, rightly or not, it was felt that the enemy's machinations might extend to tapping the Hornby post, correspondence with Lingard was kept up through Dr Brown or his sister.

Although he was seventy-one, and had been so badly wounded at Martinique in 1793 that he never went to sea again, the Admiral's health was very good, his energy and determination even better. He and everyone else frequently referred to his age (seventy was still seen as a watershed after which one lived on borrowed time), but in fact he seems to have ailed very little. He undertook a great deal of the business, which began immediately, of collecting witnesses, and gained considerable expertise in the art of taking depositions. Higgin went up and down to London to deal with the legal side, but Tatham clearly was in control, and most of the initial correspondence came from his pen, not the solicitor's.[3] It was now that he gained the strongest support of all, that of his cousin, Pudsey Dawson, a Liverpool banker with a large fortune which, along with unstinted personal effort, he was willing to use in the Admiral's cause.

There were several lines to be pursued as rapidly as possible. The will was to be challenged on whatever grounds could be made to stick: either that Marsden did not know what he was signing; or, if he did know, that he was under another person's influence and control. This

was never going to be easy: British juries were notoriously loath to
overturn a will. Before the process could begin, Sandford Tatham had
to prove that he was indeed the heir at law, and this had its difficulties
also. Was his pedigree legitimate, and was his elder brother William
dead without issue?

In the end the opposition accepted his position without making it
the subject of a subsidiary court case, but a great deal of hard work
was necessary to attain this end. There was, for instance, the little matter
of his parents' divorce on the grounds of the wife's adultery, but this
did not much affect Sandford who was born three years before the
affair. If anyone's parentage was to be questioned it would have been
Charles, the youngest, and probably the father's will, in which he
accepted all his sons, but was most generous to Sandford, would have
disposed of any doubts in that direction. Much more serious was the
missing marriage of the Tatham parents: seventy-five years had elapsed,
and it was not easy to prove that the marriage had been accepted as a
fact without demur, but this in the end was done and was considered
proof enough.[4]

Even more complicated and time-consuming was the question, not
finally settled until 1830, as to William Tatham's death and marital
status. This was more recent, but most of the evidence was on the other
side of the Atlantic. That he had cohabited with Mary Mears, his friend's
servant girl, during his residence in London while he was working on
the London Docks, was admitted. That she had a son, who in spite of
a misleading baptismal entry ('William, son of William Tatham and
Mary') was known by himself and everyone else to be illegitimate, was
also admitted. The son, William Mears, was a feeble Micawberish character, always in need of money which he seemed unable to put to good
use, several times being helped to jobs which he seemed unable to
keep. He makes appearances at intervals on the stage, and is last seen
as late as 1841, begging for enough money to fit him out for some
magical opportunity in Venezuela. Pudsey Dawson, always a soft touch,
continued to respond to his begging letters, but he had no serious part
to play on the stage of *Tatham* v. *Wright*.[5]

There are several letters of William Tatham to Mary Mears from
America about the year 1809, swearing undying love and promising to
come back and get her and the boy, but it seems very unlikely that he
had any such intention. As far as anyone knew, he was and remained
a bachelor. He certainly was not married in America, though he tried
for one lady who preferred someone else. His rumoured military career
was also fiction. Perhaps he had had some involvement in the American

Revolution, and subsequently dubbed himself 'Colonel' – a widespread habit, as Dickens remarked. When official information was sought in the 1820s, the British Consul in Baltimore found that he had worked for the government as a civil engineer, but the United States War Department could find nothing more to his name than a brief period as a military store-keeper.

His death in 1819, in Richmond, Virginia, was bizarre. No satisfactory explanation was ever offered to the family. 'About sunset of this day, while the evening salute by cannon was fired, he the said William Tatham rashly and precipitately threw himself in front of one of the guns when an order had been given by the officer to fire, and at the very instant a match was set thereto. It is clearly the opinion of this jury that the late William Tatham came to his death by casualty or accidentally, the officer exonerated from all blame.' Everyone understood it to be suicide, but suicide was a crime, and juries interpreted it as accident wherever possible.[6]

In that summer of 1826, as well as collecting witnesses and working on his pedigree, Sandford Tatham had to address himself as rapidly as possible to the important question of finance. The friendship between himself and Pudsey Dawson was not yet fully developed, nor the extent of the younger man's generosity. Going to law is never cheap, and the opposition, both Bleasdale and Wright, were widely quoted as saying that all they had to do was to delay matters as much as possible ('ten or twenty years', Bleasdale boasted in front of a shooting party) until the Admiral's funds ran out. 'Wright has said that he would soon beggar that old fool, the Admiral.'[7]

A letter to John Higgin of 31 July 1826 from a Mr Gell of Nottingham, on which the Admiral noted approvingly 'a very sensible Letter', warned 'I hope your Client has the sinews of war; beyond a Warrior's half pay. Since I came here I have seen £8000 spent on a Will cause – three trials'. The rest of the letter underlines the difficulties experienced many times in the search for witnesses: 'Isabella [his wife] was too young when she left Hornby to know much of poor Marsden and his keeper. Had Tom been alive he would I doubt not have been of use ...' 'Had Tom been alive ...'[8] The story of Wright and his dominance of Marsden now ran back forty-six years and it was the early years, when the dominance was being established, which were most likely to provide examples to impress a jury. As an advising counsel said: 'In the state of quiet and resigned submission to which Mr Marsden was reduced for many years before his death it is not likely that any striking instance of influence or control should occur frequently.'[9] Many potentially useful witnesses were dead, many had moved out of the district. Chasing them up to hear their stories needed manpower and, already and inevitably, money.

The Admiral turned first to William Dawson of St Leonards Hill at Windsor, whose grandmother had been a Marsden, and who was nearest in line to the Marsden fortune if the Tathams should die out. At the time the Admiral had no idea that Dawson had also tried to get his feet under the Marsden table by interesting John Marsden in his eight children, but he was aware that Dawson took umbrage at the Lister bid from the furthest end of the family tree.

The Admiral's side of the later correspondence has not survived, but he clearly offered William Dawson a deal if he would support the cause financially. As he said in a letter to Higgin: 'My wish is that the Estates should be continued in the Right Line – and at my time of life I must necessarily look to a successor.' [10] Dawson refused: it was too much of a gamble to undertake whatever wholehearted commitment Tatham had suggested, which was probably that if Dawson would finance the case, the estates should be entailed on his sons. He none the less told his cousin to call on him for cash, and in the end made a considerable contribution. His son Frederick became the Admiral's treasurer and enthusiastic supporter for a time, though he cooled off later when the going got hard. In the early days he supported the cause wholeheartedly, and urged his father towards generosity.[11]

There was yet another matter to be taken up without delay: the incumbency of Gargrave. Anthony Lister (now Anthony Marsden, he had changed his name as directed by the will), had duly signed his resignation. As has been said, to make quite sure that Wright knew he was above board, he had signed it at Hornby, using Roger Chester and George Smith as witnesses. The Archbishop, however, refused to accept it, giving no reason: it was strongly suspected, but not provable, that Lister had done some private engineering through his contacts in the Yorkshire establishment. Tatham conducted a correspondence with another cousin, Ambrose Dawson, incumbent of St Michael, Liverpool, offering him the lucrative Gargrave benefice if he would fight for it. Ambrose expressed himself as both grateful and willing, but the correspondence breaks off and the sequel is lost. Higgin also applied to Chester diocese, entering caveats against the possible resignation of either the Rectory of Tatham or the Curacy of Hornby.[12]

Both parties were jockeying for position. Admiral and Mrs Tatham were seen in Melling Church when they stayed with their friends the Remingtons of Crowtrees, sitting in the Wennington Hall pew. In

October 1826 notices from the Admiral were pinned up on all the church doors (except Tatham, where no doubt John Marsden Wright took it down), announcing that Wright's calling of a manor court was illegal and he intended to hold his own, but nothing seems to have come of this. A year later, the two manor courts (Hornby and Tatham) found that George Wright was Lord of the Manor under Marsden's will. On rent day in November 1826, Tatham came to the Castle Inn in Hornby with Higgin and tried to persuade the tenants against paying their rent.[13] He had the church bells rung while he was in the village, and told George Smith, who conducted the tenants' dinner, that he wanted to join them, but Smith refused.

These gestures may have owed more to naval bravado than good sense, or perhaps it was felt necessary to make some public statement of the Admiral's claim. It was an anxious time for the Hornby tenants, caught in a tug of war and needing for their own safety to guess the outcome correctly. All but three decided to pay up, and the three were formally excluded from the tenants' dinner. It was not an easy time for Wright either. In some cases he had a weapon against recalcitrant tenants: George Smith noted in January 1827, 'Thomas Procter of Castle Inn paid part of his rent to Mr Wright and his bills for dinners and posting were settled', but action against others was not so simple. William Sharp thought that the position of an executor distraining on goods for non-payment of rent was a fragile one.[14] To make the position more secure, Sharp took advice from the authorities in York. On 3 January 1827, the caveat having run out, Wright proved Marsden's will before him as the Deputy Registrar of Richmond Deanery.

These were in some ways ritual formalities before the real battle began. The plaintiffs settled down to the task of producing a body of evidence which would shake the positions of the defendants. As they piled up the depositions, sorting the likely from the unlikely, returning to the likely ones to enlarge and strengthen the evidence, discarding those with nothing to offer but a twice-told story and a half-heard rumour, it became very clear just how hard the task was going to be. It would be necessary to prove either that Marsden did not understand the will to which he set his signature, or that he signed while totally under the domination of Wright. The first was a negative which would be impossible to prove directly, and on the second Wright and Bleasdale presented a united front. Wright was adamant that he had known nothing about the will until it was read out after the funeral, and in particular knew nothing of being a beneficiary. Bleasdale, a respectable attorney of good reputation, stood firm that he had drawn the will that

WHEREAS Notice has been given on the part of GEORGE WRIGHT, describing himself as " Devisee in Trust, named and appointed in and by the last Will and Tes-"tament of JOHN MARSDEN, Esquire," that a Court Leet or view of Frank-pledge and Court Baron for the Borough of Hornby, will be held at Hornby Castle, on Thursday the 26th day of October instant at 10 o'Clock in the Forenoon ; and that a Court Baron for the Manor of Tatham, will be held at Hall Barns, in Tatham, on Friday the 27th day of October instant, at 10 o'Clock in the Forenoon : at which Courts all Persons who owe suit and service are desired to be and personally appear, and that all fines due and in arrear within the said Manors must be then paid.

NOW, I SANDFORD TATHAM, Rear Admiral in His Majesty's Fleet, and the Heir at Law of the said JOHN MARSDEN, *do hereby give Notice* to the Resiants and Tenants and other persons who owe suit and service at the said Courts, that I claim to be solely entitled to hold the said Courts, and I hereby caution such Resiants and Tenants not to do such suit or service at any such Court claimed to be held by the said GEORGE WRIGHT, until the Right and Title thereto shall be decided in due course of Law—And I *give Notice* to such persons not to pay to the said GEORGE WRIGHT, but to the legal personal Representative of the said JOHN MARSDEN, when he shall be duly authorized, any fines which are now due and in arrear within the said Manors.

Dated the 19th day of October, 1826.

Sandford Tatham.

C. CLARK, PRINTER, LANCASTER.

The Hornby Castle Court Leet (1826): Sandford Tatham's challenge to George Wright. (*Edith Tyson*)

Marsden had instructed him to draw. Unless something turned up to link them as fellow conspirators, to prove that Wright knew all about the will in advance, that Bleasdale had been his instrument in obtaining Marsden's assent to a rigmarole he did not understand, it was going to be extraordinarily difficult to produce anything to shake a hard-headed jury of Manchester business men or Cumberland squires.

Those on the ground had no doubts at all. Procter had had a number of conversations with Wright in which the latter had asked whether Anthony Lister ought not to be satisfied with Gargrave Vicarage, which should be quite enough for him and his family. Bleasdale and Wright at times spent hours, almost days, either closeted in the study or walking arm-in-arm outside. A servant, asked about this familiarity, said, as something that everyone knew, 'They are making Mr Marsden's will'.[15] The very witnesses, Procter and Edmund Tatham, knew that the codicil had been so much impenetrable gobbledygook to the testator.

But such stuff has to be made to stand up in a court of law, and there was the added difficulty that, however nefarious the will was presumed to be, its provisos did not contradict Marsden's own perceived sympathies. He had turned against his Tatham relations in no uncertain manner. He probably would have preferred to think of Anthony Lister, rather than anyone else, living in the Castle after his death. And there was plenty of evidence to show that while he lived Wright was the most solid figure in his landscape. Wright managed his life and stood between him and chaos. ('Ask Mr Wright. Mr Wright knows all those things.') Life without Wright was unthinkable. When Wright was ill, he had hovered outside the bedroom door to catch the doctor coming out, wringing his hands with despair as to what he should do if Wright died.[16] In very broad outline, it was a will that Marsden might have made. In very broad outline, led, we may imagine, by Bleasdale's careful questions ('Your cousin Tatham tried to get a commission of lunacy so that he could take your estate away. You don't want to give him anything, do you?' ... 'You wish Mr Wright to go on running the estate, don't you?' ... 'You wish to give something to your godson and goddaughter, don't you?'), it could be glossed as a will that Marsden *did* make.

Bleasdale had spent years soothing and flattering Marsden into be-lieving that they were conducting proper conversations. If Marsden expressed an opinion, Bleasdale never growled, like Wright 'Hold your tongue. What do you know about it?' They not infrequently dined alone together at Wenning Cottage, and their relationship, gentlemanly and respectful, pushing a convivial bottle between them, may have been hard work for Bleasdale but must have done wonders for poor Marsden's self-esteem.

As Tatham's party struggled to make a breakthrough, one figure loomed large in their sights. This was George Smith, Wright's clerk, who caused equal frustration to both sides, as the key witness who was never called. Opinions swirled round him, both sides tried their hardest to winkle out of him what he would say if he were set up in the witness box; neither side succeeded in extracting anything useful. In the end both were so frightened that he might damage their cause that they left him alone.

Smith was born in 1788 to William and Mary Smith of Tunstall, while Robert Procter was incumbent there. William Smith probably served as parish clerk; he is not mentioned as such in the parish register, but his name appears as witness to thirty marriages between 1793 and 1811, so he was a literate man, a little better than his neighbours. Dr Lingard said that the only son, George, 'owed his education to Mr Procter'. Whether this was by teaching him himself or by getting him into one of the local schools is not said, but George was sufficiently well educated to go to Hornby Castle as clerk in 1803, at the age of fifteen, and stayed there for thirty odd years. When he married Mary Barrett in 1819 he was described as 'book-keeper'. By the end of his life this had been upgraded to 'land agent'. A reader and self-improver, he was a great deal better educated than his master George Wright, and therefore of necessity became a very confidential clerk. He was almost certainly responsible for composing many of Wright's letters, and whether he did the same for Marsden was a question to which many people longed to know the answer and were never satisfied. A sober, competent, responsible man, of an even temperament which must have been a most useful antidote to Wright's hasty rudeness, well-liked by many and respected by all, he seems to have found his own line through the complicated situation at the Castle, and steered safely along it. He gave in his notice once, in February 1826, for June of that year, but evidently changed his mind.

Among the documentation there are two sources of information about George Smith, and both are maddeningly defective. One is the Reverend Robert Procter, as retailed mainly through the letters of Dr Lingard, and the other is his own diary, kept from 1819 until his death in 1856. Smith had always regarded Procter as a mentor and confidant, and continued on good terms with him; but after Marsden's death, whether because he rightly mistrusted Procter's confidentiality, or simply felt that silence was his only safety, he gave little away. The diary, started in 1819 possibly on Procter's advice that he ought to keep notes on everything, as they would be necessary one day, is equally reticent. It is a factual record, bald and dull, few days omitted, but few given more than a line or two. At some time it was copied into four large volumes, by various persons none of whom could read his handwriting well, and who perhaps were not local, since names of persons and places are wildly misspelt. These have not been corrected, nor have gaps where words defeated the copyist been filled.

Every diary has a hidden agenda which dictates the selection of items. Usually the key is the personality of the writer, which gradually emerges even through a factual record, outlined by the sum of his interests, attitudes and reactions. Very little personality emerges from Smith's diary and this is perhaps an indication that he was working to more than one agenda. Although his records range over his own work, life in his home, Wright and his family's activities (and Marsden's during his lifetime), work being done on the estate, events in the locality or occasionally further afield, none of these is noted consistently.

Usually he enters what he did that day ('I made up the ends of the Rental book'), but a comment on the weather ('A very cold day') or a domestic occurrence ('The other pig that we got of Nanny Turner died') can replace any comment on what he was doing in the office. Nor is it a regular record of work on the estate, although many entries deal with that subject ('E. Knowles and S. Armistead cutting up oak trees above the hothouse'). He often records the doings of the Wright family ('Miss Wright went to Lancaster on horseback and returned, Thomas Parker with her') and of their visitors ('Mr Sharp and his son came in the gig and dined at the Castle').

The question as to why the entries are selected as they are is a tantalising and in one area at least an important one. Were the notes of Wright's activities innocent, or intended as possible evidence of wrong-doing? Whatever the motive, the diary provides valuable evidence of certain things: one is the extent to which Castle resources and Castle workmen were used for Wright's house at Heysham, Wright's estate at Snab, William Sharp's house at Borwick and Bleasdale's house at Wennington. 'Richard Gibson took two carts of slate to Heysham. Robert Cornthwaite's three carts also took slate.' 'Chris Harrison came from Heysham with Kellet's carts and took back some apple and plum trees and ½ doz. Appleby Scots.' 'Enoch Knowles and William Smith [the Castle carpenters] finished the building at Borwick.' What does not appear is whether these extra-mural activities were ever paid for. It seems unlikely, although on one occasion there is mention of accounts 'between Mr Wright and the Estate'. It seems very unlikely, when we know that Wright had the only bank accounts, in Lancaster and Settle, to which Smith regularly rode with hundreds of pounds in gold after rent days.

Once the lawsuit had begun, the estate was systematically denuded of its most saleable product, timber. This was done for quick returns, it would seem, since George Smith noted of one transaction: 'Mr Burrow of Guy Hill called, Conder of Old Town and Anderton called and looked at the east end of the large wood, but did not buy it of Mr Wright. They offered 200 guineas for it but wanted two years to fell it in which Mr Wright would not agree to.'

Among the felled timber was the great elm tree avenue leading up to the Castle ('Luke Eastwood called and bought eleven Elm trees, eight cut down and three growing in Avenue'). There is no record of any replanting. The stripping was severe enough for it to be the subject of an extension of the law suit (23 January 1828. 'Mr Wright ... told me that Admiral Tatham had been amending his bill and had charged him, Mr W., with disposing of wood and appropriating the money to his own use'), but after a while this was felt to be, if not an irrelevance, at least an over-complication, and not pressed.

Robert Procter had many conversations with George Smith during the time of preparation for the trial, and faithfully reported everything to Dr Lingard who in turn reported to the Admiral – a chain reaction which was not unknown to Smith. He did not dare to brave the watching eyes in Hornby by calling directly on Lingard, though he intimated that he would have liked to have done so. Lingard also collected evidence through his housekeeper Mrs Croft, who was a great friend of the Miss Rainforths in the shop across the road, who in their turn were intimate with Mr and Mrs Smith. Along this grapevine travelled a distinct intimation that if Smith were called on the Admiral's side he would have much to say which would do the Admiral's cause no harm.

His caution had two roots. One was a loyalty to the man whose confidential servant he had been for twenty-five years. The other was a real fear that Wright would have no compunction in sacking him and, as a man with a wife and four children, he did not know where he would turn for another job. Procter assured him that if Wright felt like it he would sack him anyway; under the will there was that convenient £400 a year for an assistant, and Smith would do well to remember that Wright's son-in-law, Thomas Brancker, was a bankrupt who could certainly do with a steady income.[17]

In July 1829 Lingard reported that Procter had had 'a long conversation with G. Smith. He is very close, and indeeed low-spirited under the notion that he will be ruined. He said, however, that the time would come when all must come out. Mr P. said the admiral must connect B[leasdale] and W[right] together. "He will not have much difficulty in that, I think", Smith answered, "No, certainly, not at all". Mr P. added, "You know what I have to say, but you, I suppose, will have much more". "Yes", he replied, "indeed I have, much more". It is provoking that we cannot discover the particulars'.[18]

Provoking it remained to the end. Procter tried on one side, Sharp tried, cautiously, on the other. ('Mr Sharp also examined me at length respecting what I had to say in the Cause but did not write anything down.') Wright tried. Another report on the Procter-Lingard line: 'On the 25 Feb. 1830, Wright had been to Kirkby – and getting out of a chaise in Hornby asked Smith to walk with him. They walked backward and forward in the wood adjoining the Castle almost an hour. What passed is unknown, but may be guessed. On Smith's return his wife said to him (such familiarity as walking with Wright was quite unusual) "I saw you walking with Mr Wright". "Yes", he replied, "but it was for the last time." There can be no doubt of the fact and the reply. Hence it is inferred that Wright had sounded Smith as to the Evidence he would give and that Smith was firm.'[19]

Shortly before the trial, a 'friend of Admiral Tatham's'

> had an interview with Smith, who hoped Admiral Tatham would attribute his backwardness not to any partiality for Wright but merely to his wish to avoid the shame of his appearing in the Witness Box as a man who had betrayed one whom he had served for so many years ... He thought he would be of more service if he appeared as an unwilling Witness and the facts seemed to be drawn from him against his will tho' in reality he was anxious to detail them.[20]

The 'friend' was Lingard himself (the event is mentioned in Smith's diary as 'Mar. 13. I called on Dr J.L.'). Lingard concluded 'that Smith knew much as to constraint and influence, but they had not made him privy to any of their secret intrigues', which may be the reason, though it seems an insufficient one, why he was not called as 'an unwilling witness'. A further reason may be that he said himself that he 'did not think so meanly' of Marsden's intelligence as Mr Procter did. To the last minute both sides hoped to use him.

12

The Trial at York

It took nearly four years to bring the case to court. John Marsden died in July 1826, the cause of *Tatham* v. *Wright* was tried at York Assizes in the spring of 1830. Both sides had retained distinguished counsel. James Scarlett, recently appointed Attorney General, represented Tatham; Frederick Pollock, for Wright, though younger, was perhaps the brightest star on the northern circuit.

Meanwhile, the Hornby Castle estate began to bleed slowly to death. Although there were still ten servants and workmen at the Castle when in July 1829 George Smith handed out half-crowns to celebrate John Marsden Wright's marriage, the place was less and less used. The Wrights lived almost permanently at Heysham; the Lister Marsdens remained, apart from an occasional shooting party, at Gargrave. In the summer of 1828 there was a four-day sale of most of the contents, and thereafter only a few rooms were kept habitable. Windows were blocked up and the damp ran down the walls.

Hornby village was blighted; not only from the continuing uncertainty but from the absence of patronage and trade. The inhabitants, those who could move, began to leach away; there were other contributory reasons, but the population between the censuses of 1821 and 1841 dropped by a third.

In the spring of 1827 a commission was appointed (two members for the Admiral, two for Wright), and sat for three months in Lancaster, making forays into the country to interview witnesses who could not or would not make the journey. There was a second commission in the following year. The lawyers confabulated endlessly and expensively in London. Bills were filed on either side, one to establish the will, one to challenge it.

When it seemed good to them, both sides used delaying tactics. In February 1827 Wright tried to sub-poena Tatham, for what purpose is not clear, but, warned by Higgin (he was at the time in Lichfield, reletting his house and disposing of the furniture), the Admiral took evasive action, which he clearly enjoyed.

Your letter was just in time. Herbert [his servant] and I got on to the Birmingham road unperceived and in a few minutes I was on board the Express going 9 Knots an Hour for Birmingham. In half an Hour Mr Hinkley's clerk was at the door. Is the Admiral at Home? No. Where? Gone which road? Towards Lancaster via Stafford. Can a Horse catch him? Don't know. Herbert was quite up to the thing. Whether the clerk took a Cruize by Moon Light to enjoy the Cool Breezes or not I know not.[1]

The purpose was to dodge the sub-poena by disappearing for a few days. As Higgin explained to his client, if the action were delayed until the vacation began, 'it will be impossible to bring their artillery to bear until next November'.

The intervention of four legal vacations a year, during which all activity seemed to cease, became a cause of immense frustration. Another was that both sides wanted the best of the legal profession to act for them, and busy lawyers not only can pick and choose, they can also take their time. Thomas Cuvelje, Wright's London solicitor, wrote to Sharp in January 1827:

It is impossible to get Counsel of any eminence to lay aside all other Business to attend to that which they think does not press for a few Days. I could very easily have procured the Drafts of the Answers and the Bill long before this if I had put them into the hands of some young man who had little to do and therefore had had little experience.[2]

It was a painful and costly lesson to be learnt by both sides. In April 1828, nearly two years after Marsden's death, Tatham was borrowing the large sum of £3000, and so far no definite progress had been made.

By the autumn of 1828 the Admiral's side were only just ready to send their case to counsel for an opinion. It went in November to Samuel Duckworth of Lincoln's Inn, who in spite of much prodding from Higgin ('I sincerely assure you that I have the greatest reluctance and sustain the most painful feelings whilst I find myself obliged to address you the language of complaint'),[3] failed to send his reply for six months, months which were further complicated by the diversion of Higgin's attention to his own bankruptcy. This was sorted out within a few months, but meanwhile, anxious in case there was distraint on his office, he had sent all the Admiral's papers to his father to be locked in the strong-room at Lancaster Castle.

When Duckworth's opinion finally arrived in May 1829, it was a model of percipience and clarity. As the solicitors kept saying, if you wanted the best counsel you had to wait their pleasure. The opinion was in two parts: Tatham's right to bring the case and the best case to be brought. On the first, he advised that the position of heir at law was sufficiently proved, but that there was still some doubt as to William Tatham's death without lawful issue. On the second point, he advised that there was satisfactory evidence to obtain an issue 'devisavit vel non', but not enough to obtain a special issue as to fraud, control or undue influence. On the simple will issue, he felt that John Marsden's weakness could be sufficiently proved by his lack of information; his incompetence to fill any of the usual offices taken by gentlemen of his position; his failure to manage either his estate or his household in the smallest particulars; and the uncertainty over whether he could even pay bills or write letters. Duckworth's private opinion was that Marsden could probably have been responsible for a simple will, but not a complex one. However, this distinction, he said, had never been put to a jury before, so it would be a doubtful starter, and they must look at the question of fraud and control.

On this issue it would not be difficult to prove Wright's influence over Marsden and Mrs Cookson, his total control of the property, the servants and even the guests, the fact that his family were installed in the Castle and his children educated at Marsden's expense, and that he held the only bank account for all monies. The weak link, said Duckworth, was the link between Bleasdale and Wright. Could Wright be proved, in the face of his own and Bleasdale's strong denials, to have used his undoubted influence also to control the will? The opinion ended sombrely. Unless Bleasdale could be shaken by cross-examination or further evidence found for their collaboration, the jury would probably find for Wright.[4]

After this opinion, efforts were redoubled to strengthen the weak places. Dr Lingard scoured his numerous acquaintance in Hornby and elsewhere for possible additional evidence. 'I have almost daily notes from Dr Lingard', wrote the Admiral, 'Nothing escapes him.' To make sure of the evidence relating to William Tatham, Captain Robert Barrie, a younger naval friend and colleague, stationed on the Great Lakes in Canada, volunteered to get leave from the Admiralty and go down to the United States to collect the necessary affidavits at first hand, and thence beg a lift to England by some Royal Navy vessel. He arrived just in time, almost days before the trial.[5] It was worth the trouble. The opposition agreed to accept Sandford Tatham as heir at law.

Meanwhile Wright's party had put much effort into changing the venue from Lancaster Assizes to York. They saw it as a move to get a fairer trial, to escape what Sharp called 'the general Prejudice existing in Lancaster', but Tatham was convinced it was a move to cause him further trouble and expense. It was not going to be convenient for either side to transport the documentation (a cartload of boxes had to go from the Castle the seventy miles to York); or the witnesses, many of whom were old, and would need not only transport but board and lodging at the other end.

Lingard continued to report activity up to the last moment, and George Smith continued to be an unknown quantity. He was reported as saying: 'I don't think I shall be called at all, neither party can tell what I shall say, and therefore they will be afraid to call me.' Lingard also reported a visitor to Hornby Castle ('an opulent butcher ... on Shrove Tuesday') who had found Wright sorting out and burning large quantities of paper.

Giles Bleasdale was a sick man, but was determined to go to York 'if he creep there on his hands and knees'. Edmund Tatham had suffered 'a fit' but 'Mr P. and the Misses P. will do all in their power to get him to York'. 'Will Miss Whaley make a good witness? Should she not accompany her father to keep him sober?' The need for chaises and horses brought a brief new prosperity to Hornby as all the world passed through on its way to York. Some went willingly; some, who had never travelled so far in their lives, with the gravest misgivings; some from lighter motives. 'Mr Murray means to be at York through curiosity.' He was not the only one: the cause was now celebrated throughout the country.

Robert Procter, always a nervous character, had been under pressure of a severity amounting to blackmail. His debts to Wright had been mounting up for fifteen years, and now tallied over £1200. In 1828 Wright had demanded security. Shortly afterwards he sent for Procter and he and Sharp examined him closely. 'He was asked, could Mr M. have made the will. No. At the word Sharp looked aghast. Wright in a passion said: By God, you'll make a pretty figure in the box. You attested the execution when you thought the testator incapable. They'll trim you, sir.' They tried again on another occasion, when, finding him still firm, Wright 'burst into tears'. This moment of weakness did not prevent him thereafter issuing demands for his money back, and threatening reprisals. A month before the trial the whole sum was paid, through Francis Pearson, a Kirkby Lonsdale attorney, who was never retained but did some useful work for the Admiral on the sidelines. The payment was recorded by both Lingard and Smith, but neither source suggested the name of the rescuer.

Sharp was also doing his best to pump Smith, and not getting very far. He made one last attempt at Hornby, pleading that if they did not get a verdict for the will the Wright family, and he specifically cited 'the young people' whom Smith had known since they were babies, would have their lives blighted. Smith continued to maintain that he would tell the truth but that he was not going to disclose what that truth was until he was in the witness box. He did however tell Sharp, who professed extreme surprise, that Marsden had never audited his own accounts. 'Not audit his accounts? Who did?' 'Mr Bleasdale did it.' 'Is it possible? I assure you this is the first time I ever heard it.'

The trial began on Friday 2 April 1830 and lasted until Friday 9 April, which happened to be Good Friday. There were thirty-five witnesses lined up for Wright, and sixty-one for Tatham. The York inns were full: the Black Swan bursting with Wright's witnesses, the Admiral's scattered through the town. The Admiral himself was lodged in the suburban village of Acomb.

Robert Procter and Edmund Tatham were not called, Wright's party depending on Bleasdale alone as a witness to the will. Whether it was admissable to depend on one, while the other two were not only alive but standing by, was a nice legal point. George Smith was not called. He attended two days of the trial, Friday and Saturday, and on Sunday was summarily sent home. It was reported that even when the post-chaise was waiting at his inn, he lingered as long as he could, as though hoping that someone from the Admiral's party would come for him; but nothing happened, and he returned to Hornby.

He had had time to hear most of Wright's case, including the speech with which Frederick Pollock led off, which was received with surprise and some consternation. The shorthand writer's copy of this speech does not survive, but there are plenty of references to it. Years later, Dr Lingard reported from a judges' dinner he attended at Lancaster:

> Pattison talked of the long duration of the cause, of the great annoyance it was to the judges, and of Pollock's imprudence and obstinacy, which he said was the cause of its duration. At York, at a consultation on the evening before the trial, it had been resolved to make during the course of the trial some offer of a compromise, and on that account to do and say nothing which might prevent it taking place. Judge then, said he, what was our surprise the next morning, to hear Pollock, soon after he had begun his opening speech, make an abusive attack on the Admiral, which at once put all hopes of a compromise out of the case.[6]

Why Pollock should have behaved so was never made clear, nor why he continued in the same vein at every succeeding trial. Lingard had dined with him not long before, and had sent a reasssuring message to the Admiral that 'Pollock will oppose you as a gentleman'. Instead he castigated him for the iniquity of taking statements from Rigg, the Hornby Castle gardener, without the permission of his master, Wright, and probably also for not protecting the character of his aunt Sarah Cookson. At a later trial he ranted:

> The Admiral has not scrupled to rake up all the gossip, and all the slanders of the surrounding country; all the rumours and gossip of the kitchen, even so far back as fifty years ago – to rake up all the imputations he could collect against his father's sister, even to the age of sixty years, she being an old woman, fit to be his grandmother. But says the Admiral Tatham 'I value not that old woman's reputation; away let reputations fly, light as air, let me but have the Castle'. I trust, gentlemen, this will be to him a castle in the air.[7]

(*Pickwick Papers* was not written until 1836, but this is precisely the language of Serjeant Buzfuz.)

Most of the York evidence is only available in summary from the Judge's notes, no verbatim report having survived. In the case of Giles Bleasdale, however, the shorthand-writer's copy was read at a later trial, Bleasdale having died in the meanwhile. It was a masterly performance. The Judge, with a partiality he should certainly not have shown, commented in his summing-up: 'I have known Mr Bleasdale ever since I was in the law and I will say he has gone through the world with a character he by no means deserves if the will be not genuine.' All good liars stay as close to the truth as they can, so it may well be that much of Bleasdale's evidence was accurate, but it has been noted earlier that he perjured himself in at least one important statement.

He said that he had stayed several times at Wennington Hall, and had frequently met Marsden in London.

> He never came to London, I think, without his coming to visit me, and we always dined together when he came to London repeatedly.
> How long have you known Mr Wright? – From about eight or ten years after I knew Mr Marsden. I did not know Mr Wright till I had visited Mr Marsden at Hornby Castle. I never had seen him.[8]

Bleasdale knew the importance of convincing the jury that Wright was uninvolved in Marsden's will-making as well as the opposition knew that they had to prove his involvement. This particular statement is made with a clarity and emphasis quite at variance with the rest of his presentation of an old man with a bad memory, cudgelling his brains

to give honest answers. Even in print, the presentation is very convincing: but for that single circumstantial lie, it would be overwhelming.

Pollock gently drew out of him the history of all Marsden's wills with
which he had been concerned, from the one which was in existence
when he first came upon the scene.

Do you recollect who was chiefly to be benefitted by that will? – I have
been endeavouring to recollect, and I think it was Mr Anthony Lister,
the father of the present Mr Marsden.

Do you remember whether any of the family of the Tathams were
benefitted by that will? – I incline to think that Mr Harry Tatham (as
they called him) was named in the will, but in what way I cannot satisfy
my mind: I think he was mentioned in it, and it was from a particular
circumstance that I remember that.

What was the circumstance? – It was this: that upon a subsequent
occasion in cancelling his will (for I made several, and he himself constantly cancelled them and threw them into the fire) he said 'There go
the Tathams', and if it had not been for that I should not have remembered that his name was mentioned; I do remember that.

Well, upon the occasion when you were first applied to, did you make
him a will? – I had little to do, as far as my memory serves, to the best
of my recollection, it was merely changing the trustees the first time I
made one. I believe there was a change of trustees; as it was an entailed
property, it followed the outline of the former.[8]

Counsel led the witness through the various wills made at one time
or another for John Marsden, until the series, starting in 1815, in which
Wright was appointed sole trustee. This appointment, on which the
whole will hinged, was presented as nothing to do with Wright, and
not even Bleasdale's own idea. It came from a completely impartial
source.

Do you remember ever making him another will? – When he spoke to
me about a further will I was dissatisfied with the plan of the former
one; I followed Mr Barrow's idea, and it did not carry conviction to my
mind that it would be the best mode that could be adopted, and I am
ready to state my reason.

Did you consult with a conveyancer in London? – In consequence of
doubts in my mind I did consult a conveyancer in what way they could
be removed.

Who was that? – Mr Richmond, a young man I employed.

What was the alteration that he suggested? – After a long consultation,
and making himself master of the subject as much as I was myself, he

suggested the idea of Mr Wright being appointed trustee; he suggested the plan upon which the present will is drawn.

How many wills have been drawn upon that second plan suggested by Mr Richmond? – There have been three wills upon that plan.

In all those wills was Mr Wright made trustee? – He was.

When the new wills were made, did you always destroy the old will, or keep it? – The depository of the duplicate was desired to bring it with him, and he did so; and the moment the new wills were executed, the old one was put into the fire.

Did you keep the drafts of the old wills? – The draft when Wright was a trustee upon the new plan, I certainly did keep it.

Where is that draft? – Upon my word, I do not know ... I thought it was here in York, and I had it with me when examined in Chancery ... I thought I had left it in Lancaster ... I could not find it ... I searched for it, and sorry I was.[8]

The Admiral's side believed, but it is uncertain on whose information they believed it, that in the first part of the missing draft there was an interpolated line in Wright's handwriting. If that were true and the draft had been produced, it would have provided the watertight proof they sought. But it was not produced, and Bleasdale's examination continued to build up, answer by answer, a picture of the upright attorney, bumbling a little in his old age, but of unimpeachable honesty.

Cross-examination did not shake him, although a series of non-sequiturs in answer to questions about disposing of draft wills should, one feels, have been pounced on by counsel. But James Scarlett (who, originally retained by both sides, had kept them guessing until the last minute, when he agreed to act for the Admiral), though a brilliant counsel, was not famed for his skill in cross-examination; or it may be that at this point Bleasdale was taking refuge in his deafness.

Did you keep the drafts? – With regard to the drafts of what are called Richmond's wills, I cannot tell what became of them, but I kept them out of the way, that curious clerks might not pry into them, to know how Hornby Castle was going. I sealed them up, and forgot that they existed, with Marsden's name upon the back of them.

You took instructions in writing, was it? – No, it was in pencil. I think I should have put them into the fire afterwards, as I had no motive for keeping them. I never expected any inquiry.

Did you never expect any inquiry? – Never; I can give you the history of that. I had heard a great deal about Marsden being incapable of transacting his own business, and that a commission of lunacy should be taken out against him, when he was selling Wennington Hall and buying Hornby Castle. I did not expect any inquiry of the sort. There was a good deal of talk, but I considered that I might be reflected upon, and I did that which he wished me to do.

I should have thought that was a reason for you to keep the instructions? – No, they were the loose idle talk of the country; the loose stories that I heard were idle ones. I never thought it necessary to keep them for my justification. If I had considered this as a regular business, I should have kept regular papers and accounts of it, and laid them by, but considering this was gratuitous on my part, an act of friendly feeling, I kept no memorandum whatever upon the subject.

Then you think the only occasion when a solicitor should not keep drafts of a will, or the instructions, is when they are gratuitous? – They are generally pinned to the drafts.[8]

We do not know whether there were any nasty courtroom surprises for Wright. There were certainly some for Tatham, not least the production of William Dawson's correspondence; in the easy tones of kinsmen who knew each other well no suggestion could be heard of Marsden's incompetence.

The ninety-odd witnesses were led through their evidence more or less successfully, those for the defendant (Tatham) having the less comfortable experience because Pollock was a fierce cross-questioner. As far as social class went, Wright's list was considerably the more impressive, and this, in a world where a gentleman could be labelled dishonourable for interviewing another gentleman's gardener without permission, counted for a good deal.

Of servants, Wright called John Nutter, who had been Marsden's servant but was now an innkeeper in Galgate; Roger Chester, who had followed Nutter from 1819 to 1826 and continued as Wright's butler; Edward Smith, Lister's butler at Gargrave; John Gregory, Lister's coachman; and Edward Dawson, servant to William Sharp. It would seem that neither Nutter nor Chester were asked to testify to Marsden's soundness of mind, only to domestic arrangements, and in cross-examination they both underwent a barrage of questions as to their treatment of Marsden: failure to answer his bell, addressing him as 'silly old fool', bullying him. Threatening to tell Wright when he was recalcitrant. To everything both of them returned flat, uncircumstantial denials, even to denying any knowledge of fellow servants whose accusations were being quoted. Neither gave a convincing performance.

Of shopkeepers and others of the same sort who would have had common business transactions with Marsden, there was Robert Hudson, a hairdresser, William Preston, a watchmaker, John Langshaw who taught and sold music, all of Lancaster. There was no one from the estate except James Hird, a farmer who had only arrived in Hornby in 1825; John Russell, a carpenter of Kirkby Lonsdale who had once been asked by Marsden to replace a piece of wood which had been knocked off the moulding of his bedroom door; and George Banks, a farmer, who had been George Wright's tenant in Wennington since 1795. (George Banks was closely cross-examined because it was said that since he had been in York he had said to someone at the Black Swan that Bleasdale and Wright had been 'getting up the case for thirty years', but he denied this.)

Two medical men were called: William Marsden of Skipton, who had attended Marsden three times at Gargrave in 1825, and Thomas Howitt of Lancaster, who attended him at Heysham in 1824 when he had his first stroke. Neither had much information to give beyond the fact that on the subject of his own condition he was able to give them perfectly adequate information.

Several parsons were called: the Reverend J.M. Hodson, who had been Curate at Tatham Fells Chapel for two years and occasionally did duty at Hornby; the Reverend John Garnett, Assistant Curate of Hornby for three years from 1797; the Reverend R. H. Beaty, Curate for some years at Tatham Fells. All these dined from to time at Hornby Castle, as local clergymen expected to do with their patron. Thomas Yates Ridley was Rector of Heysham and knew both Wright and Marsden well. He had acquired the position by marrying the widow of the last Thomas Clarkson, who had the living in her gift, and was considered (by the opposition at least) to be a doubtful character completely in Wright's pocket.

William Sharp and John Taylor Wilson, another solicitor, represented the legal profession. Sharp's evidence was long and circumstantial and, as the judge pointed out, probably the most important apart from that of Bleasdale. He had been doing Hornby Castle business since 1804 – all the business except Marsden's wills. He had dined there and slept there constantly. To prove Marsden's independence, he testified to an occasion in 1823 when he and Wright tried to persuade Marsden to agree to an arbitrator in some Chancery suit and Marsden would not budge in his refusal. He reported frequent conversations tête-à-tête with Marsden in the evening after Wright had gone to bed, and he maintained that Marsden had been interested and involved in the proposed improvements at Hornby Castle:

He shewed me what he was going to have done, he went and put his foot at the place where he wished to increase the wings of the Castle, he shewed me where the stakes were to be put to have it extended – there was however nothing of that improvement done. He also shewed me the plans and he said he had approved of one as it was a very florid architecture – those were his own words. By that I suppose he meant the minarets upon it were more gothic in their structure and more like a chapel.[9]

This was indeed strong evidence, and, as reported, Sharp gives the impression of one who believed what he said. He obviously admired Wright greatly for his competence and his skill in management. He certainly owed a great deal to Wright, personally and professionally. It was extremely important to him, as to all the other legal men, that the cause with which he was so identified should be won. It may be, witness the over-elaborate letter he wrote on the occasion of Marsden's death, that he was one of those people who can convince themselves of their own arguments as they go along. It has been previously said that he thought Marsden never came to Lancaster without calling on him, and would pick him up in his carriage and take him out to dinner. In the York evidence, when the point to be made was Marsden's idleness over business matters, he said that he did not believe that Marsden had been to his office more than twice or at most three times in twenty-two years. At York also he told a long circumstantial story of Marsden's refusal to invite Dr Lingard to his table because the priest was a Jesuit and also a tattler, 'telling at Murray's table what he hears at mine'. 'I recollect', said Sharp, 'a conversation about Dr Lingard about a year and a half before Mr Marsden's death when I told him I had met that gentleman.' This places the conversation in 1824, but Lingard had given up going to the Castle in 1817 and David Murray had died in 1822. (His son, who came to York 'out of curiosity', did not live in Hornby until 1840.)

The final group of Wright's witnesses one may call the 'parlour visitors' and these, as chosen, were impressively respectable. They included Peter Hesketh Fleetwood, the current High Sheriff, who had gone to Hornby for the shooting when his family rented Wennington Hall; James Clarke, the Recorder of Liverpool; John Bradshaw of Halton Park; John Fenton Cawthorne, the Lancaster MP, William John Lushington, whose brother was MP for Carlisle. All testified that from their experience Marsden was able to conduct the ordinary affairs of life, though most did not go as far as Mr Richard Fayrer, who maintained that he was 'in a sound state of mind if ever man was', or Cawthorne, who asserted, 'I rather think he was a man of quick parts'.

Then came the Admiral's witnesses, who presented, taken as a group, a much closer view of Marsden, but from an angle much nearer the ground. Some eighteen of them had been 'in the service' as they said, either indoors or outdoors, either at Wennington or Hornby. Many of the names are already familiar: Ann Seward, Robert Humber, John Smith, Betty Sedgwick, George Mashiter, Ann King, William Whittam, Jane Hill, Cecilia Bouskill, Mary Taylor, Margaret Nixon, William Thompson, Eliza Kilshaw, Richard Rigg, Enoch and William Knowles, Thomas Crosfield, James Richardson. William Mason had been servant to Lister, Robert Park to Bleasdale, Thomas Wright to Mr Bell of Melling. There was a farmer, William Procter of Roeburndale, and a farmer's wife, Elizabeth Kitson, who clearly had considerable grudges against Wright. There was Edmund Layfield the Hornby shoemaker, William Coulson the tailor, William Warbrick, the chaise-driver from the Castle Inn, Thomas Blackburn, nailmaker, who was also the organist of Hornby Chapel. There were painters and joiners who were employed from outside, not in the direct employ of the Castle. There were early neighbours of Marsden, notably Mary Denny of Wennington, now of Wray. (Their evidence has been heavily used in the earlier chapters of this book, as well as that of many others who did not get as far as the witness box.)

The overwhelming impression is of lively verbatim reportage and, in the case of those actually selected to appear in court, first-hand experience. The impression of people who, because they were mostly illiterate, had accurate verbal memories is strong, their picture of wild, weak-minded idiosyncrasy on the part of John Marsden, and of harsh and rigorous control on the part of Wright, can hardly be gainsaid. But their evidence could only prove the likelihood of Wright's manipulation of the will to his own and his family's advantage, not the fact. It had very little to say directly as to Marsden's ability to understand or approve the testamentary disposition of his property.

There were other witnesses whose evidence was more germane to that matter. There was Thomas Cookson, a relation, who had frequently stayed with Gillison Bell at Melling, and had always taken the opportunity to call at Hornby to keep an eye on his unfortunate second cousin. There was Dr Ambrose Cookson, another relation and expert in mental deficiencies; and Dr Wake, Physician to the York Lunatic Asylum, who had not known Marsden, but could tie up many of his traits with his own knowledge of 'connate imbecility'. There was Dr Campbell of Lancaster, grey-haired now, but remembering Marsden's early years. There was a group of witnesses who remembered Marsden in his schooldays, including blind John Willan who as a young usher had tried to teach him to count three score quills. There was a highly respectable group of youngish men: the Reverend Robert Gibson, son of Charles Gibson of Quernmore Park; John Hamilton Parr, a Liverpool solicitor; John Hindle, JP and Deputy Lieutenant. They had all been schoolboys with Robert Procter, when Marsden used to hang round their playground and come to their dancing lessons at the Castle Inn, and ask them up to the Castle for a feast once or twice in the year. There were a few genteel neighbours: the Reverend John Tatham of Melling; the Reverend Thomas Butler late of the Ridding; Dr Lingard; Alexander Nowell of Underley Park at Kirkby Lonsdale; Reginald Remington, gentleman of Melling; Mrs Mary Atkinson and Miss Emma Tatham, who had taken tea and played 'Commerce' with the Wright family and John Marsden; and Matthew Atkinson, Mary's husband, JP and Deputy Lieutenant of Westmorland, who used to come a-courting to Hornby.

The Judge was Sir James Alan Park, aged sixty-seven, who has been called 'sound, fair and sensible', but was also notoriously bad-tempered. The case bored him, and he showed that it bored him, complaining that he could not think why it had been moved from Lancaster to York, and that it really should not have taken so long. 'We must all of us most grievously lament that we have been detained six days on this question' is a fairly clear indication of bias. If the case could have been so easily resolved, it must have been because he believed the challenge to the will was frivolous: given the extreme difficulty of overturning a will, he could not have meant the opposite.

He gave unpardonable personal references for people known to him. Lefevre 'was known to Mr Brougham and myself ... He was not a man likely to lend £27,000 to a fatuitous man'. 'Mr Baron Bolland is a very fine and classical scholar and is well skilled in the arts and sciences. He has a great knowledge on works of Art and so forth and I should say that Mr Baron Bolland would not have liked the society of an idiot.'

He pointed out clearly enough that John Lushington's evidence (the Lushington brothers appear to have been a couple of sporting spongers, though only one of them was called at York) was suspect because it contradicted almost everyone else's – Lushington claimed to be a good musician and reeled off the numerous pieces he had played as duets with Marsden. Park also pointed out that John Fenton Cawthorne's evidence, which was contradictory to most other witnesses, just might have been influenced by Marsden and Wright's parading into Lancaster at election time at the head of fifty committed Tory voters ('One would think Mr Cawthorne supposes that every man who supported him at his election is the most sensible man in the world').

Most of Park's summing-up, however, was coloured strongly in favour of Wright's witnesses. Quite clearly he felt that they were intrinsically more credible than the largely working-class group on the other side, and this message came across from his first words, that evidence was to be 'weighed, not counted', to the last:

> Ignorant persons and enlightened persons will form very different opinions upon subjects of this kind. Ignorant persons, servants, and those in their condition who form their judgement in the conversation of the kitchen circle are very apt to form erroneous opinions upon matters of this kind; and this will be the case even without throwing in the additional ingredient which takes place in those circles – the loose suspicions and prejudices by which their judgements are often biassed and carried out of their true courses.[10]

But Tatham's 'broadcloth' witnesses did not fare any better. By the time Park was summing up their evidence it was late on the last of six gruelling days – the court was sitting ten hours a day. The learned judge was clearly very tired, and cross. He dismissed the schoolboy witnesses because they were too young to have had sound judgement. He dismissed witnesses whose knowledge of Marsden was gained during their visits to Hornby Castle. 'This is an instance of another gentleman [Remington] who although he dined frequently at Mr Marsden's table at Hornby Castle, he comes here to say he was a person of weak intellect and completely under control.' Of Thomas Cookson, who had testified to weakness and imbecility: 'Now it appears really singular that any gentleman should go to the house of a man so situated.' Of Dr Lingard: 'How a man of his calibre of learning should go and mingle in company with a gentleman of this description, is certainly a remarkable circumstance.' Alexander Nowell, who said that he had only been inside the Castle once in his life, but took opportunities of meeting Marsden to try and assess his deficiency, because he was interested (Nowell had trained as a doctor and had had the experience of sitting on the jury in the Portsmouth case), fared no better. 'It appears that this gentleman gives this opinion of Mr Marsden's understanding from a very slight acquaintance.' And Matthew Atkinson ('I have been invited to Hornby Castle at various times but invariably refused those invitations') got even shorter shrift. 'Now this gentleman never having been at Hornby Castle for the purpose of eating and drinking takes upon himself to say he thought Marsden totally incapable.'

The jury was out until one o'clock in the morning, when the Judge called for the foreman, who reported that they were unlikely to agree. The court was adjourned until noon next day. At two p.m. the jury returned a verdict for the Wright. The will was upheld.

13

Stalemate

Although the tone of Park's summing-up had been a partial preparation, the verdict was a stunning blow to Sandford Tatham, as one can read in the subdued dignity of his reaction. He left York immediately, and wrote the same evening to Pudsey Dawson, whose role as supporter was rapidly growing into that of executive manager. The Admiral was on his way to London, where a young relation Thomas Gorst offered him and his wife modest lodgings in the Temple. The purpose of the letter was to ask that all outstanding bills should be paid in full.

> It will not be convenient for me to keep my servant James Townson who indeed has been on the lookout for a place for some time past. He is an Honest man with many good qualities ... I think if I give him £10 and all cloaths he will be satisfied and I would have him so for he has done his best. I would have Elizabeth Parr my wife's maid immediately return to her friends ... I do not know the exact sum due to her but whatever she requires I wish her to have it. To make them easy in respect to Mrs Tatham and myself I can with truth assure them I have not felt my mind more at ease than at this time conscious of having faithfully discharged the Duty I owe to my Family and Society. Nor is my Wife in the least degree affected by the unfavourable decision, and if my Letter is not so well pen'd as heretofore attribute it to the true cause that I am writing with a painfull cramp in my hand which renderes it difficult to write in any way.[1]

A few days later, with characteristic resilience, he was able to express himself in his usual direct naval fashion about 'the Mandarine who presided – the office of a Chairman of petty sessions on the filiation of a Bastard is beyond his capacity',[2] and his friends no doubt were thankfully assured that there was plenty of fight in the old man yet.

The recovery was helped by such support as that offered by the party workers in Lancaster. John Bush was a shopkeeper, possibly retired, at least with enough time on his hands to enable him to act as a runner for Higgin, collecting depositions. Matthew Gardner was another – 'an active and intelligent man and I have much dependence on him'. With wobbly spelling but unimpeachable sentiments they wrote to dissuade the Admiral from having his furniture at the Dalton Square house sold off publicly. Bush said:

> My reason of thus requesting it is that your friends hear may not be struck dumb by it as they are very numerous. Where you had one previous to trial you have ten now and if your sale goes on it will attend to give your Enemys an oppertunity to burst forth with their slanderess imputations which at present is kept down by most or all of your Friends exclaiming against a partial Judge and a perjured Jury. I am tould Wrights are not very cumfortable and that they are afraid the Admiral will not let them alone although they have wone, this last was of Mrs Wrights saying she frets much and says all their friends have disownded them servants and others. The next I have to observe to you during the week trial at York is that very little Buisness was attended to in Lancaster, and on the Friday the gent[lemen] hear proposed to open a subscription for the purpose of opening the public Houses and having an ilumination, if you had got a verdict which they quite Expected although the Judge was against you they expected the Jurey to do their duty ... As for my own part I feeled myselfe so much disapointed at the Judges conduct and Jourys verdict I scacely know how I got home, and all this week I have been very poorly but sincerly hopes you and your Lady health will not suffer by this raskaldy proceeding.[3]

Matthew Gardner added a postscript: 'Admiral Tatham Sir I quite concor with Mr Bush as it will sertently give an opening to is antagonists and make them talk much about it I will send you a perticler Account of what I have paid to the Witnesses in A little time as I have not seen them all yet James your man is of the same opinion as we are respecting the sale.'

Such whole-hearted support was encouraging, but it must have been bitter to hear of three deaths, two of them directly related to the trial. Edmund Tatham had a second stroke and died within a few hours of returning from York; and old Mary Denny, who had insisted on going in the last stages of illness, had also died. 'In her road home I am tould she said she was happy at what she had done and would die contented and did not care how soon.' Robert Procter had lost not only his brother-in-law but also his wife in the same week and was prostrated. Giles Bleasdale had also shown considerable determination to conquer illness but Bush at least wasted no sympathy on him: 'I have been tould old Bleasdale is likely for death. I hope the Devil will fetch him before he resigns his last breth and all such like to share the same fate.'

The priorities were clear: to seek a retrial immediately on the certain grounds of the judge's misdirection and the possible grounds of at least one venal juryman; and to clear away the costs of the York trial.

Pudsey Dawson, though a strong supporter, had as yet his reasons for keeping a low profile. He was the senior member of his own branch, and a cousin of the William Dawsons. His grandfather and William Dawson's father had been half-brothers, the one a rich Liverpool merchant and the inheritor of most of the Yorkshire estates, the other making his fortune in London. As a merchant and banker himself, and eldest son of a merchant father from whom he had inherited in 1816, Pudsey was more than comfortably rich, and he had also married twice and well. His first wife had died of consumption, leaving him with one son, Hugh Pudsey, an Oxford undergraduate aged now twenty-one but not in good health, indeed suspected of his mother's disease. He had married again in 1821. His second wife was Jane Dawson, a very remote cousin of the Dawson clan, by whom he had no children, but two sisters-in-law, whom he cheerfully included in his family. He was now fifty-two and, as he comes across from his letters, an intelligent, level-headed and tolerant man, capable of deep attachments but unlikely to let his heart rule his head.

Pudsey from the beginning had been entirely on the Admiral's side, having known him, though not intimately, all his life. His father and Sandford Tatham had been good friends, the great merchant house on Rodney Street, Liverpool, always open to the sailor cousin. Their letters were at first formally addressed 'My dear Sir', which soon broke down to 'My dear Pudsey', 'My dear Admiral', and as the years of shared endeavour went on the relationship developed into that of a father and son. Pudsey's sympathies had been strong on the Admiral's side from the beginning, but there were reasons why he was slow to get involved. After the York result he wrote to Higgin:

> The peculiar delicacy of my situation closes my lips and locks up my pen – until I know how the good old Admiral's pulse beats and how he sets his Horses with my Cousins in London. If it depends upon anything I could do, say, or urge, the matter should not rest. And if I am enabled either by myself or others to give an impulse to the right cause, it shall only be under an understanding that there is neither bond, fetter, or engagement, either direct, or implied, upon the Admiral's inclinations ... To you I write in perfect confidence, and I know I am safe in your hands.[4]

For the cause of this honourable reticence it is necessary to look at the family tree again. The Admiral needed an heir, and had already expressed his intention to follow the 'right line'. But there might be difficulty, and the makings of a bitter family row, in the choice of that right line. Both families descended from the original William Dawson of Langcliffe who had died in 1762, having married twice, first Jane Pudsey and then Elizabeth Marsden, by each of whom he had a son. Pudsey and his son Hugh Pudsey were of the elder line; William Dawson of St Leonards was of the second wife, but the one who had brought the Marsden connection into the family. With the law regarding a wife's possessions as it was then constituted, the original William had a legal title to the inheritance of both his wives, and could do what he liked, but it had always been customary in such cases for a man to split his estate and let the second wife's inheritance go to her children. In this case, where there was no actual inheritance as yet, the Pudsey Dawsons might be thought to have more legal right to be the Admiral's heirs, the William Dawsons to have more moral right, and a fertile ground for family feud it might turn out to be, which Pudsey wanted to avoid. Therefore, although all his instincts were on the side of re-entering the legal lists, he held back until he knew which way the Admiral himself wanted to go.

There was very little doubt about it. Within a few days the Admiral was writing with all his old zest: 'in the first place we must have all accounts collected and get our Debts paid, and next consider the ways and means to raise the means and replenish the Amunition and at them again.'[5]

His troops re-formed with eagerness. John Lingard took up his position again as chief local reporter and bolsterer of morale. The Admiral urged Pudsey: 'Should you go to Lancaster, I wish much you should be acquainted with Dr Lingard and in communication with him. I am sure you will like him when you know him, he is a most honourable high-minded man, most liberal and in every sense of the word a perfect Gentleman, just what a man of his high attainment should be.'[6] He was right, and first acquaintance developed from mutual respect to a very firm friendship which lasted to the day of Lingard's death.

Higgin's office was showered with communications offering new evidence, new witnesses, good advice. There were persistent rumours that the jury had been got at, or had been swung at the last moment, when they were all battered and exhausted, by a man called Eeles or Eccles who boasted that he had sworn never, ever, on any jury, to take the side on which Brougham was counsel. Ten of them were said to have

My Dear Sir

I thank you for the information, and also for the trouble
which you have taken with my parcel. We must wait with patience
till next term.

Wright is at Wenning Cottage;
probably preparatory to the rent
day next monday.

Will a letter reach the admiral
directed to him at Cheltenham? If so,
do not answer this note. If not, be
so good as to send me his address.

I am told that Mr John Thompson
used to tell a story of Mr Marsden
being persuaded to eat a part of
a tallow candle, while he was at
Lancaster free school.

I am, &c,
Most truly yours
Friday.   J. Lingard

Letter from John Lingard to John Higgin. (*Lancashire Record Office*) been put up at the Black Swan and mingled freely with Sharp and the Wright witnesses. (This was later cut down to two, who had been lodged in an entirely different part of the inn and mixed with nobody, but the suspicion that Sharp meddled with the juries rightly or wrongly continued to rear its head to the very end of the Cause.) Matthew Gardner had a tale to tell of a conversation overheard on the top of a coach, but something better than such stories would be needed to get a retrial and that something could only be Park's misdirection.

Henry Robinson, attorney, and Higgin's agent in York, was very busy trying to sort out and pay all the bills, helped by Thomas Gorst, who had elected himself Pudsey Dawson's unpaid assistant. He was about twenty-eight, with quite enough money of his own not to need to work, a little, bouncy man, cheerfully darting about the country wherever he or someone else thought he could be useful. As he was of that sociable sort which is welcome in any house and takes endless trouble for its elders ('a very good fellow', 'one of the best lads living'), he was an invaluable lieutenant, not least because he was far less noticeable than either Pudsey or the Admiral, who both kept well away from Lancaster. The venue of the last trial had been shifted to York because the Admiral was accused of advertising his cause, and they did not want the next one to be in London, or Carlisle, with all the attendant expense.

Money was the bugbear. Pudsey undertook the responsibility of financing any future trial, but the Admiral had to shoulder the burden of the last one, up to April 1830, and it is a tribute to his toughness that he was not broken by it. Pudsey's resources were to be channelled to building up a fighting fund for the future, but he was keeping publicly very quiet about that, as he kept quiet about all his involvement. The ensuing two years were a financial nightmare, as two main props crumbled: one was a failure of support in the William Dawson family; the other the financial weakness of John Higgin.

It should be said that apart from Frederick, who went up and down in his estimation, and had to be defended by Pudsey ('He is at the bottom a very good fellow'), Tatham had little time for any of the William Dawsons. Although his early correspondence with William Dawson himself had been courteous, it was unlikely that the Admiral would have much in common with a man who had written 'those foolish letters' to his subnormal cousin, especially since their unexpected production in court had done a good deal of damage to the case at York. 'It was Madam's doing', and indeed Sophia Dawson seems to have been an unattractive woman, hiding selfishness behind a display of anxiety for her family.

William Dawson died in 1829, the eldest son William in 1830, when the widow reneged on her husband's promises of help to the Tatham cause, although it must be said that these had been dragged out of him largely by Fred's intervention, and he, he said, now had no influence with his mother at all. She was now able to plead the difficulties of widowhood and, she might have added, the anxieties of an upper-class mother with four daughters still unmarried, the eldest over forty. If, as was thought, it was she who had urged on her husband to try and get some part of the Marsden fortune to add to his own, she was not the woman to be generous when that dream faded. Pudsey plugged away in letter after letter, pleading the necessity and the justice of family support for family honour. He did not get very far. She countered that she had bills of her own, and that her money was in the hands of trustees:

> Unaccustomed to demands of this sort, I, having no funds to draw upon, shrink naturally from contingencies that may involve me. I do not therefore like to make a promise, at the same time I hope I may have it in my power to spare something from my April quarter – but not to any extent. This January I have all my Xmas bills to settle. St Leonards may be unlet and at any rate the Roof will require £200 at least laid out upon it. With these things before me, I can neither be prompt nor so liberal as you seem to expect.[7]

Both the sons, Henry and Frederick, did what they could, and in the end the Dawsons provided some £3000, as Fred, when relations had cooled, pointed out rather sharply to the Admiral. But the Admiral pencilled an unrepentant note on the letter to the effect that this was small against his expenses. He and Pudsey expressed their frustration to each other in references to 'Lady St Leonard's' and the 'Duchess of Manchester [Square]'. On a rare occasion when Tatham called on her, she 'said little about my affairs, she seemed too much occupied with her own'. 'If I am successful, St Leonards will be open to receive me, if otherwise I risk a *Not at Home*.'

An even more serious, because more uncertain, cause of stress was the relationship with John Higgin. His legal work was good: he had prepared the case well, he worked hard, and indeed had to be restrained from running up and down to London too often owing to the expense. But, 'It seems to me', said the Admiral, 'that he is one of those whose pocket is under the influence of a constant Emetic'.[8] He had already suffered one bankruptcy, and seemed to be slipping towards another. As the sterile months went by, while the Cause seemed to be hopelessly bogged down in the hands of Counsel who could make money out of delay, Higgin's demands for his bills to be paid grew louder.

His original position had been that 'he was so zealous in the cause he desired no more than his bare expenses knowing how I was situated', but his personal needs became more and more pressing. 'Can nothing be done to raise the wind and stop Higgin's mouth who I have no doubt is so very hard run that I fear to endanger his solvency?'[9] The letters from Lancaster grew shriller ('Most reluctantly and under the pressure of necessity *the most urgent* I am *compelled* to address you on the subject of my account'),[10] until the Admiral himself admitted 'So very very sick am I of his handwriting and so averse to break the seal of his letters'. On one occasion Mrs Higgin wrote on her husband's behalf, she said entirely without his knowledge, but the clients doubted this since the letter contained a vague allusion to the impossibility of carrying on the Cause without funds, which they regarded as blackmail.

It was inevitable that, as relations were strained, suspicion grew that Higgin's desperation for money was blurring the edges of his honesty. 'Deeply as we are engaged it is no pleasant thing to feel want of confidence in the integrity of your agent.'[11] The financial responsibilities were split between the Admiral and Pudsey, and they began to suspect Higgin of playing off one against the other and getting money from both; not from any real dishonesty, he probably had every intention of making all straight in the end, but to plug some desperate present hole in his personal finances. His anxieties had their effect on his work. 'Cash with him goes quicker than he can find it, and will in my opinion always do so, so that when he should be devoted to the interests of his clients exclusively, his Brains are in Committee on his own ways and means.'[12]

However uncomfortable it might be, they were yoked together as colleagues until the end of the Cause, whatever and whenever that might be. As Fred Dawson rather callously pointed out, there was no need to take too much notice of Higgin's cries for help: his whole business would collapse if the Cause collapsed. At the same time, the Admiral's party could not get rid of him and start again with someone fresh. They would lose an irreplaceable body of knowledge and, what was worse, they might drive him into the enemy's camp.

It was a bad period for all of them, worst of all for Pudsey. He had withdrawn his son, Hugh Pudsey, temporarily from Oxford, and sent him on a voyage to Madeira for the sake of his health. Quite unexpectedly, in the summer of 1831, he died there of some sort of seizure, though it was a shadow of comfort to find from the autopsy that he was so riddled with tuberculosis that he could not have lived for more than a few months in any case. It would not have been surprising had the fire gone out of the father, now deprived of a son to follow him, but he took the opposite course and worked harder: 'I have been engaging myself, as much as I could, with tenants, and improvements, and buildings, and occupying my mind, and still there is a vacuum that never in this life can be filled'. But even as he described himself as 'in health tolerably well – but sick at heart', humour emerged in the postscript: 'I have had a very flaming letter of fashionable condolences from the Duchess – on sky-blue paper – heavenly minded woman!!!' [13]

As a background to these personal events the legal mills were grinding, from 1830, through 1831 and 1832, at speeds varying from slow to very slow and full stop. In spite of his success at York, it is probable that Pollock, who had once confided to Dr Lingard that he wished he were on the other side, was not totally confident. He was largely instrumental in making moves towards compromise. The suggestion bandied about was that the Admiral should be offered Wennington Hall and £2000 a year for life, but it never came to an actual offer. As Sharp said, 'I am quite sure from the disposition of the Admiral that in case such a thing were offered he would treat it with indignation and contempt',[14] in which he was perfectly correct.

Immediately after the York verdict there had been great hopes for a speedy motion for a retrial. This was heard by the Master of the Rolls in July 1830, but postponed by him until November. He refused to consider Park's summing-up, but studied only the notes on the evidence: 'Upon the whole, therefore, I am of opinion that this verdict is consistent with the weight of evidence in this case and notwithstanding the powerful observations which have been addressed to me, I must refuse this new trial.' Sharp was in London to hear the appeal because 'I do really think that my feelings are so wrapt up in the success of the Cause that whether I do any good or not it would almost kill me not to be in the scene of Action'. He reported the result back to Wright in high spirits. 'I'll warrant us "We'll fight and we'll conquer again and again" and I trust they will always find me in the front to protect the Character and Property of my sincerely respected Friends!' [15]

The Wright camp had now two wins to its credit, and Dr Lingard reported some managed rejoicing in Hornby. 'Mr Wright came to Hornby yesterday. The ringers were ordered to be in attendance. They rang for the greater part of the afternoon, were regaled at the Castle with bread and cheese, ale and spirits, and received a sovereign for their loyalty to the Lord.'[16] George Smith, unfathomable even in private, left a blank in his diary.

In the spring of 1831 Pollock made another attempt to get the parties to compromise. Dr Lingard described the background to the attempt.

Pollock came here on the Sunday at an early hour and requested me to walk with him to the castle. I was surprised, he much more so. He expected to see a princely residence, and found a ruin. Nothing could appear more desolate. With the exception of the kitchen inhabited by Blezard and his wife, and a bedchamber where Wright slept, we saw not a room that had an atom of furniture in it. The walls were running down with damp, and in some places covered with green vegetation. The paper had fallen on the floors, the canvass on which the paper had been fastened, had rotted into holes. The rooms themselves (I mean the best, those in front) were low and ill proportioned, and the parts of the castle which I had never seen before, in the state in which they existed in the reign of Henry VIII. Everything was so different from what he had expected, that Pollock could hardly believe his eyes. He appeared to doubt all that he had been told about it, and repeatedly questioned me about the rental. I told him that now it was somewhere between three and four thousand pounds but I knew nothing more. He paused and said, I do not think it probable that the whole is worth more than £110,000 or £120,000. Why it will be all spent in law. Nothing more passed. I was never out of his company till he left, and am sure that he had no conversation with any one else on the subject. On the Thursday, as he went through to York, he called again to breakfast. We had a good deal of conversation. He said: there is a mortgage of more than £30,000 on the property, the expenses of the last trial will amount to £15,000, if there be another trial in London the expense will not be less than £20,000. There go about £65,000, more than half the value of the estate as far as I can learn. If *we* get a verdict and keep the estate, my client will lose one half, if the admiral get the verdict, the cause will not stop there, one or two more trials must come on, and when these are over, what will he or his representative, or the conqueror, have left? I have turned the matter over in my mind and have come to the conclusion that it would be better for both parties to come to some amicable arrangement. And for this purpose I have determined to stop at Gargrave as I pass, and propose the matter to Mr Lister. If he refuse, I must do my duty, but if he follow my advice he will make the proposal, not, however, through the attorneys, for it will always be their interest to continue the litigation ...

Keep all this to yourself, but act upon it as your prudence may suggest. I certainly think that he is afraid of Mr Procter, as he repeatedly said that, if he could but cross-examine him, he thought he could neutralize his testimony. In my mind the conclusion was favourable to you. If an arrangement be made, it will, I trust, be both honourable and profitable to you, and, if the cause proceed, I augur well of it, for it was plain to me that Pollock's *confidence* of success was much abated.[17]

Nothing came of Pollock's initiative, and the cause did proceed. The appeal from the Master of the Rolls to the Court of Chancery was brought up in April 1831, postponed through May and June, finally decided in November, again against the Admiral.

In the same month Giles Bleasdale died, and Wright's strongest support had gone, for although the enthusiastic Sharp had been and continued to be the leading attorney, making up in hard work for what he may have lacked in experience, there is no doubt that the earlier stages of the Cause had been master-minded by Bleasdale from his long experience of London legal practice. When he finally took to his bed, the two Miss Wrights, Margaret and Dorothea, moved in to nurse him, and it was reported that 'his servants never saw him alive again'. The inference was that Wright was making sure there were no death-bed confessions, but the Wright girls had always been the old man's companions and he had treated them like favourite daughters. In his will he left some £4000 of his considerable fortune to his own relations, and all the rest, at least three times as much, to George Wright and his family.

The possibilities of the first trial being exhausted, it now remained for the Admiral to bring a trial by ejectment, but it took another fifteen months, and an immense and costly preparation of new evidence in affidavits, to get this to the point at which the Court of the King's Bench ordered a hearing. The spring of 1832 was the point of lowest morale for the Admiral's side, perhaps for the other side as well. Six years had gone, money had vanished like water down a drain, and only the eye of faith could see whether any advance had been made at all.

There came a moment in the spring of 1832 when the Admiral actually had to escape from the lodgings at Cheltenham where he and his wife were living and vanish for a few days to avoid arrest. At the last minute Pudsey stepped in to arrange things with his bankers, which he could have done at any time before, but had been very unwilling to do as long as there was a faint hope of persuading or shaming the Duchess into clearing the last of the 1830 debt. There would certainly be no hope of getting anything from her for anything incurred later, and he had been loath to use his fighting fund. Tom Gorst, who had some property of his own, provided £1000 from the sale of a farm, and at last the old Admiral was free of debt, a situation for which he was truly grateful.

'Thank you, my liberal, kind and honourable friend and kinsman, you have set me at liberty.' At the same time, it must be said that he felt quite a boyish pleasure in his jaunt to Bath. 'Here I am in a snug bow-windowed room a small Bedroom and very excellent Bed and Bedding with attendance and all for 2 shillings per day, indeed the Bed is the best I have met with on the Journey, the good woman below a ci-devant Ladies Maid keeps a little shop, a young girl attends, no other lodger or any intrusion.'[18] On the way he had got off the coach six miles out of Bath to visit a famous spring, and walked into town 'without feeling the slightest inconvenience'. He was now approaching his seventy-seventh birthday.

In order to bring a trial for ejectment, which was the usual way of trying a disputed title to land, it was first necessary for the claimant to take physical possession of the land claimed. In fact by this time it was no longer strictly necessary, the possession often being replaced by a series of legal fictions in court, but whether Higgin thought it would be safer to go through the older method, or whether he and the Admiral shared a romantic soul, it was so organised, and they appeared to enjoy their escapade.

All I have to do is to go to Hornby make an Entry which I believe is done by granting and executing a Lease upon the premises before competent witnesses. I then have to do another little act and sign etc. [this was a codicil to his will] which altogether will not require many minutes and then take myself off without having any further intercourse with Lonsdale ... It is not necessary to enter the Castle, if it was empty and the door open, a Barn, Shed or the open Air anywhere on the premises will do.[19]

The operation was smartly and secretly carried out when it was known that Anthony Marsden was not yet there for the shooting, which was the only reason for which he visited Hornby, where he was deeply unpopular. 'I hope he found "Sandford Tatham 10th September 1832" on the Door when he arrived at the Castle to add to the Comfort he must have felt from the greeting he met with when he enquired his road, a feeling so universal that it must strew roses on his path whenever he goes there.'[20]

While he was on this very rare visit to the neighbourhood, Tatham found out that the Hornby churchwardens were raising money for a new clock and, after some deliberation as to whether it would be too ostentatious a move, he sent them £5. Dr Lingard wrote to thank him. 'Your friends are charmed and exult. Wright has been asked and surlily replied "Let them put a clock if they choose. What have I to do with it? I don't live at Hornby". He seems to have forgotten that he *did* live at Hornby and feathered his nest there.'[21]

At last, in January 1833 the court of King's Bench ordered the case of *Tatham* v. *Wright* to be heard in Lancaster at the Spring Assizes before a special jury from south Lancashire. The Judge would be Sir John Gurney, recently appointed a Baron of the Exchequer, an independent, Methodistical, severe man, whose honesty no one doubted. His appointment solved the question of venue: before his appointment, Lancaster had seemed an impossibility, the only two available judges on the circuit being Park, who had been on the bench at York, and Baron Bolland, who had been a witness for Wright.

With three months for their final preparation before the April Assizes, both sides must have swung into action with equal determination but, as ever, we can only follow the activities of one. Pudsey Dawson immediately came up from Sidmouth, where he rented a house every winter with his frail wife and her two sisters. The Admiral remained in his lodgings at Cheltenham. It was now out of the question, as he readily acknowledged, for him to do more than sit on the sidelines, guard his precious life, and send his often sharp and perceptive comments through the post, although hearing that Pudsey had a bad cold he did offer himself as a stand-in for the London conferences. 'I am not your equal, but I will do my best, and I think not be humbugged.' A coach journey from Sidmouth to London in the middle of winter and a bout of flu was no light undertaking (on one occasion it was 'a most delightful and easy journey – only seventeen hours on the road'), but all was well, and for several weeks Pudsey 'fagged like a Turk' in London, working so hard that he had not even time to see his own relations.

Higgin of course was with him, his expenses paid up to date. 'I have succeeded in stopping Higgin's craving maw for the present, I *hope*.' But poor Higgin's inability to manage money had become a fact of life, which Gorst kept under control by a severe scrutiny of his expenses, and 'I must do him the justice to say he is indefatigable'.

Pudsey reported from his round of consultations a good meeting with Scarlett; although they had never regretted the huge sums spent on retaining Scarlett, they often wished he would take the sort of interest in the case which Pollock showed on the other side. This time 'he seems really eager to grapple with the case and to make every effort to surmount the great difficulties thrown in the way by one verdict and two appeals'.

From London Pudsey went north, still pursuing last-minute potential witnesses. On the way for the first time he travelled between Liverpool and Manchester 'by Rail Road and got to Manchester to Breakfast (thirty-one miles in eighty-eight minutes)'. From there he went on to Marshfield, Miss Dawson's house in Settle which the family used as their Yorkshire home, until Pudsey's new house at Stainforth should be finished. And from there to Lancaster for the trial, still sending back signals. 'I have a pleasant letter from Henry Dawson – he sends me £200 – but not a word from the Duchess. Frederick is better but very crusty at times, though really hearty in the cause. Gorst has thrown £500 into the bank – a little hero!' [22]

Lancaster was seething. 'The Town is like a Fair – though it is Passion Week' ... 'The lawyers like a flight of rooks darkening the air, not a horse to be had in the neighbourhood.' And still the unknown factor: 'George Smith has been acting very mysteriously. He will not be called unless actually necessary. I fear he is a tool – but perhaps I may injure the man.' [23] Almost simultaneously Sharp was writing to George Wright in acute alarm as to the contents of Smith's examination which his son John had seen in London: 'Smith must be managed delicately and I have no doubt you will in talking to him use the greatest care and discretion. You will of course keep him up to some future expectation. You will I know excuse my great anxiety in writing this letter.' [24] Two days later George Smith was summoned to Heysham and stayed the night, but needless to say his diary is silent on what passed or what 'future expectation' may have been held out to him.

The trial itself, to the acute disappointment of the hundreds who crushed into the court and circulated in the streets waiting for a verdict, was aborted after three days. Wright's side knew this was going to happen, because it was by Pollock's engineering. Whether the other side anticipated it as at least an option is not certain but, considering the impossibility of keeping secrets in the freemasonry of the legal profession, probably they did.

The defendant's (Wright's) side of the case was heard almost in full. The witnesses were called. The first one who claimed John Marsden's competence, the solicitor John Taylor Wilson, was hissed by a large and partial audience which had to be sternly restrained by the judge. George Smith, yet again, was not called.

On the third day, which was by coincidence again Good Friday, the will was put in. As at York, only Giles Bleasdale's evidence, of the three witnesses, was called. But, since York, Bleasdale was dead, while Robert Procter was alive and in court. The discussion as to whether all the witnesses to a disputed will should be called, if humanly possible, had been prominent at York, and decided in favour of Wright – in favour, because by then it was widely known that both Procter and Edmund Tatham would be hostile.

Scarlett protested: 'I object to his having a right to read that will unless he produce the best evidence that can now be produced to prove it. The rule of law is that if the witnesses to a will are all dead the law admits the proof of their handwriting, but if any one of those witnesses is alive then he must be called to give his evidence if he be within the kingdom.' Pollock countered with the argument that he should not be required to call a hostile witness who could be cross-questioned by the opposition. The learned and often impenetrable argument lasted two hours, when Baron Gurney closed it: 'In this case I decide that the living witness should be called.'

Pollock promptly put in a Bill of Exceptions which would have the effect of shifting the matter to a higher court once again. The Judge accepted but directed the jury that the plaintiff was entitled to a verdict, and the verdict was duly brought in for Tatham, with one shilling damages and forty shillings costs.

A goal for Tatham, but this verdict had the curious result of pleasing both sides. Sharp wrote a note to Wright: 'Pollock and all our Counsel are in high spirits ... It is what was explained to you when you attended the consultation.' Pudsey wrote to the Admiral the same afternoon, with messages from all his 'gang' – Higgin, Bell (the London attorney), his brother-in-law Anthony Littledale ('my aide-de-camp'), Gorst and Henry Robinson. 'Read Higgin's inclosure and then say "Well done Pudsey!"' The verdict might not have advanced matters much but it would go far to reverse the impression of the three contrary verdicts so far chalked up. And they could not help feeling that Pollock had taken refuge in a delaying action, which could only mean that far ahead he saw ultimate defeat. 'We have got the weather gage of the pirates and they begin to tremble.' There were even rumours, with very little foundation, it must be said, of unconditional surrender. Even the Admiral, who for all his vigorous language was remarkably calm and considered in his thinking, was on this occasion euphoric – 'Well done, Pudsey!!! Where indeed could we have found your equal' – but continued cautiously: 'I am gratified by all the accounts I receive and highly approve of your Prudence and prompt restraint on the expression of public satisfaction. The course you take is best for us – cool and quiet and silent as far as our triumph must be the order of the day.' [25]

14

The Trial at Lancaster

In spite of their own sense of elation and relief, Pudsey Dawson and his troops acted swiftly to damp down any euphoric outburst on the Hornby estates. If any of the tenants took it into their heads to celebrate prematurely, for instance by withholding their rent, the principals might find themselves tangled into minor lawsuits on the grounds of incitement. 'We were able', said Dr Lingard, 'here and at Melling to restrain the public manifestation of the general joy; at Wray people acted as they thought fit and spent the night in carousing and drinking your health.'[1] The Admiral heaved a sigh of relief that his ebullient friends the Barries were stationed on the Great Lakes and not at their English home near Lancaster: 'The *Lancaster Gazette* and a letter from Swarthdale put the Commodore's house in an uproar ... fortunately for us the Lady was on Lake Ontario had she been at home Kellet Bells would have given a merry Peal before your Message could have prevented it and the Country at Night been set in a Blaze.'[2] The self-denying ordinance was a wise one: 'They [the opposition] are vexed and mortified beyond measure that we have not set up, or attempted, some rights of possession or ownership.'[3]

Morale had received a welcome boost, but it was a victory gained on a legal technicality. The verdict had to be either confirmed or rejected by a higher court, and even then the result would still be a purely technical one. So the process was far from complete: but temporarily at least things looked bright – even Higgin was in everybody's good books, and Pudsey was in better spirits than at any time since Hugh Pudsey's death. He was lodging with Higgin while he was in Lancaster and was reportedly 'the life of the party', spoiling the children disgracefully. A week after the verdict, he could not resist going over to Hornby to see Lingard, with Gorst and Henry Robinson and two of the Higgin girls, and they managed to have a look at the Castle.

For the first time in my life, I crossed the Threshhold of the Gates which were wide open, and walked up to the Terrace. The Doors were all closed, and, I believe, nailed up – it rained – the party sought shelter in one of the outhouses. The old woman passed through the yard, and saw us. The Doctor begged to be admitted if only to the Kitchen fire. With much fear and suspicious trepidation we were shown into the Kitchen. She said repeatedly to the Doctor 'I hope no harm will come to me'. 'Who are these Gentlemen?' 'I have positive orders from *Mr Wright* and *Mr Smith* to admit nobody whatever'. The Doctor assured her we were friends of his, and had no intention of doing *her* any injury. She let us see the Eagle Tower – I mounted to the summit. It was a glorious prospect and the sun burst out and favoured us – but the Eagle did *not* sing.[4]

A side effect of the trial was that George Smith, whether he realised it or not, had lost his credibility as the witness whom everybody courted. A week before the trial he had 'called on Mr Sharp at the King's Arms and afterwards on Mr Higgin who gave me three sovereigns for my expenses', but something during the latter interview set alarm bells ringing. Afterwards the Admiral gave instructions that he was 'not to be thought of by us, except our case become desperate. Higgin would tell you what happened when Smith called on him for his Expences'. Pudsey concurred: 'Depend upon it, Geo. Smith is a traitor – I heard something of him from Procter (late of the Castle Inn) which almost induces me to think he has *had his price*'.[5] Sharp's urgent recommendation to Wright ('You will of course keep him up to some future expectation') seems to have worked.

On the credit side was the discovery of a new and valuable asset in the person of Mr Cresswell Cresswell, junior barrister, a man in his late thirties and soon to replace Scarlett as the northern circuit leader: 'A most indefatigable, intelligent and zealous advocate who has taken up the Cause with spirit, looking to the success of his labours in it as certain stepping stone to fame'.[6] He was not a good speaker, but an industrious and very fast worker, of an extremely clear mind and forceful personality, who was fascinated by will cases.

The trial had once more taken its toll of witnesses. Roger Chester, Marsden's servant and then Wright's butler, who had got himself into such a fearful tangle of denials at the York trial and had presumably repeated the performance in Lancaster, died a week later. 'Never looked up after the trial', the Admiral had heard, '... much disturbed in his mind.' The word suicide was not mentioned.

Scarlett recommended not trying to argue the Bill of Exceptions before the Michaelmas term, so in the summer of 1833 there was comparatively little to do. The Tathams spent the summer in Wey-mouth, sniffing the sea breezes. The Admiral, to his great pleasure and his wife's alarm ('The Channel is as bad to her as the Alps were to Aunt Harriet – she can never cross it'), had a trip to the Channel Islands and Saint-Malo, to stay with one of the Lowther relations. Neither of them forgot the Cause for long: the Admiral pumped his cousin, but James Lowther was a forgetful eighty-year old who had dined once at Hornby, as he believed, but did not remember much about the occasion except that 'he thought Mr M. silly. Mr M. sat sniggering in a corner of the room'. Pudsey did some homework: 'I thoroughly mastered the Bill of Exception – that is to say, as far as it was comprehensible, for a mightier mass of, to me, unnecessary jargon was never compiled to puzzle and "obfuscate" a plain question.'[7]

November brought further delays – the sitting of the Court of Errors was put off until the spring, and Pudsey momentarily gave way to depression. 'I have never felt really mortified and wounded until now – for it really does appear, as if everything, Courts, Judges, Counsel and the Devil himself, were all equally under Pollock's filthy thumb.'[8] What hurt the most was that Bell, Higgin's London agent, had known since April that this was the most likely thing to happen. 'Why did they not tell me so eight months ago, and prepare me in part for the disappointment which they knew, by their own admission now, *must* come.' The Admiral responded with a healthy fury against all the legal personnel, particularly his leading counsel.

> After the Verdict at Lancaster, I did not expect the hearing on the Writ of Error would have been put off beyond Trinity Term, but to reconcile me to disappointment I was then told Sir James Scarlett thought it better to put the argument over the long Vacation, as he should take the Papers down with him into the Country and be completely master of the Case. Now that Michaelmas term is nearly over we find out that we had no reason to expect it could take place this term and the probability now is that Trinity Term will again come round and find us just where we are now and Sir James Scarlett may then have another long vacation to study the case, the whole of which if he has ever given his attention to it he hath by this time entirely forgotten.[9]

Neither frustration nor depression lasted long: if either of the partners had been subject to such moods their campaign would have crumbled long since. By mid January Pudsey had lobbied and argued and interviewed and pressurised, and as he said double-thonged, everyone to such good effect, ably seconded by Higgin, that the case did get a hearing before the Master of the Rolls, a hearing which went against them, but left the parties free to take their case once more before a jury. 'Consequently we are just where we were on the 1st April last – and to trial again we go ... Higgin is very low. Gorst would be so, but I won't let him. I have neither sighed – nor suffered my hand or my heart to quiver.'[10] The Admiral too had found fresh reserves:

> As I had no expectation from the beginning of the verdict being con-firmed, I am not in the least put out of the way by the Judge's decision ... A Jury, not points of law, is the only way to get satisfaction ... Remember me most affectionately to Gorst and tell him to take example from a tough old Sailor, who, let the wind blow as it lists, never loses sight of Hope and the severer the Gale the firmer he treads the decks.[11]

The twists and turns of the case were closely followed, as ever, in Hornby. Lingard reported that when the case went before the Master of the Rolls, the Farleton pitmen refused to go to work, and assembled on the road to intercept the post. Had the news been favourable, 'they would have come to Hornby and probably have done mischief, as they talked of turning Dickinson out of the Castle Inn' (the old landlord, Thomas Procter, had expressed his sympathies too loudly and been ejected). There was, said Lingard, 'general gloom among the inhabitants. They said that the Devil was on Wright's side'.[12]

The new trial was fixed for the Lammas Assizes, August 1834, in Lancaster, with a jury from the Salford and Manchester area. Public opinion saw this as the definitive contest, best out of three. Wright had won at York, Tatham at Lancaster; now here was the decider, at Lancaster again.

National sympathy was with the Admiral, but national expectation of an outcome favourable to him much less so. On the whole the Bar was for the Admiral, but the judiciary against him. To defend the honour of a family against upstart intervention was admirable, but to challenge the sacred right of property by querying a man's will was to challenge the whole establishment, and it was the establishment from which not only Bar and Bench, but also juries were drawn. The French Revolution and the Napoleonic Wars had shaken the foundations on the Continent, and raised many fears in England. Many people felt that they lived on the crust of a volcano, whose minor eruptions from time to time, whether they came legally as Catholic Emancipation or a widening of the suffrage, or illegally as Luddism or Chartism or Trades Unionism, or simply as urban riots, needed a very firm stance. Not that the case

A

VERBATIM REPORT

OF THE CAUSE

DOE DEM.

TATHAM *v.* WRIGHT,

TRIED AT THE

LANCASTER LAMMAS ASSIZES,

1834,

BEFORE

MR. BARON GURNEY AND A SPECIAL JURY.

———

BY ALEXANDER FRASER,

OF CLIFFORD'S INN,

THE ACCREDITED REPORTER IN THE CASE.

VOL. I.

LANCASTER:

PUBLISHED BY WILLIAM BARWICK;

AND BY ARTHUR FOSTER, KIRKBY LONSDALE.

SOLD IN LONDON BY SIMPKIN AND MARSHALL; OLIVER AND BOYD, EDINBURGH;
BANCKS AND CO. MANCHESTER; AND MARPLES AND CO. LIVERPOOL.

1834.

Title page of the printed report of the 1834 trial.

was seen consciously in these terms, but with hindsight these terms had some bearing on its course.

The case came on at Lancaster Castle, in August, at the end of the Criminal Assizes, the court being transformed into a Nisi Prius court and transferring to the Shire Hall to hear the civil case with a special jury. Lancaster, as usual, was packed with 'the fashionables'. There were all the regular Assize events but 'the Cause' was the great draw: the balls were well attended, but Morecambe Regatta was a poor thing, as it fell on the second day of *Tatham* v. *Wright*.

So great was the interest that the shorthand writer's verbatim report was printed and published: as the flyleaf says, sold not only in Lancaster and Kirkby Lonsdale but in London, Edinburgh, Manchester and Liverpool. It is not an easy book to find nowadays, but time was when no Lancashire country house library would have been without one, and so great was the demand that a sixpenny pamphlet version was produced for the common reader.

It has to be remembered that legal reports then combined the vicarious thrills of the Sunday tabloid with the human interest of the soap opera. They were at once totally convincing and more bizarre than reality, lifting the lid in the name of truth from the boiling pots of low life and high life quite as effectively, and with something of the same smugness, as the *News of the World* in its palmiest days. *Tatham* v. *Wright* was a classic of the genre, and although now almost completely forgotten, the excitement it generated outlived memory of the facts.

To read the book of the 1834 trial is to be aware of the intensely dramatic nature of the contest. The real protagonists were invisible, except by reference. Tatham was in the midlands, watching for the postman. Wright was in the seclusion of his Heysham home. The Reverend John Marsden Wright, who, one gets the impression, was as detached from the whole affair as filial loyalty would allow him to be, was going about his parochial duties. Anthony Lister Marsden was in Gargrave, where his wife, who had longed to live in a castle, was dying. His son, on whose life-expectancy so much of the will turned, was in court for the first day and then called home to his mother's death-bed. Pudsey Dawson was among the spectators, with two of his brothers for moral support: the Reverend Ambrose, to whom the Admiral had held out Gargrave Vicarage as a long-term investment; and Richard, whose family, since Hugh Pudsey's death, were closely concerned in the final outcome.

The changes made by the past four years in the list of witnesses have largely been noted. Bleasdale was represented by his evidence at

York, Edmund Tatham was dead, and Robert Procter, after the decision of the Court of Error that the living witness need not necessarily be called if he were hostile, could be ignored as a witness to the will. It had clearly been decided thereafter by the Admiral's side that, although they would have loved to cross-question him as a defence witness, he was too old and too feeble to be called for the plaintiff. Pollock's cross-questioning would have destroyed him utterly, and probably done more harm than good. Smith, it has been noted, was no longer regarded as reliably honest. Roger Chester was dead, and his York evidence was read, but it was too self-contradictory to have greatly impressed the jury. (One may recognise which witnesses carried most weight by the care which opposing counsel took to discredit them, a phenomenon well known in political circles. Thus poor old Mary Denny, judging by Pollock's denigration, was still a powerful witness even on paper.)

A witness who carried great weight for the defence was William Sharp. He was sixty, and the last four years had told grievously on his health. He had had his first stroke after York, and another later, and was still subject, under stress, to spasms. He had lost, and then recovered, the use of his right arm; sometimes it was almost back to normal, sometimes it went numb again and the pen floundered in his hand. His eldest son John, in his early twenties, had taken over much of his father's work, but William was still in charge. In one of Wright's very few surviving letters, written in this year, he expressed complete confidence: 'You have the management of the cause and whatever you think right should be done, do it and it will satisfy me, as whatever you do I am sure will be for the best.'[13]

It is hard to fathom Sharp. He was largely regarded as an upright citizen, and even the opposition never saw him as a villain like Bleasdale. Some of his activities were shady, particularly what seem to have been well-founded accusations of tampering with witnesses and juries. His evidence in support of Marsden's competence, based on a longer and more intimate acquaintance than that of almost any other witness ('For thirty years. I was above twenty years his attorney, from 1804 to the period of his death'), is both convincing in its delivery and unbelievable in its content. Somehow one hesitates to call him a liar as it is possible to call Bleasdale a liar. Sharp undoubtedly put loyalty to his clients very high on his personal list of virtues, and even after thirty years he had never outgrown his pleasure in his confidential intimacy with Hornby Castle. Skilled in the law, he was perhaps not very intelligent: his evidence often reads as though he had convinced himself of the truth of his own answers but was not quite listening to the implications of what he was saying.

On this occasion he was several hours on the witness stand, where he was allowed to sit, owing to his weakness. Most of his evidence, under Pollock's examination, was straightforwardly tedious, to do with the multitude of written material necessary for the defence's case. He was calm, competent and clearly well in control of all the details of the case. When Scarlett took over the cross-examination, he met a stonewall. The man who had been so intimate at the Castle, who had recited with pride all the gentlemen and dignitaries he had met, who had dined there, he thought, a hundred times a year, who knew his client so intimately ('Mr Marsden and I used to sit frequently chatting for an hour and a half in the evening after Mr Wright had retired'), seemed to have great blanks in his knowledge just where one would have expected information, blanks which did not seem to trouble him at all. He had received quantities of letters from Marsden, but never saw him write anything; he had seen George Smith frequently but had no idea whether he lived in the house and had never been in his office; he had talked to Marsden frequently on 'legal and equitable' matters but had no idea of the size of his estate or its value; he had no idea what money Marsden had, or where he kept it, or who kept the accounts. Finally, driven into a corner on the subject of Wright's control, he spoke an unpalatable truth. One cannot imagine Bleasdale being so caught.

Now [said Sir James Scarlett], you describe Mr Marsden as a person you knew very well, and very intimately; did you ever transact any business without Mr Wright's authority? – I transacted business under his direction certainly.

You do not understand my question; did you ever transact any business for him without the authority of Mr Wright? – Oh, yes, I have, certainly ... I know he gave directions to send for a writ for Murray after he pulled down the wall.

As you did not approve of that business you declined it? – I did not approve of it.

Did you ever transact any business for him without the authority of Wright? – I do not know that I did without his knowledge.

Did you ever transact any professional business for Marsden without the authority, concurrence and instructions of Mr Wright? – I do not think I ever did.[14]

The court erupted and the Judge had to intervene: 'If there be not the most strict silence, I shall not suffer anyone to remain here.'

The contrasting styles of leading counsel must have added to the courtroom tension. Sir James Scarlett at this time was a man of sixty-five, and by far the most successful advocate of his day, earning, it was said, not far short of £20,000 a year. He was not what could be called an eloquent speaker, but he could analyse the evidence before him and lay it in front of the jury with absolute clarity. He appeared the perfect gentleman – handsome, dignified, with a fine voice – speaking off the cuff and yet never missing a trick. He was not a great cross-examiner, and appeared to disdain an easy verbal victory, but he had a habit of getting verdicts unrivalled by anyone else at the time, and his pursuit of a point, illustrated in the extract above, repeating and refining his questions so that the witness in the end had to give a straight answer, was very typical. His analysis of the will, showing clause by clause how it worked for Wright's family and left the Listers hamstrung and power-less, was brilliant, as was his analysis of Bleasdale's evidence, showing up every weak point and self-contradiction, but intellectually, without linguistic or emotional fireworks.

In his analysis of the will, with which he closed his speech, evidently regarding it as his strongest card, he began by tacitly accepting that Marsden might have been able to make a simple will, and using that acceptance against the opposition:

> I venture to say, that if Marsden were really and truly competent to select the objects of his preference, and if he could do that which he meant to do, or according as some witness said, he meant to leave handsomely to Lister, and something to Wright; then, I say the man who prepared this will for him has betrayed him. I do not mean to speak of the technicalities of it; those are left to the lawyers to arrange for him; but the effect or object of the will, is what the testator himself ought to understand and comprehend. Now I say, that no one who reads this will can do so without seeing, that the man who concocted it or prepared it, meant to put Lister, who was said to have been the main object of Marsden's bounty, in such a predicament, that if he dared to hold up his hand, Wright could suppress him; for the fact is, it is Wright, and not Lister, that has the absolute dominion over the property left by this will.[15]

He embarked on a carefully detailed analysis of the will. The whole of it is worth reading, the following is a paragraph.

> He is to permit the tenant for life, Anthony Lister, to occupy the house, grounds and park, and to keep them in repair at his own expense, so that Lister will have the pleasure of remaining in the mansion-house,

having the benefit of the pleasure-grounds and park, but you will observe, it is to be at his own expense, while George Wright is to let and demise, cultivate, work and manage the whole property, as he shall think fit, or as he may imagine most accordant with the views of the deceased, and for this management he is to have £1000 a year, together with £2000 a year for the payment of debts and legacies. He is to have a right to deduct from the residue £1000 a year for himself, but not to be considered as a satisfaction of any sums due from Mr Marsden to him, and exclusive of all costs, disbursements, and expenses, in performance of the trusts of the will. He is thus to have during the whole term of twenty-one years the entire unaccountable control and management of the whole estate, including the timber, the mines, the coals, the farms, the rebuilding of farm-houses and offices, and, in short, he may dig, pull down, rebuild and do anything he pleases except the capital mansion itself; he may grant leases according to his own pleasure, so as in other words to condemn Mr Lister Marsden, who is nominally to have the estate, to keep within the castle, without having the free use of it as to building or rebuilding, or even repairing his own mansion, that sort of management being entirely according to the pleasure of Wright. Nay, more, he may open and dig quarries in any part of the estate wherever he pleases; he may even open a coal mine under his drawing room window, so as to render Hornby Castle uninhabitable. He is to have the sole uncontrolled power and to demise and lease – to employ agents, attorneys, auditors, stewards, or bailiffs, and to pay them such sums of money, in the shape of salaries or allowances of any sort whatever, just as he may choose, without being in any manner accountable to the persons here represented as being in possession of the estate.[16]

He continued to build the case, detailing all the pressures which could be brought to bear on the Lister Marsdens, to an inevitable outcome. 'Will he not say to Lister Marsden "Is it worth your while to live here? I shall not permit you to hunt, nor shoot, nor fish". Certainly he could do so, and certainly it would not be worth John Lister Marsden's while to retain it under such circumstances, and therefore he would consent to sell it for a few thousands.'[17] It was closely-reasoned, low-key argument, but not without some emotional content, of a kind which had won him the verdict many times before.

Frederick Pollock, fourteen years Scarlett's junior, was as different as he could be. His preparation was different: he had worked unrelentingly on his client's case, rolling up his own sleeves, where Scarlett left things to the last minute, relying on his own brilliant grasp, and often giving the impression that he was not really interested.

When the case was in court, where Scarlett was low key, Pollock was high. He worked on his jury like a conductor with an orchestra. Where it was necessary simply to produce evidence, as in the immensely long series of deeds, bonds and letters produced to prove Marsden's competence as a man of business, he could be straightforward enough. But where appropriate, he could and did produce every mood and colour. (It will be remembered how Dickens's Serjeant Buzfuz drew depths of emotion out of a note to the landlady 'Don't bother yourself about the warming-pan'.)

Pollock, in his twelve-hour opening speech to the jury in Lancaster (as it was an action of ejectment, the usual order was reversed, the defence leading), let himself go in tremendous purple passages supporting his own witnesses and undermining his opponents. In particular he shredded the character of Robert Procter, perhaps to make sure that the opposition would not dare to call him, and that of the Admiral, whom he presented as a greedy schemer, always hovering on the edge of the Hornby property, but not daring to move during Marsden's lifetime. Everything was coloured in with the broadest of brushes, and evidence which did not suit his case was flicked aside.

One of his methods was to exaggerate his opponent's case until it looked ridiculous. He made much of the 'plot' which would have been necessary had Wright intended to get a will in his favour. Could it possibly have been hatched so many years ago (the number of years varied at different mentions, but sometimes stretched to the full sixty-eight of Marsden's life)? Was it possible that the conspirators could have implicated so many respectable people? He reached his total by counting all the signatures to all the business papers in which Marsden had been involved:

> Now in this stage of the case I beg to state that the parties who have been implicated in these different transactions, amount in point of number, when added together, to no less than one hundred and seventy-nine. Many of these parties were concerned twice over; but notwithstanding that, there are one hundred and seventy-nine different parties concerned in those instruments, some of them as executing a bond, or rather receiving a bond from Mr Marsden; or executing a mortgage, or concerned in other instruments. There are no less than fifty-eight attesting witnesses to these instruments, and adding all those together will make a total of two hundred and thirty-seven persons.[18]

And having paid lip-service to accuracy with 'Many of these parties were concerned twice over', he continued to flourish the magic number of two hundred and thirty-seven (which on at least one occasion was rounded up to 'between three and four hundred persons') throughout his case.

The full documentation is no longer there to be checked, but from what there is it is a reasonable conclusion that the signatures of Mrs Cookson, Wright and his clerks, Bleasdale and his clerks, Sharp and his clerks, would cover some 90 per cent of the signatories. But Pollock's vast 'conspiracy' was introduced so often that it became, as such things do, familiar and acceptable by mere repetititon.

The contrast of style may be underlined by quoting the last paragraphs of the speeches which Scarlett and Pollock addressed to the jury. Scarlett had been summarising the evidence of Marsden's weakness which the jury were to consider:

> If you be of opinion that he could not comprehend great subjects, nor subjects of this sort as to arranging the interest of the individual he meant to provide for, then the law would say he was not of sound and disposing mind and memory. Then if you doubt that, the next question will be, was his strength of mind sufficient to resist the influence of the gentleman who had got the entire control of him; not only in regard to all his desires, but also of his purse, his estates, and his property of every description; but also of his person, aided by a skilful attorney, the intimate friend of that gentleman; and who was playing into his hand, in regard to the will he had made. If you be of the opinion that that will was made under that sort of control, then you will say it was not his will, as Bleasdale had got it prepared and executed; and had introduced into that document, such provisos as to leave Wright entirely as the person to be ultimately benefitted. That is another ground for your thinking that although he were capable of certain acts, yet he was perfectly under the control of Wright. If he were actually so imbecile as not to understand it at all, or if he were capable of understanding certain things, and not others; or if he were unable to resist control, then the plaintiff, whom I represent, will be entitled to your verdict.[19]

Pollock, in a voice grown hoarse with overuse, or possibly emotion:

> Gentlemen, I hardly know how you feel upon this subject; but I own, at the close of this, my address to you in reply, I feel some of that deep responsibility, which nearly overpowered me as I was turning round to address you. I cannot think of the tremendous and perilous consequences, in point of stake, and in point of character to so many persons, some of whom have passed away with honour and credit, while others still exist, without my feeling the greatest anxiety in regard to your verdict.

When we find that so many individuals attesting the acts of Marsden, and thereby giving evidence of his acts, and attesting the truth of the whole story; I feel I cannot think any otherwise of that consideration which I cast upon you. I must naturally entertain the most anxious feeling upon the subject, and with which I should scarcely be able to bear myself up, were it not in the entire confidence and persuasion that I have, that your verdict will prevent any title being shaken, and will restore tranquillity to any one who had a doubt about it; or rather that it will purge from any stain of suspicion, the hundreds of persons who are supposed to have been implicated in this foul conspiracy. That your verdict will be a satisfactory one, I must heartily pray to God – that it will be a just one, I cannot entertain a doubt. Gentlemen, it is for you to say how it is to be; my confidence in this, as it were in my own cause, is of no sort of importance; but I may be merely allowed to say, that I have conducted the whole of this case, from the beginning to the end of it, in the true spirit of prayer, that may God enable you, gentlemen, to do justice between these parties.[20]

Baron Gurney summed up very much more fairly than Park had done at York, and omitted none of the telling points on either side. His direction, however, veered towards Wright's case, mainly because he could not bring himself to disbelieve the evidence of the two important legal witnesses, Bleasdale and Sharp. To anyone who reads through the whole body of evidence, the fascination of the case lies in its knife-edge balance. It is extremely difficult, if not impossible, on the evidence as given, to decide whether the jury made the right decision. As it happened, they did not take very long: after three hours, they returned a verdict for Wright and the will.

15

The Last Trial

Public opinion, tending as always to see things in black and white, saw the 1834 verdict as another clear case of judicial misdirection and an unsatisfactory jury. Matthew Atkinson, one of the Admiral's most respectable witnesses, lately High Sheriff of Cumberland, had voiced an opinion just before the trial, wishing for a jury 'of country gentlemen, as these Manchester gentry have little regard to heredity, descent or family distinction – but many would consider Wright an uncommon quick discerning fellow in having thus cajoled and cheated the rightful owner – as all in the way of Trade'.[1]

The verdict was a crushing blow for the plaintiffs, and yet perversely the defendants, after the first rejoicing, may have been the ones to see the shadow of ultimate defeat. There was something unnerving in the way their opponents melted away after the verdict, just when they ought to have been coming cap in hand to seek some arrangement. There should have been soundings about settlements: instead there was silence. And the Admiral had vanished completely, which occasioned much anxiety on the other side.

He, in fact, aware that it was other people's money which was chiefly involved, and immovable on the subject of coming to terms with Frederick Pollock, with whom he felt a more bitter personal enmity than with George Wright, was reconciled to the thought of defeat. He would not write direct to Pudsey, because of suspicions about the mail: the country post office, like the modern telephone system, was vulnerable to tapping. Instead he wrote to Tom Gorst: 'When a ship is on shore it is not the Part of a good Mariner to sit down on the deck and moan over her Misfortune till the Ship goes to peices; but in the first place to sound round her and ascertain the probability of getting her afloat and safe into a Harbour, and if he finds that impracticable to save all he can from the wreck.' And after further consideration, 'I much doubt if we have any chance of redress by proceeding further. I was indeed so convinced that *the Bench* was hostile to us that I could not bring myself to believe that we had a chance of a verdict except from a highly gifted and Independent Jury.'[2]

Before this message had time to reach Lancaster, he received a letter from Pudsey (addressed, for security reasons, to Mrs Tatham) reporting that they were collecting affidavits respecting the conduct of the jury, in deepest, deadliest secret. Gorst was doing much of the work ('What an excellent little piece of sterling stuff is that man'), and the letters of support had been pouring in. Pudsey was quite cheerful, as he always was when there was work to do, and assumed so firmly that the battle would go on that capitulation was not mentioned again. The Admiral and his wife set off for the south coast, to Sandgate, and then to Dover, leaving misleading directions behind them, and considered, even at the cost of 'Madam' having to cross the Channel, wintering in France. He told Gorst that he did not want anyone to know where they had gone (there was always the danger of arrest for costs), but explained that they had quite enough money for all future needs: half-pay of £450 a year, a little estate at Colton in Staffordshire let for £100, cottages and house in Lichfield, although these were at present unlet and apparently unlettable.

In November James Scarlett was made Lord Chief Baron of the Exchequer, a political promotion which had been expected for some time, but his clients did not really regret his going. They had never, they felt, had his whole-hearted interest, as the other side had had Pollock's. That was clear enough from his delays in getting down to his brief, and the fact that both at York and Lancaster he had made his speech and then quitted the court, leaving the rest of the operation to his juniors. They much preferred to be left with Cresswell Cresswell, whose conduct at Lancaster had impressed everybody.

Scarlett's last action on the Admiral's behalf was to move for a new trial, on five counts, which Sharp reported to Wright:

1. The conduct of the jury, two of them having been seen to go to Mr Sharp's house during the trial, and one of them having accompanied Mr Charles Lister Marsden to dine at Mr Birkbeck's at Poulton.

2. That the letters to Mr Marsden to which there were no answers or acts done were not evidence.

3. That the verdict at York was not evidence.

4. That one of the jury stated after the verdict was given that he had read the trial at York and had made up his mind to give a verdict for the will.

5. That the Court of Exchequer Chamber on the Bill of Exceptions were wrong in their decision as to not calling an attesting witness to the will.[3]

The court disallowed the fourth clause, on the grounds that what jurymen might say after a trial was too chancy an area altogether, and the fifth because the Court of Exchequer decision had not been appealed at the time and must therefore be considered final. However, they allowed the first three as grounds for seeking a new trial, though the dinner story was later dropped, having apparently originated with a chaise driver who, innocently or not, had misidentified his passengers. Sharp did not deny the callers at his house, though he insisted that one of them just happened to be a keen collector of letter-wafers, and he (Sharp) had promised to give him some, which was either false or, if true, a piece of uncharacteristic stupidity; but the poor man was very ill throughout the trial, crammed with opium to get him through his ordeal as a witness, and this particular slip in the end carried little weight.

Among the Admiral's vociferous supporters was Commodore Barrie, returned from Canada. He was in London and had had an interview with the King, not primarily on that subject, but William IV naturally took the part of a fellow sailor and sent kind messages. 'I have followed the proceedings with interest. He ought to have had a verdict. Tell him to bring his case before the Lords and then he will get justice.'[4] Barrie thought this a hopeful idea and was prepared to lobby as many of their lordships as he could claim acquaintance with; unfortunately that very week, on 16 October 1834, the Houses of Parliament went up in flames, preventing his good intentions.

The law, as usual, crept slowly along its appointed paths. *Tatham* v. *Wright* was put on the list which allowed it to be considered for a new trial in November 1834, only three months after the Lancaster verdict, but it was eightieth in the queue and there were only certain days in each term when new trials were considered.

Dr Lingard acquired an interleaved copy of the trial report and went through it painstakingly, making notes for the barristers holding a future brief. Meanwhile Sandford Tatham, in his winter retreat, was working on a great refutation of all that he felt in the trial to have been untrue and unfair to himself and his family, particularly of course Pollock's unrestrained attacks on his character. In the end it ran to 200 pages, and he had several copies made. Written by a man approaching eighty with nothing to refer to but his own memory, it is a remarkable piece of work.

Meanwhile, that winter of 1834–35, they had further trouble with Higgin, 'the needy cormorant of Morecambe'. Pudsey reported 'His accounts – folios – have come in, and my eyes they are *woppers*. I thought it as well to come up [to Lancaster] with all my own vouchers and to save time and correspondence'.[5] But Gorst said that some of the trouble was of Pudsey's own making. Pudsey found it difficult to think ill of Higgin for long. 'I am disposed to think he will do what is right and correct – I wrote firmly and liberally to him – but his want of regularity I fear has led him to expect a balance of at least £1000 more than he will find himself entitled to.'[5] Gorst said that Pudsey must stop his bad habit of giving out little sweeteners of £50, and refuse any more advances until the accounts were finalised. 'May luck attend you in your attack and crown your efforts with success; all depends upon your own firmness; keep copies of your letters.'[6]

Gorst himself had a trip to Lancaster and Hornby and brought back interesting gossip. Lister Marsden and Wright were said to be quarrelling over a bill for £18,000 which was claimed as Anthony's share of the costs. 'Marsden, poor noodle, advertises in vain for friends to call, he had not the last time he was at the Castle a single visitor except Mr and Mrs J.M. Wright. Even Batty and Fleetwood Hesketh kept away.' He reported that 'a little new furniture has been put into the house of the plainest and most ordinary kind, principally of unpainted deal: the dining room table is like a common kitchen dresser, and the beds without a rag in the shape of a curtain'.[7]

The Admiral and his wife went to Boulogne for the summer of 1835, where there was a large English colony, and took lodgings in the well-named Rue des Vieillards. He reported the celebration of his eightieth birthday 'without any apparent diminution of Health, Spirit, or Intellect'. He was as determined against compromise as ever. 'I have I trust to this late period of life maintained the character of strict integrity. I will not now for any worldly advantage sully it.' Dr Lingard had sent an encouraging report on his notes. 'I have read your MS with interest and pleasure, you have completely demolished the fictions employed in his speeches by Pollock and I hope that if we have another trial you will allow the MS to be seen by your Counsel.'[8] Tatham responded that counsel would be welcome, but to keep it away from Higgin.

Sharp in his turn was asking for money from Wright ('I am very poor'), and increasingly anxious about the possible death of the Admiral, which would have prevented them recovering their costs. 'I have not the least doubt but that they will raise all the Powers that can be in Heaven and Earth to get a new Trial so as to stave off the costs if possible by the death of the Admiral.'[9] Although Wright had sent him £500 on account, he had undoubtedly sunk a good deal of his own money in the cause.

Twelve months after permission had been granted to seek a new trial, the case was still creeping painfully up the list. Young John Sharp, only twenty-four but now the more active partner, reported from the Gray's Inn Coffee House in November 1835:

> The Court have made such very slow progress with the new trial list that the motion still remains so far distant from coming on that, unless the Court take new trials again this term after today, I fear it must stand over until next Term. It is now *nine* off, therefore the Court have only disposed of thirteen in four days. I shall possibly be able to ascertain tomorrow whether it is intended to take new trials again this term. I fear it will not. And that we shall therefore be compelled to go over to next term. If in the meantime the Admiral dies, we shall lose our Costs. It is really excessively annoying to be thus put off from time to time, however I fear we have no help for it and must bear it all with patience.[10]

The Admiral's health would have been less of an obsession if they had known where he was and in what case; but it was not until January 1836 that William Sharp heard that he was abroad and reported the fact to Wright.

> I was not aware that the Admiral had already gone to France, altho' I am not in the least surprized. For if you remember more than twelve months ago I mentioned to you that I was sure the Admiral had gone to the Dorsetshire Coast for the purpose of getting over the moment it was necessary to avoid any proceeds we might take against him for costs, but altho' he is and may continue in a Foreign Country I hope we shall be able to get hold of his Pension in case of our discharging the Bill for a new Trial and the costs are not paid by Pudsey Dawson or some one, as from the conduct of the Admiral and his Partizans they are not entitled to the least favor at our Hands whatever public feeling or opinion may be.[11]

They need not have worried on one score at least. 'The old Admiral', as he described himself, 'notorious for his elastic step and upright person' was enjoying Boulogne, where he was quite a personage among the English community. Pudsey went to visit him and found him in excellent form.

In the spring of 1836 at last the new trial was set for the next summer assizes at Lancaster, and interest centred on who would be the Judge.

From the moment he was identified as Mr Justice Coleridge, there was a sigh of relief in the Tatham camp. Here at last was a representative of a new generation of Judges, and they hoped for great things. John Taylor Coleridge was only forty-five and very recently promoted to the King's Bench. He was a nephew of the poet and a friend of the literary establishment, spending more time on literary pursuits than on his profession. But if this background perhaps made people like Lingard feel more comfortable, he was no dilettante as a Judge, and he had one advantage which they felt that both Park and Baron Gurney had lacked. 'His fairness of temper', says the *Dictionary of National Biography*, 'often caused him to be selected as an arbitrator.'

In the run-up to August, a sense of inevitability, almost of exhaustion, seems to have settled on both parties, the kind of feeling that with hindsight can be interpreted as a premonition of the result, although at the time it is felt as an inability to get excited or even very anxious. George Wright's son William was dying of consumption at the age of twenty-seven, and perhaps because of this his father seems to have lost interest. When Sharp asked him for instructions on an important matter, he replied 'Do what you think best', which responsibility Sharp sharply refused to accept, even though he concealed the refusal under his best flowery manner:

> My dear Sir, It is on all occasions a great gratification to have the concurrence and approbation of those who entrust the management of any affairs to one but in the Hornby Cause, which embraces so vast a Property and in which so much of Character is involved the responsibility is great and almost overwhelming, that it makes me most anxious to have the expressed approbation or disapprobation of those who are so immediately and personally interested in the Question as yourself. I hope and trust I have always done the best for my clients and my exertions and anxiety in this Matter have almost been beyond my strength, seeing and feeling that the Character property and comfort of my most particular Friends and their connexions are at stake. The Matter is no ordinary one therefore, my dear Sir, do let us have your expressed sentiments and feelings with regard to indicting the several scoundrels who have so palpably perjured themselves. I hope and trust nay I am sure you will give me Credit that I will do the best for my Clients and I should like and I hope to have your expressed opinion as to this Proceeding against these men which Sir F. Pollock advises.[12]

Frederick Pollock had recommended, rather wildly it would seem, that the chaise driver who had sworn to a member of the jury going out to dinner with young Lister Marsden, should be indicted for perjury. 'The expense would doubtless be considerable but it might have a great effect in deterring some of their infamous witnesses.' (Pollock was commonly reputed not to mind spending his clients' money as long as it would last, although this reputation does not fit with his earlier attempts to move towards a compromise.) Another counsel's opinion scotched the idea: the chaise driver had undoubtedly driven two customers where he said he had driven them – if he had mistaken their identity no jury would convict him of perjury.

As the summer of 1836 advanced towards the trial, Dr Lingard commented on the silence in a letter to Pudsey. 'We hear nothing of the plans of your adversaries. It is surprising how little is said about the trial in comparison with the sensation which it created in former years.' [13] He himself was quietly optimistic: 'It is my persuasion that he [the Admiral] will be victorious at last.' He was delighted to have a letter from the Admiral himself, 'who is certainly a wonderful man', and answered at once.

My dear Sir, Seldom have I been more gratified than I was, when on opening the cover, I saw your handwriting, and learned from it that you were again in England, well, in spirits, and prepared to fight the old battle over again. You will have to fight under you the same men, as hearty as ever in the cause, and more confident of the victory.

I am of your opinion that the cause has hitherto been mismanaged. There were many omissions on the part of your counsel, as it appeared to me. But I cherish a confidence that Mr Cresswell will undertake it with greater attention to those parts of Pollock's speeches which require to be answered. The length of the trial is against you. What has been said by your counsel is forgotten by the time Pollock rises to declaim, and confound, and mislead the jury. Nor do I know how that can be remedied.

I agree with you that you should have someone at the table, whose only object should be to attend to the discrepancies and doubtful assertions of the witnesses. There is another thing which I also think expedient. In his opening spech P. made a number of unfounded assertions which he never attempted to prove, but which were all calculated to prejudice the jury against you. I will endeavour, and I hope someone else will do the same, to make out a catalogue of all these falsehoods from the printed trial, and put it into the hands of one of the junior counsel that he while Pollock is speaking may mark with his pen each of them that is repeated by P. Then I conceive that your counsel in his speech would have a good opportunity of shewing how your adversaries attempt to bolster up their case with these falsehoods by going through them seriatim, and remarking on each that it has not been proved, and is not true. Would not this be likely to shake the credit of P. with the jury? . . .

All your friends are well in this neighbourhood, and in hopes of victory. Wright is also well; he appears to me as if he paid his devotions to the bottle – this from his colour – but others do not think so. Hornby is gradually sinking into a miserable hamlet. There is nothing to be done in it. The last May day we lost about thirty-six men women and children, who are gone to seek their fortune elsewhere.[14]

Wright in fact had always been remarkably abstemious, but he may have relaxed a little in his later years and under the long strain. Sharp had recently written to him about 'a pipe of Choice and very curious old Port' which the shipper was saving for him: 'If Mr Wright wants a Pipe I should be very glad for I consider him a better judge of Port Wine than almost any of you.'

The case of *Tatham* v. *Wright* came on again on 29 August 1836, at Lancaster Assizes, before Mr Justice Coleridge. Sir Frederick Pollock led for the defendant and Mr Cresswell Cresswell for the plaintiff. The case lasted for eleven days. No verbatim report has survived but the newspapers did their best. Two issues of the *Lancaster Gazette* had almost everything else squeezed off its pages, although the reporter complained how much had to be left out.

Pollock, as before, threw out a number of unproved and unprovable suggestions as facts; as a starter he suggested that 'The party on the other side was nominally Admiral Tatham, but that that gentleman had a particle of interest in the matter, or had any more to do with it than himself or any one of the jury, was very doubtful indeed', and wound himself up, as before, to a passion concerning the 'odious, filthy, disgusting and scandalous attack upon the character of Mrs Cookson', and ended with a peroration which, at least in the version of the reporter toiling behind him, had so little logical foundation that it reads like a self-parody:

Sir Frederick then drew to his conclusion. He alluded to the sort of inquisition held upon Mr Marsden's incapacity, and said the question involved was repugnant to the Christian religion, which cut down the pride of wealth and intellectual distinction – forbade one erring being to pass his fellow sinner by with 'I am holier than thou', and as they heard in the lesson of last Sunday denouncing the man who dare say to his brother 'thou fool'. Of all pride the pride of intellect was the most intolerable; and against the principle these proceedings would seek to establish, he would lift his hand and voice.[15]

It does seem that both the judge and the opposing counsel had his measure very much better than those of the earlier trials. Coleridge was very firm on the subject of letters which came under the rejection rule: the very rule which had got the Cause to this its fourth trial. Several times Pollock tried to introduce certain letters: each time Cresswell pounced like a terrier and Coleridge upheld his objection. Then it was the turn of plaintiff's counsel, and it is clear that someone had been doing exactly what Dr Lingard had recommended, and made notes on Pollock's wilder flights of fancy so that they could be picked over and refuted by Cresswell, who did a cool and efficient job.

Once more the argument had been used of the numerous signatories to Marsden's business papers – far too many to make conspiracy possible or credible. This time Cresswell had his own figures ready. 'His learned friend dwelt on the numerical amount of parties to the deeds. Of the deeds *to* Mr Marsden he would say nothing, because they proved nothing, the parties not having occasion to know anything of Mr Marsden. Of those *by* him there were only twelve to which Wright was not an attesting witness ... of the twelve exceptions, his attorney Mr Barrow was witness to six, Mr Dowbiggin [Sharp's elder partner] to three, Mr Sharp to two, and Mr Hailstone [Wright's Bradford solicitor] the other.'

> He did not dispute the estate was well managed but they had not been presented with any rental, or anything to show the value of the estate, or how the accounts were settled. They had not called any one to prove the accounts between master and man ... And yet Mr Wright had a clerk, who was still living at Hornby. There was a trial at York, and that clerk was taken there, but he was taken away again, and never examined – that clerk was not produced that day, and who, he asked, could so well tell the secrets of the Castle ... It was because they dare not call him.[16]

At this point a loud cheer from the body of the audience was sternly rebuked by the judge. It would not be entirely fair to rely on a summary from a newspaper which was sympathetic to the Admiral, except that the jury's verdict supports the opinion that Cresswell was much more effective than Pollock, who clearly overused his time-honoured tactics. Another reporter mentions that at one moment, referring to his client Anthony Lister Marsden and the loss of his wife, he swept his gown aside to show the said client sitting behind him, sobbing into a large white handkerchief: the audience broke into unsympathetic titters.

One part of the trial has survived: the judge's summing-up was printed in full. True to Mr Coleridge's reputation, it was a model of clarity and restraint. He first cleared the air of the sulphurous descriptions levelled at the principals on each side by the other. He summed up all that Pollock had said about the Admiral and pointed out that, even if it were true, it had no real bearing on the case. He outlined the facts of Wright's career, which were by no means reprehensible, and pointed out that the jury must consider not the fact, but only the means, of his advancement. He told them to clear their minds of pressures based on possible evil consequences resulting from one verdict or another. He underlined the central point of their deliberations – the will:

> It is not a necessary consequence because a man can take part in a general conversation, can say how do you, or talk about the weather, or matters he may have seen in a newspaper, or because he may have written a complimentary note on the marriage of a friend. It would not be enough, because he had performed the simple transaction of borrowing or lending £100 that he was therefore competent to make a will: he certainly might be able to make a simple will, but not one disposing of a great deal of property to persons which, under the circumstances, must be of a very complicated nature. Therefore under all circumstances, a man must, to make a will, be of a disposing mind and memory, and in proportion to the complicated nature of it, his disposing mind and memory ought to be increased. You will have to consider the will by and by, and the division of property under it, but the consideration must not be pushed too far. The question is this: was Mr Marsden's mind free from disease? Had he any delusion? Was it madness of any kind? Had he sufficient memory and understanding to know the general state of his property, and his family – his own station in life – the relation he bore as between master and servant in any act that he was doing – the nature of the instrument, if explained to him, in plain and familiar language (for no man was bound to understand the technicalities and forms) but if the will was read over to John Marsden, in plain and familiar language, was he capable of understanding it? That is the first question. The next is, was the mind brought to act; for a man may be capable of understanding a will, but that will may never have been brought to him. Now although this particular will may not have been explained to him, if the will in 1810 had been so, if he merely wished an alteration of putting in C. D. for A. B. and all the other parts

remained the same, it was not necessary that it should be again read over to him. The next question is did he execute it of his own free will, for the term 'last will', implies that it should be his own free act – an act of his volition: therefore if a man be under such control, if there be what the law calls duresse upon him, if he does a thing because he cannot help it, or is intimidated until he does it, it is folly to talk of that being his will. But you must be cautious in your inferences of improper influence, for in nine cases out of ten, in every will, a certain influence is used by a beloved wife, or a favourite son, or by an intimate friend, and still the testator may remain a free agent: and therefore I desire the question to be taken in its fullest extent, before you say that anything like control or influence was used prohibiting him from being a free agent.[17]

And so on, stripping off the verbiage and laying out, not so much the facts presented to them by either side, as the considerations by which the jury should approach those facts, for, as he said, there was advantage in such a long trial. 'We may take it for granted that so far as ability and zeal can sift the matter to the bottom, we have all the evidence that could be obtained to enable us to bring the matter to a decision.'

The summing-up was brief by comparison with what had gone before: it took four hours. The jury retired and took the same length of time to present their verdict. They declared for Tatham and against the will.

16

Lord of the Manor

Most of Lancaster's population appear to have gathered in the narrow streets round the Judge's Lodging, waiting for the verdict. When they heard it, they went happily wild. The band came out and paraded the town all evening. The Hornby inns no doubt sold more beer than usual, but the Hornby estate population was once more strictly reminded that the case was not at an end, and that it would be positively dangerous to rejoice too soon.

George Smith noted 'I fastened up the windows at the Castle and superintended the loading of Mr Marsden's goods and took the Keys of the Castle'.[1] It may have seemed a significant action and he may have noted it for that reason, but in fact it was no more than the regular closing down after the ritual opening up for the grouse shooting, which had this year been extended to take in the Assizes.

The tenants were confused and anxious. They wanted to end up on the right side, almost to a man they rejoiced that at last it seemed as though that side would be the Admiral's, but there was still some need to hedge their bets. Higgin was asked about the coming Court Leet: could they still be fined by Wright for non-attendance? Higgin told them that, legally, those who had been paying up over the last eight years must continue to do so. Dr Lingard preached patience, patience, for a little while longer.

After so long it may have come as no surprise that the little while stretched to another year and a half. At first Pollock was enthusiastic about the possibility of another trial in two years' time, but Judge Coleridge had left little foothold for accusations of misdirection, and on this occasion there was no hint of persuasion having been applied to the jury by either side. The only way forward for the defendants was by a Bill of Exceptions on the admissability of certain letters which Coleridge had not allowed because they resulted in neither actions nor answers, and on this a Writ of Error was brought in the Exchequer Chamber of the House of Lords in the beginning of 1838.

Meanwhile a subsidiary action had been brought to the 1837 Summer Assizes to recover the mesne profits from Wright. An acquaintance of the Admiral's wife reported meeting the Miss Wrights at Matlock 'who told her that they and their brother wished their father to give up the Castle to the heir at law but he replied he would keep possession as long as he can'.[2]

Pudsey, as almost always, was the most optimistic of the Tatham alliance, perhaps because he knew that, as long as his will held, he could outlast the opposition financially. ('My dear Admiral, say not a word, I beseech you, on the subject of resources. Make yourself easy. Gorst and I will manage that matter.')[3] From the winter retreat at Sidmouth where his sisters-in-law had built a handsome house, from Settle which was his constant pied-à-terre in Craven, from his sorties to his family at Bolton-by-Bowland and to London, he sent cheerful messages to the Admiral, who stayed quietly in Cheltenham, husbanding the strength that he was determined to keep intact for the final act of the drama. 'We have nothing to fear!!! Skirrow [a barrister friend] told me yesterday, putting his hand on my shoulder: "I have the best authority for saying it, Dawson, the verdict will not and cannot be disturbed. Go home and be patient".'[4]

The gossip he picked up about their opponents he retailed with a pleasure that sometimes fell short of the magnanimity in victory and defeat for which he had become renowned. 'The Vicar they tell me is now *cut* and *despised* by both sides. Poor Devil!!! It is nothing more nor less than he merits.'[5]

'Lady St Leonards' was declining into senility: 'Madam is in that nordling, fatuous state (the effect of pride and pomp upon a silly weak mind) that her signature cannot be considered valid!! So ends her strange eventful history!!!'[6] 'We hear today from Lancaster that Wright is very low and sulky and no one dare go near him. I hope he won't hang himself – it would give us much trouble.'[7]

The somewhat ruthless tone, and the proliferation of exclamation marks, are not typical. But if an element of gloating is understandable, he had also to be anxious, as was everyone, about the durability of the old man, now past eighty-one, and suffering the debilitation of bronchitis and cold weather. He was clearly not the man he had been; and letters were Pudsey's only way of keeping his spirits high. Sarcasm at the expense of their enemies was occasional: filial love and enthusiasm were frequent.

I shall indeed rejoice, it will delight my heart and amply repay all my anxious moments of the last eight years – to lay at your feet the title deeds and keys of Hornby Castle – to see you quietly and calmly passing the rest of your days in the happy conscientious knowledge of having done your duty not less by your own family than by the Public.[8]

But the Admiral, in some ways the toughest of them all, was dispensing his own kind of moral support. 'I still think the decision will not be for us except there should be ad interim more than one change on the Bench ... You will of course be prepared and not shook by the judgment being against us.'

Meanwhile Higgin was having his own problems with the Corporation of Lancaster who 'could not get on with him', apparently more politically than personally. At the beginning of 1837 he parted company with them as Town Clerk, Coroner and Magistrates' Clerk. 'I don't know', said the Admiral,

> whether I should condole with or congratulate Higgin, for it seems if he had continued in office, to get anything by it, it must have been by dint of wrangling, and after all hardly a compensation for his time and trouble: who the present corporation are I hardly know even by name; on all these subjects however it behoves *us* that is the assailants of the Castle to be silent on local or national politics *mum* for we know not yet how much remains to be submitted to the good People of Lancashire. We must excite no enmity either of Whig or Tory – therefore in the Borough squabbles of Lancaster or the County politics we shall do well to keep out of the scrape and offend neither party.[9]

Apart from those areas where he felt his family honour had been touched, Sandford Tatham's level-headed common sense was his greatest attribute: he often preached the necessity of keeping out of politics until the Cause was over, particularly to Pudsey, who was a paid-up member of the Conservative Club, whereas he himself inclined to the Whigs, provided he agreed with their tactics. 'Now ... don't you put my name down on the Tory list – proceedings so highly reprehensible I shall always repudiate from whatever Party they come, and when Whig Ministries do shabby things, I call them a shabby administration. So you have my Politics, *Multum in Parvo*.'[10]

Higgin wrung compensation of £100 a year out of the Corporation and was free to devote more time to *Tatham* v. *Wright* and to his other great interest, the railway which, having reached Preston from Birmingham, was on its way to Lancaster. The Admiral, retailing this news, showed that he did see himself, from time to time, actually in Hornby Castle. 'It would be of great advantage', he said to Pudsey, 'to have it continued to Bentham', and thought he would gladly take a share in such an enterprise 'when in a condition to do it'.[11]

Through 1837 they were working for a Writ of Entry to the estates, even though the appeal would not be heard until early in 1838. Plans had to be made, though it seemed like tempting providence. 'This is reckoning our chickens with a vengeance', said Gorst, admitting to being 'nervous and anxious'. None the less he was jollying the Admiral along in his expected role as Lord of the Manor. It would have been against human nature to abstain, and they all feared the quite probable outcome of the Admiral's death before he could enjoy his success.

The Admiral himself was the restraining influence: 'For myself I have no anxiety, satisfied that all will be right at last, though it prevents our [himself and his wife] fixing permanently, which certainly at our time of life would be a great convenience, and save us much trouble.'[12]

So they spent the summer of 1837 in Birkenhead, near to Pudsey's brother Richard, and closer by many hours' travelling if it became necessary suddenly to go north, 'for the excellent Doctor tells me that the good people of Lonsdale will not be satisfied if the Lord of the Manor does not *make the Entry* in person'.[13] But for the winter of the same year, when it became clear that 'the Grand Entry' could not take place until after the result of the appeal, they returned to their old winter quarters, Cheltenham, in 'perhaps a larger House than is necessary for our comfort in compliance with the mandate of that positive gentleman Thomas Mee Gorst Esquire that the Lord of Hornby should not be disgraced by a shabby Residence without a *good Bed* for a friend'. Berkeley Lodge had plenty of room for friends to come and stay: 'Indeed it may be usefull in breaking us in a little for acting the Lord and Lady of the Manor if your exertions should be successful in placing us in the old Chateau.'

The appeal came on in February 1838 before the twelve Law Lords. The point of law upon which it hung, as is so often the case, seemed a very slight one compared with the huge weight of the complete case. Were certain letters which Pollock had insisted upon using to be counted as evidence or not, since there was neither answer to them nor any evidence of action by John Marsden upon receiving them? If the verdict was for Tatham, it was the end of the case; if for Wright, the whole thing could be resuscitated, retried, and 'go on to Eternity', said Gorst despairingly.

Their Lordships delayed the promulgation of their verdict from February to May, while the protagonists weighed up the likely opinions of the twelve judges. There was no doubt that old James Alan Park and

Gurney would be for Wright, since they had presided over trials at which the letters had been admitted. There was no doubt either that Bolland would side with them. 'Bolland is a sinner – having twice been witness to have the indelicacy to adjudicate in the cause is shameful!' Coleridge and James Parke were equally certain to be on Tatham's side. Of the others, Williams, Paterson, Alderson, Bosanquet and Littledale might be for Tatham; Tyndal and Vaughan would most likely be for Wright.

The verdict was given in May and, cliff-hanging to the last, the result was six all. 'Joe Littledale has deserted,' wailed Gorst, 'otherwise it would have been seven to five as we all along supposed ... It remains with the Chancellor to decide the point.'[14] But, on 7 June, 1838, the Chancellor upheld the verdict of the lower court, and the news flashed round the country as fast as the stage-coaches could run.

On the 8th the Admiral was writing to Pudsey, 'To you will fall the task of carrying my wishes into Execution and it is a great happiness to me to reflect, I cannot place them in more honourable or more able hands'.[15] And at pretty well the same hour in Sidmouth Pudsey was writing to the Admiral, 'May God in his mercy give you health and strength to enjoy the noble possession which the just and triumphant decision of the Lords has this morning laid at your feet ... I am very cool and quite collected ...' (which his handwriting certainly was not).[16]

John Lingard reported the Lune Valley's reception of the news:

The victory, God be thanked, is at last yours. We have all been drunk with joy, bells ringing, flags flying, healths drinking, etc. etc. ... Mrs Croft, whom you cannot know, but a well-wisher at Hornby [his house-keeper] had prepared a blue flag with your arms, the cross on a white field, which from the moment the news arrived, has been flying on the tower of the chapel. Mrs Higgin sent up a day or two after two flags, the union and another which are flying on the tower of the castle. Several individuals both here and in the neighbouring hamlets have also sported blue flags. In fact I know not whether you and the queen are not the two most celebrated characters at the present time ...

Your friend Wright last Thursday had an accident. He was on board a small sloop or some kind of boat, delivering coals for him, amd in expressing his passion at something that did not please him, advanced a foot too far, and fell down the hold. He is home, now able to go about, but with two black eyes and large patches on the forehead and nose.

Mr and Miss Procter are well, the first is grown several years younger in consequence of the good news. At Melling your friends are also in high spirits ...

Excuse the above for I write in great haste to save the post, and mention whatever occurs to me at the moment. But be assured that of the thousands who rejoice at the success with which it has pleased God to reward your efforts, there is no one who can do it more sincerely than, my dear sir, your obedient servant, John Lingard.[17]

At Kirkby Lonsdale, Alexander Nowell sent a couple of guineas to the bellringers but they could not get into the church – history has nothing to say of the Vicar's sympathies, but he may have been a Wright supporter. Nothing daunted, and anxious to earn their money, the ringers turned out the band and gathered outside Dr Batty's door (Batty was the Hornby Castle doctor who, though he had dined out for years on 'silly Marsden' stories, had appeared in the witness box for Wright). Here they played endlessly 'Dainty Davie', the simple country dance that had been quoted so often in court as the only tune Marsden could ever get to the end of, that he had spent whole days playing in his library, sometimes stopping to address himself in the mirror: 'Very well played, Mr Marsden'. 'Shall I play it again?' 'Pray do'.

What, one wonders, would that innocent catalyst have made of all that had happened in his name? It is impossible to know, but it is a feature of the whole story that his wishes, and even his rights, were totally disregarded in the battle of titans for which his death had fired the starting gun. His competence was the key, but the struggle was over something quite different – money, land-ownership, family honour, power, fear of social upheaval, stability. What John Marsden actually wanted, what he had a right to do with his own inheritance, was only occasionally in evidence, and then as a mere lawyer's pawn. Nobody else thought of it at all. Unless, perhaps, the Admiral did. All through the trials he had castigated Anthony Lister Marsden for his 'mean, dirty truckling ... to Wright, to his eternal disgrace'. But before the end of the year of triumph Pudsey was writing in some surprise that he had heard in a roundabout way 'of your great liberality and very handsome conduct to Mr Lister Marsden, your giving him, what he did not deserve, the advowson of Gargrave, and for which he had expressed himself greatly indebted to you and very sensible of your kindness to him and his family'.[18]

Meanwhile, the summer of 1838 was a busy one. 'It will make you young again', said Lingard to the Admiral, and in some ways so it did. Before the final result, Tatham's letters, though not unhopeful of the result, were full of his determination to shed his responsibilities and pass everything to Pudsey as soon as possible. He even revealed that he was uncharacteristcally haunted by the thought of losing his mind and falling under the influence of 'a Bleasdale or a Wright'.

Success wiped that fear, and with a surge of new energy he stepped into the waiting shoes. '*I must take the helm*', and he fired off a stream of letters, whose practical commonsense in dealing with a situation so totally new to him reflected not only the soundness of his own mind and his naval training, but would have done justice to a man half his age. 'The short time Messrs Gorst and Higgin were with me', he told his troops a week after the result, 'gave me no time for considering either what they proposed, or what might occur to me as necessary; I therefore now give a few Memorandums'.

The appointment of George Armistead as Bailiff of the Lands, Woods etc. and to reside in the Castle in the same way Blezard did, I suppose: I think him a very proper man for the situation, and I think he may act as Lord's Bailiff also – of course such part of the Castle as is requisite for his Family must be made habitable, if it is not so now: the rest of the house to remain *shut up* till I give Directions ... I will not have any room prepared or anything done there.

If James Richardson had still held his situation with Sir Henry Mainwaring I should not at present have appointed any Gamekeeper but as it is I shall not object to his being engaged.

If it is necessary to have a Carpenter at present in constant employment Enoch Knowles is the Man I should chuse.

I do not know on what terms the gardener holds the gardens or what rent (if any) he pays for them. If he pays rent and there is any bargain to supply the occupants or managers at the Castle with Fruit etc. it must not be made a pretence to plunder him of the most valuable part of the Produce as heretofore.

I inadvertently consented to have the glass in the Hot Houses and conservatories replaced, but before any order is given I desire to know what will be the expence. I have at present no money to spare, nor do I know when I may get a shilling from the Estates and till I do no expence whatever must be incurred in any operations.

As to hothouses and conservatories I have no passion for them, they are a heavy expence producing at least to me neither pleasure nor profit, and as far as I am concerned I should be glad to see them sold and taken away: Pines, Vines and altogether such things are a very foolish display of ostentation and nothing better.

Let the new house at Tatham remain in statu quo till I give directions.

If Bleasedale's Cottage is in our possession let me know what rooms it contains, and if a good roomy bedchamber for Mrs Tatham and I, say the length Breadth and Height of the largest, it might be convenient to occupy it pro tem: till a better is provided.

I wish to know the state of the Collieries and Quarries and if tenanted or how worked, at present, that due attention may be paid thereto: before any promise or encouragement is given to offering tenants. After due investigation we must consider what arrangement is best in respect to them. I am not determined the Castle Inn is to be discontinued or not.

The repairs of Hornby Chapel must be attended to, a Vestry meeting should be held and if I am not able to attend Dr Lingard will have the goodness to be my representative. Everything should be well done, without ornament and fripperies. I am disposed to contribute liberally but I should like to have the plans and know the *extent* of the cost beforehand.

Mr Pearson had been making some application about the tythes. I do not understand the matter (never having attended to it) but I will not be any impediment to what is proper, my wish being to aid in everything beneficial to the country.

Mr Higgin to be the steward of the *Manor Courts* etc. and to hold the Courts as such and admit tenants. In respect to the Estate *till other arrangements are made* I shall take them under my own immediate Direction all Applications and Communications respecting them to be made direct to me for my Decision and I will *order* what I think proper to be done.

If Mrs Tatham can without inconvenience be ready to accompany me, I intend to proceed to Liverpool in two or three days and to make that place my sojourn a short time – I did not intend immediately to go to Hornby, wishing first to have all preliminary matters settled, so that I should have less to do; but should my presence be necessary, or a constant communication with my attorney be required: I shall immediately be on the spot and take my part, feeling myself in every respect fully equal to the Task, and requiring no other Assistance except my legal Adviser.

There are some minor considerations. First the Fisheries. I would not have the rivers poached by *strangers, no intrusion*: but the Inhabitants to have the full Liberty of Angling, even the Labouring Class should not be debarred from catching a dish of Fish for their Families in an evening after working Hours, but this does not give Liberty to trespass on any man's fields without his permission and the grounds round the Castle of course must not be intruded on.

Messrs Lingard and Procter, and Mr Murray will have all the accomadation the Manor affords and if the good Doctor at any time desires to be supplied with Fish or Game in the season, the gamekeeper will attend to it and supply him, and I wish the rector of Tatham within his parish with a Friend who may be his Visitor to have the same indulgence. I have no objection to his knowing I have desired it. The gamekeeper must be told not to interrupt him.

I desire that the rooks which may be on the Estate may not be shot or disturbed. I have always had a sort of Friendship for them and wish to protect them and the same with the Thrushes and Blackbirds (whatever the Gardener may say) and all singing Birds. I have a very great partiality to them. As to the Old Eagle which has *given over singing* and the Little one *which has not begun to sing* do what you like with them.

Sandford Tatham   16th June 1838 [19]

It was typical that the Reverend John Marsden Wright was to be offered an olive branch in the form of permission to fish. With those who might have been drawn into the affair rather than participating actively, bridges were to be built. 'Above all things I dislike the thought of exulting and crowing over a fallen adversary, there is something so *Dunghill* in it.' He heard that young John Sharp wanted to meet Gorst personally. Why not? 'We have not received *from him* any personal offence.' George Smith was told that there was no reason why he should not continue to keep his house cows and harvest the fog (the second hay crop) in the Avenue meadow in front of the Castle. Smith also received a personal invitation from John Higgin to join one of the dinners being arranged for the great entry day. It was arranged even with George Wright that he should keep Bleasdale's house (the Admiral insisted on its being renamed 'Tatham Grove', he disliked 'Cottage' as an 'old-maidish' term) as a tenant for the rest of the year.

There must have been distress and bitterness here and there; supporters were to be rewarded, which meant opponents being ousted to make space, but there was no regular campaign against them (even Dickinson, Wright's sycophantic tenant of the Castle Inn, would not necessarily be asked to leave), and the intention was clearly to restore a workable, efficient and harmonious state of affairs. Lingard, who had managed over thirty years to do exactly that on the religious front, was no doubt a valuable adviser. The Admiral expressed his appreciation of the Doctor with several fine cheeses sent in at intervals from the midlands.

He found it more difficult to be generous to Higgin, who had worked so hard and on the whole so effectively during the whole twelve years. He could not be faulted on industry, loyalty and enthusiasm – but his money sense was disastrous, and the Admiral found this very hard to forgive. He had only recently warned Pudsey again:

> All I have to say further to you as to your *associate* in London is what the policeman might say to you when entering the passage at Drury Lane Theatre – Take care of your pocket, Sir, for I see a man very likely to try a pluck at it.[20]

He was quite willing to have Higgin Steward of the Courts in Sharp's place, but baulked at appointing him Steward of the whole estate: 'I do not think him a proper person to manage about land and letting farms, *receiving rents.*' Higgin had applied for the post; he was so much the obvious candidate that refusal would have been a public slap in the face. Gorst embarrassed the Admiral, no doubt deliberately, by recommending Higgin to his face, when they were both in Cheltenham. Pudsey persuaded as well, undertaking to keep a close personal eye on estate matters, which, having been a landowner all his life, he was far better equipped to do than either Higgin or the Admiral. Before the end of the year Higgin was appointed at a salary of £300, but for the moment, whatever his official position, he threw himself happily into the business of the Great Entry, which he and Tom Gorst were stage-managing with relish.

They had time for their preparations, as the 28 June that year was earmarked for Queen Victoria's Coronation, and it would not do to let the two celebrations overlap. In fact, not much happened in Hornby for the Coronation: unlike the neighbouring village of Wray, where the mill-owners staged the festivities; or Lancaster, where the corporation and gentry arranged dinners and processions and great doings. Hornby had no industry, and for twelve years now no resident landowner. There was a distribution of mutton among the poor families, and sixpenny vouchers for free drink changeable at any of the public houses. Otherwise, Hornby accepted the beginning of the Victorian Age very quietly, saving its energies.

Friday 3 August was as fine a day as one has any right to expect in the north west in August: that is to say, it rained a little in the morning in a half-hearted fashion, and then cleared up. It was as well that it was not too hot, as the road from Lancaster was thick with people from an early hour. Anyone who could find a wheeled vehicle did so, of course – 'carriages and four', the *Lancaster Gazette* reporter remarked, 'barouches, chariots, landaus, curricles, gigs, omnibuses, cars, horsemen and every description of conveyance' – but many hundreds were happy to walk the ten miles, enjoy the day and walk back again. 'Lancaster,

Kirkby Lonsdale, Burton, Milnthorp, Sedbergh, Settle and Gargrave all helped to swell the stream, not to mention the adjacent townships and parishes.'

The carriage procession formed in the broad street of Hornby village, which was bright with evergreens and 'various fanciful devices'. It set off for Melling, the next village, where it was to meet the Admiral and an entourage of close friends, and return in triumph. The Vicar of Melling, John Tatham, had claimed the right to start the procession off from his house, not so much because of his name, the cousinship being very remote, but because Melling was the mother church of Hornby. The Admiral, however, was not staying there but four miles away at Nether Kellet, with Admiral Barrie. It might have been even more appropriate for him to start his triumph from Marshfield in Settle with Pudsey Dawson, but Settle was sixteen miles away, and fatigue was a consideration. As it was, Mrs Tatham was thought too delicate to sustain the day's festivities and stayed at home.

Although, since he became famous, a portrait print had been circulating (drawn and produced without his knowledge), there must have been huge curiosity to see the Gallant Admiral, as the papers invariably called him, in the flesh. He had hardly ever been seen in Hornby, having set foot in the park once in connection with the plea for ejectment in 1837. That Friday afternoon John Higgin showed him round his Castle for the very first time.

The people who lined the road could not have expected anyone younger than this very old man, tall, thin, somewhat frail in appearance. The first chapter of the story had been written in 1780, and they had heard it from their fathers, or even their grandfathers; the surviving characters were all old men. John Marsden had been sixty-eight when he died in 1826. George Wright, who needless to say stayed quietly at home in Heysham, was almost as old as the Admiral. The Reverend Robert Procter, last of the three witnesses to the will, was now nearer eighty than seventy and in delicate health. The Admiral had wanted him to conduct the service of thanksgiving in Hornby Chapel but he had not felt up to it. 'Mr Procter', explained John Higgin, 'has not preached during the last two years, and he is very reluctant to ascend the pulpit again, under an apprehension that he might find himself unable to go through the duty.' Relieved from the necessity of taking any public part, he was well able to enjoy the day, sharing a carriage with Dr Lingard.

Pudsey Dawson must have been pointed out with nearly as much interest as that accorded to the Admiral, particularly by the locals who knew that, as heir to the estate in the not too distant future, he would have more influence on their lives than Sandford Tatham himself. His reaction to the day must have been mixed, the triumph shadowed by thoughts of his son's death. But his brother Richard, a shipowner and merchant of Liverpool, whose young son Richard Pudsey would be Pudsey's heir, provided more than one man's share of conviviality. To him, as the newspaper said, 'the harmony and good humour of the meeting was greatly indebted'.

The long procession included at least four bands, of which the Bentham band aroused interest for its grand mix of tartan, topped off with cavalry epaulettes and the feathered hats of an infantry regiment; their playing, it was noted, was much more coherent than their uniform. Among the carriages filled with the Admiral's friends, relations and supporters, the bands marching or perched on their wagons, the cheerfully undisciplined footsloggers, banners waved here and there. Some were white and purple with anchors embroidered, some bore suitable slogans: 'Justice triumphant', 'Justice is at length obtained'. The ladies, and the omnibuses, and nearly everything else, were decorated with blue rosettes, Tatham being a Rear Admiral of the Blue.

So from Melling into Hornby, the Admiral's carriage with the horses out and 'the populace' drawing him 'in triumph' processed to what the newspapers naturally called 'his patrimonial estate'. This was of course not true, but it was no time to quibble, or to remember that all the patrimonial estates had been sold, nominally to finance the acquisition of Hornby, but in reality to build up George Wright's personal fortune.

'From the battlements of the Castle waved the flag under which Admiral Tatham last sailed as a naval officer. The Union Jack was also proudly waving from the Castle, and from the tower of the Church streamed a blue flag, having an anchor painted on one side and the Maltese Cross on the other.' Over the Castle gates there were flowers and evergreens, silk banners screaming 'Welcome Home', and an elegant transparency painted by Mr Hutton of Lancaster, representing Justice with her scales, trampling on a figure 'writhing in the embrace of serpents', which some took to be Envy and others Oppression, but which was undeniably being trampled. The association was further pointed by a 'noble three-decker' in the background. Higgin and Gorst, and many willing hands in Hornby, had not spared their efforts.

As the Admiral's carriage passed through the gates, a gun was fired. The gentry who had been invited to the Castle followed up the avenue. So did the rest of the crowd, or as many as could find space. At the top of the steep drive the Admiral stood up in his carriage to address them. There were tears in his eyes and surely not in his alone. It had been a punishing twelve years and they deserved their triumph. 'He sincerely thanked them for the kind and affectionate reception which he had met with at their hands. He was now come among them where he hoped to end his days.' And he added that he intended the fishing on his estates to be free to his tenants, which was very well received. Then the grandees went inside, and the crowd milled about until an announcement was made that there was free beer down at the Cross, which cleared the area.

Inside the Castle, the boarded-up windows had been reglazed, and long tables laid out in the hall, but even in August it must have been cold and dank. The Admiral was much touched to see that the one portrait which had been hung on the empty walls was that of his mother. This had been in the possession of his elder brother and Admiral Barrie had fetched it back from America as an unexpected present.

The place was otherwise unfurnished and not remotely habitable, but the excitement of the people crowding in created a temporary warmth, and the tables were handsomely laid with an 'elegant cold collation' supplied by Miss Noon of the Royal Oak in Lancaster, the acknowledged local caterer for all big occasions. There were seats for fifty. When the ladies had finished their lunch, the gentlemen waiting behind their chairs sat down in their turn, and more than a hundred people got something to eat and drink.

Then came the speeches. Pudsey Dawson proposed the Admiral's health in his usual modest style. The Admiral's reply was saltily naval, and the reporter omitted some 'terms of great severity' on the character of Sir Frederick Pollock. On the other hand, he was generous to John Higgin, having 'during an intercourse of twelve years ... always found him most gentlemanly in his conduct and talented as a professional adviser'. This was a fair tribute, although it by no means represented their bumpy and often bruising relationship. Apart from his disastrous money sense, Higgin had enviable qualities of enthusiasm, resilience and devotion to the purpose in hand, and he seems never to have borne resentment for the snubs he received. His happiness in the happy outcome of the great Cause was complete and unfeigned.

Admiral Sir Robert Barrie proposed the Counsel. Everyone regretted that Mr Cresswell, widely regarded as having tipped the scales to victory, was on circuit and had to be represented by Mr Starkie, his junior, who made 'an eloquent and impassioned speech' about the case in general and his client's tenacity in particular. This went down very well, representing as it did exactly the quality which had won the hearts of the

British public. There were cheers, and more cheers, and 'See the Conquering Hero' from the band, and fluttering handkerchiefs from the ladies.

The Reverend John Tatham proposed Pudsey Dawson, who characteristically replied in a couple of sentences, and passed on the compliment with a toast to 'The Witnesses'. Dr Lingard replied and was 'greeted with gratifying marks of the respect in which he was held by the meeting'. Then the Admiral was on his feet again to propose the health of the clergy present, no doubt thinking particularly of the clergy not present. John Wright of Tatham, whose church was in full view of the flags snapping from the Castle tower, had tactfully taken himself and his family off to Heysham for a short break. Anthony Lister Marsden was keeping a very low profile at Gargrave.

John Higgin had his health drunk, Tom Gorst had his health drunk, everybody from the Lord Lieutenant downwards had their health drunk, and finally the ladies had their health drunk twice, once as 'the Lancashire witches' by the Admiral, on his feet for the third time, and again as 'the widows, wives and maidens of the banks of the Lune', all with three times three and musical honours.

There was dancing in the large drawing-room upstairs for the gentry, and dancing in the village, where the tenants had their own dinners and balls at the various inns. Even George Smith joined in, and entered in his diary: 'We had twenty one persons to tea etc.' The Admiral was taken home by his friends at six o'clock, but Hornby went on drinking and dancing for a very long time, only pausing to watch the fireworks which were let off from the Castle tower in the twilight. It was a day to remember.

17

Summing-Up

Although Sandford Tatham had his inheritance for less than eighteen months, and that was longer than he or anyone else had expected, it is pleasant to report that from his letters they were months which gave him a sense of fulfilment, and a good deal of honest enjoyment. The legal wrangling, as they tried to drag the title deeds, and still more the money, out of Wright, continued unabated, but Higgin and the arbitrators were doing that. There was much to do before the Castle could be actually lived in, and from Cheltenham the Admiral busied himself with enthusiasm in the business of getting the house itself and the estate into something like tolerable repair. 'In agricultural matters,' he wrote to Pudsey, 'I may find it best to ask your advice and assistance, but I think everything else I can manage very well.'[1]

On agricultural matters, Pudsey tramped the ground: 'on foot from 10 to 6, on the Camp House and Priory Farms, I believe in every field west of the High Road. More shameful neglect and mismanagement I never could have thought possible'.[2] He imported the bailiff from his own Yorkshire estate as a temporary help, and Higgin moved in to Giles Bleasdale's cottage, working assiduously and shuttling up and down to Cheltenham to consult with his employer.

The Admiral was now suffering not only from his bronchitic ailments but also from extreme old age. The bells rang at Hornby to celebrate his eighty-fourth birthday. His gentle, patient wife had had a fall and damage to her hip had left her permanently lame. They celebrated their golden wedding in the spring of 1839, and it was perhaps for this occasion that Pudsey was commissioned to look at furs in London and reported on 'Sable Capes from £8 to £20 (splendid). Real Ermine Capes £5 to £12 (very handsome). Chinchilla Capes £4 to £10 (too much like scabby rabbit)'.[3] Mrs Tatham chose an ermine one for £10 2s. 6d. and Gorst delivered it on his next visit.

In October 1838 the Admiral had some sort of attack ('It went off in a day or two but was very alarming'), and his courage almost failed at the prospect of living in the cold and distant north out of reach of his own doctors, but a month later resilience asserted itself, and he was writing 'The Castle becoming my residence for the remainder of my life I now deem indispensible, not as a Matter of Choice but what circumstances render absolutely necessary'.[4]

Through the winter of 1838 and spring of 1839 the builders, joiners, decorators were at work under Higgin's eye. Mrs Higgin was coopted to organise the furnishing. 'Dr Lingard and Mr Procter have been up and are much pleased with what is done and doing, and I trust when you visit the Premises you will give us credit for our Talents in our respective departments. "Director, Sandford Tatham, architect and chief manager John Higgin junior, and Susan Higgin upholsterer".'[5]

In the event the Tathams did not move into Hornby until the beginning of August 1839, and there were great plans on foot to celebrate this second entry by a shooting party for the 12th. 'I think the Castle will be full and the Moors covered with sportsmen.' They had intended to move out again 'for warmer winter quarters' by the beginning of November but this did not happen. There are no more letters so we may conclude that Pudsey did not leave them alone again. The fact that they stayed through the winter can only mean that the Admiral's health deteriorated too much to make a move possible. However hard the plasterers and decorators had worked, Hornby Castle must have been wickedly cold and damp for an old man with bronchitis.

Admiral Sandford Tatham died at Hornby Castle on 24 January 1840, and was buried according to his instructions:

> I most positively direct that my remains be not subject to the folly of funeral pageantry, but that the same may be committed to the Earth and at such time and place as my dearly beloved wife shall direct in as quiet and private a manner as possible and that no Expence be incurred which can decently be avoided. It is my desire that everything be plain and Frugal.[6]

An unobtrusive brass cross in the floor of Hornby Church, next to that of John Marsden, confirms that his wishes were carried out. Mrs Tatham went back to her relations at Leicester for the remaining two years of her life, and the Pudsey Dawsons moved permanently into Hornby Castle. In one respect only, Sandford Tatham mistrusted his heir, as the codicil to his will showed.

> And I hereby request and solemnly charge the said Pudsey Dawson ... as a sacred and indispensible duty ... to society in discountenanceing fraud and protecting the just rights of Families and Individuals to claim

and sue for at law or in equity and to do and use his ... utmost endeavour to recover from the said George Wright and his sons and daughters respectively and from the representatives of the said Giles Bleasdale and all other persons whomsoever all houses building lands goods chattels monies or other estate or property which in the judgment of the said Pudsey Dawson his heirs executors administrators or assigns may have been fraudulently or illegally obtained from the said John Marsden.[6]

Of the other players in this drama, John Higgin junior died in 1847, having, it may be presumed, continued to work for Hornby Castle to the end. His descendants continue and his law firm, under a different name, flourishes on Castle Hill in Lancaster. Tom Gorst, the cheerful and ever-helpful aide, never married, in spite of the Admiral's attempts at match-making with some of Pudsey Dawson's nieces. He changed his name to Lowndes when he inherited an estate from a great uncle, and died a bachelor at the age of fifty.

The chief counsel of the case all continued with illustrious careers. Sir James Scarlett, appointed Lord Chief Baron of the Exchequer, Privy Councillor, Serjeant-at-Law, and created Baron Abinger of Abinger while the Cause still continued, died suddenly on circuit in 1844, aged seventy-four. His younger opponent, Frederick Pollock, became Robert Peel's Attorney-General, then took over Scarlett's position as Lord Chief Baron of the Exchequer, and remained in it for over twenty years, during which, says the *Dictionary of National Biography*, he was noted for his 'learned and luminous judgments'. Age and the changing culture of the mid-Victorian period no doubt toned down his Pickwickian rhetoric. He died 'of old age' in 1870, aged eighty-seven. The young Cresswell Cresswell, who had been eager to make his name by victory in *Tatham* v. *Wright*, won far greater fame as a Judge in the new and experimental divorce court, in which he presided until his death in 1863. 'He adjudicated upon a thousand cases, and his judgement was but once reversed.'

George Wright died in 1848, at the advanced age of ninety, and lies in a family tomb in Heysham churchyard. It took the gravediggers three days to hack the cavity out of almost solid rock. The funeral was meagrely attended, by his doctor, two or three neighbours and his Heysham tenants; and George Smith, who noted only 'a hearse and two mourning coaches'. But we presume he died content, having fulfilled his ambition to found a family of gentry; in spite of losing the lawsuit he had kept the greater part of his wealth. He seems to have had to sell nothing that he had acquired, and as late as 1843 he was still adding another piece of Heysham land to his estate, for which he paid £3500. His will cites the Lower Snab estate at Gressingham, land at Danby in the North Riding, Heysham Lodge and its estate, and more in Poulton, Bare and Torrisholme, Arkholme, Over and Nether Kellet, Bentham and Kirkby Lonsdale. He owned well over a thousand acres, most of it left to his eldest son, the Reverend John Marsden Wright, with a comfortable nest-egg of £4000 to each of his unmarried daughters.

He had no descendants except through his eldest son. William had died during the lawsuit, Henry was a hopeless alcoholic, who died unmarried not long after his father. The two daughters who had married before the lawsuit had no children, the other two did not marry. A photograph remains of the eldest, Margaret, a formidable woman who may well have been her father's right-hand.

One would like to know more of John Marsden Wright, Rector of Tatham for half a century, inheritor of his father's land and money, founder of a prosperous and typical Victorian family. His picture shows him prematurely grey-haired and extraordinarily like his father, but with a benignity missing from George's expression, which even the portrait painter James Lonsdale, setting out to please, could only make tight-lipped and austere. John Wright's daughters married respectable local gentry, his sons included an army surgeon and two civil engineers. The clan as it spread achieved almost total amnesia as to where its prosperity began, and only the vaguest memory of its forebears having once been involved in a lawsuit.

It was never felt that the well-respected Rector was tarred with his father's brush; indeed in the months after the victory there are suggestions that he had had no idea of negotiations going forward between the parties ('incredible as it may appear'). It has already been said that as soon as the verdict was final, the Admiral was making gestures of peace by his inclusion of John Wright in the list of those who should be allowed free fishing. Two months later, Higgin having moved into Giles Bleasdale's old house with his family, Pudsey Dawson reported to the Admiral: 'The Higgin family went to Tatham church and occupied old Giles' seat. Mr John Wright, they told us, was highly gratified by their going, tho' he was very much unnerved while doing the duty'.[7] Thereafter the Wrights and the Higgins were on affable dining terms, and a few months later Pudsey himself met John Wright and his wife at dinner, possibly at Wenning Cottage: 'I found him mild, quiet, and much at his ease – of course no allusions to anything which could annoy.'[8]

John Marsden Wright died in 1875 and was buried at the east end of the church he had served well. He evidently had no ambition to retire to Heysham Lodge, although it was lived in by grandchildren and great-grandchildren of old George until well after the First World War.

William Sharp, Hornby Castle's devoted solicitor, also lived on to old age, once the extreme stress of the case was off his shoulders. It was said that he and George Wright parted company with acrimony in the aftermath of the case, and George Smith reported a running battle over £2000 owed to Sharp, which had still not been paid at the end of 1845. The firm by then was entirely in the hands of young John, who kept the old house in Dalton Square before he built himself a handsome new one at the Crook o' Lune, called The Hermitage. William continued to live in style and comfort behind the high walls of Linden Hall in Borwick, a pleasant villa whose extensions were planned by Webster of Kendal and built by Hornby Castle workmen. His descendants live there still. He died in 1857 and was buried at Warton. John ran the family firm until 1879, greatly respected and trusted by his clients, who put up a window to his memory in Halton Church.

And George Smith, the man who could have spoken but never did? He, it seems, was treated with civility ('Mr Higgin came in the afternoon and gave me leave to angle in Roeburn, Hindburn and Lune'), though it is not recorded that he ever came face to face with the principals in the case except once: when as he was walking from Lancaster, he was overtaken near the aqueduct by Higgin and Pudsey Dawson, who gave him a lift and 'set me down at my own door'. He was not hustled to leave his house, and it was May 1839 before he moved to Wray village, where he worked as a free-lance land agent to various local landowners, was employed by the Ordnance Survey mappers, did some work on the Little North Western Railway through the Lune Valley, and continued to act from time to time as confidential clerk to George Wright. In 1840, having gone with Higgin to London on business concerned with the mortgages on the estate still unresolved, he recorded the coming of a new era, in that he made the return journey within a single day: by the 9 a.m. mail train from Euston to Birmingham where he dined, caught the 2.45 p.m. to Parkside and thence to Preston where he arrived at 7.30, and thence by the Lord Exmouth coach to Lancaster, arriving at 10.30 'and staid all night at the White Lion'.

In the later years it is clear from his diary that he retired progressively. The last entry is in May 1856. In the thirty-three years which the diary spans, the nearest he ever got to a personal comment on the rights and wrongs of the case is an entry in 1841: 'I attended Mr White's [the Vicar's] lecture at Wray Church – subject the Unjust Steward'.

The Reverend Robert Procter outlived the Admiral by only a few months and died aged eighty. It is recorded that he bequeathed his pet guinea fowls to his good friend across the road because 'he knew Dr Lingard would look after them'. Lingard himself minded about Procter's death more than perhaps the difference in their intellectual powers and pursuits would suggest. He wrote sadly to a friend: 'My neighbours drop in succession into the grave, and there are scarcely any left who can come to sit with me on a winter evening, or whom I can visit then.'[9]

But, in fact, one of the neighbours who had recently dropped into the grave being old Mrs Murray next door, she was replaced in the same year by her son (he who had attended the York trial 'out of curiosity'), his lively young wife and two engaging children. Mr Murray was something of an invalid, but Dr Lingard soon wore a path through the gardens, taking a daily short-cut to play a hand of whist, and when Pudsey Dawson replaced the Admiral at the Castle, he found that his last years were as rich as any that had gone before, and his spirits were soon as high as they had ever been.

He continued to say his Mass and conduct his parish business in the good old-fashioned way of his youth, in his brown coat and breeches, and with none of the new-fangled flummery from across the Alps. He had, he said, no objection to Italians carrying on thus, but why import things into England? Gothic architecture for one (he never could come to terms with Pugin), and dog-collars, and black frock-coats, and calling people 'Father', and processions, and splashings with holy water –

> all of them practices in themselves certainly unnecessary, in their consequences, as far as I can see, calculated to confirm the prejudices of well-educated protestants, and prevent them from considering the essentials of our holy religion; and yet all advocated by men whose judgement I respect, and of whose zeal and sincerity I can have no doubt ... the best thing I can do is to keep myself to myself, and leave others to follow their own judgements without any interference of mine.[10]

He died, after prolonged ill-health, very quietly, and was buried, as he wished, at Ushaw. The College also has the Lonsdale portrait which he thought was his best likeness. The secular clergy of Lancashire put up a tablet to him in the Catholic chapel at Hornby, but across the road there is a more striking memorial – probably the only tablet in the country put up in a Protestant church to a Catholic priest.

In memory of John Lingard D.D., the learned author of the History of England and of the Antiquities of the Anglo-Saxon Church. He died at Hornby xviii July MDCCCLI aged 81 and was buried at Ushaw College Durham. 'Quis desiderio sit modus tam cari capitis?' This tablet is erected by his friends and associates.

Among whom Pudsey Dawson was certainly the first. No doubt he also chose the Latin tag which, slightly misquoted from an Ode of Horace, roughly means 'How can we measure our grief for one so much loved?'.

Pudsey himself lived on at the Castle until 1859, losing his invalid wife soon after Lingard's death. Although he died at Hornby, he is buried in St Alkelda's, Giggleswick, the church of Langcliffe Hall, his family's ancient estate. During his tenure of Hornby Castle, he did everything that became a gentleman and landowner, but so unobtrusively, as was his fashion, that very few echoes have come down the years.

He undertook a wholesale programme of improvement, first rebuilding farmhouses and cottages, then a new vicarage, and finally calling in the architects Sharpe and Paley to remodel the dwelling part of the Castle, in the style of Henry VII. He became High Sheriff in 1845, as a landowning gentleman was expected to do, and he took particular interest in the Little North Western Railway, cutting the first sod at Bentham in September 1848. Where the Lancaster road was bridged on his land near Hornby, the bridge carried his 'Cat and Rat' crest, long since moved to a position in Hornby village over a drinking trough.

He collected and tidied up the accumulation of material regarding the Cause into eight large tin boxes. Much of it is confused, but the Admiral's letters to him, and his to the Admiral, he sorted and docketed with filial care.

He was, it would seem, a good employer, a good landlord and a good friend. The Admiral would have approved his activities in all but one respect: he failed signally to squeeze enough money out of George Wright, and when he died in 1859 the estate, though in prosperity a totally different place from that which he had inherited, was still heavily mortgaged. His nephew Richard Pudsey Dawson, who had other estates of his own, sold it in 1860 to a rich industrialist from Yorkshire, John Foster of Black Dyke Mills, who was a sufficiently rough diamond, it has always been said, to arrive with the purchase price in bags of gold coin.

So ended the eighty-year saga of Marsden, Tatham and Wright. It only remains to mention one other of the characters. Anthony Lister Marsden continued, by the generosity of Admiral Tatham, as Vicar of Gargrave to his death in 1852, and was followed in the same appointment by his son Charles John, who lived until 1903. Whereas the Wright family totally forgot any pretensions they may have had, it seems that the same is not true of the Marsdens, in whom the memory of lost glory seems to have rankled for a hundred years. Efforts to trace the family of Charles John have failed, although it seems probable that he only had female descendants, and that they died without issue. Recently, someone who remembers vaguely that her grandmother was born a Marsden, but remembers nothing else about her, not even her married name, recollected that, probably in the 1930s, she was taken by this grandmother to visit another old lady in Lancaster; and that the second old lady, who was somehow related, flourished a bundle of documents in front of the child and said with sufficient emphasis for the occasion to stick in her mind, 'Of course, by rights we should have had Hornby Castle'.

Notes

The records of *Tatham* v. *Wright* in Hornby Castle are contained in eight tin boxes. These have at some time been numbered 5, 6, 7, 8, 9, 10, 10A, 11. Each box contains a number of brown paper parcels, and each parcel a number of smaller packets or individual items. There is no catalogue. The three-figure references therefore are to *box* (first) *parcel* (second) *package or item* (third), but the second and third are notional numberings only, with the exception of the packets of letters, which are marked by numbered slips of paper tucked into the string securing them. A copy of my working catalogue is now held with the collection.

Chapter 1: John Marsden

1. For the genealogical details of the Marsden family the two main sources are the Marsden/Tatham pedigree (Hornby Castle, 11.1.1) and Admiral Sandford Tatham's manuscript (Hornby Castle, 11.7.2), written during the trial to prove that he was indeed the heir at law.
2. Hornby Castle. Among the muniments is an eighteenth-century manuscript book detailing the estate as it was bought by the Marsdens from the Morleys.
3. Lancashire Record Office, probate records (WRW), will of Henry Marsden of Wennington Hall, 1742.
4. Hornby Castle, 11.5.9, Sandford Tatham to Pudsey Dawson 23 February 1834.
5. Public Record Office, Chancery proceedings, C 12, Trinity 1769 to Hilary 1772.
6. Lancaster Record Office, RCHy 6958 (uncatalogued collection). The main evidence for this episode or episodes is in a letter (undated) of John Lingard to Sandford Tatham relating what he had gathered from informants, and also reporting what he had heard John Marsden say about it. In another undated letter (Hornby Castle, 11.5.18) to Sandford Tatham, he says that the Reverend Robert Procter is anxious as to whether he should make the story public in his evidence.
7. Alexander Fraser, *A Verbatim Report of the Cause doe dem. Tatham v. Wright: Tried at the Lancaster Lammas Assizes 1834* (Lancaster 1834), i, p. 356. Evidence of John Willan, ex-usher at Kirkby Lonsdale School. The explanation of the strange '*doe dem.*' in the title of the book is complicated. At common law a freeholder who had been wrongly dispossessed of land could bring an action for its recovery. Such actions were known as real actions (the plaintiff re-covered the *res*, the subject of the dispute. There actions were slow and costly and could only be brought in the Court of Common Pleas. The remedy was

not available to leaseholders. Originally a leaseholder who was wrongfully dispossessed could not recover the land from which he had been ejected but only damages for trespass. By the sixteenth century the King's Bench, which was the court with jurisdiction in trespass, had fashioned a remedy (the action of ejectment) by which the dispossessed lessee could recover not merely damages for trespass but also the land which had been leased to him. The remedy in ejectment was cheap and speedy and eventually, by means of legal fictions, it was made available to freeholders. A freeholder (P) who claimed to be entitled to land in the possession of D would bring an action against D in the name of an imaginary plaintiff (John Doe). The writ would allege that P had leased the land to John Doe and that John Doe had been unlawfully evicted by D. This was quite untrue but the defendant D was not permitted to dispute the lease and, in order to defend the action successfully, had to prove that he, D, had a a better right to the land than P. Such actions were styled *Doe d. Smith* v. *Brown* or, more fully, *Doe (on the demise of Smith)* v. *Brown*, demise being another name for a lease. The action was abolished in 1852. I owe this information to the kindness of Dr David Bentley, QC.

8. Hornby Castle, 6.1.2, deposition of Joseph Gardner of Lancaster, ex-servant at Wennington Hall.

Other sources for this chapter: *Victoria County History of Lancashire*, ed. W. Farrer and J. Brownbill (London, 1913); parish registers of Melling, Gisburn etc.; Lancaster Record Office (MF/27), Hearth Tax Returns, 1664; Admissions Register of Gray's Inn; J. A. Venn, *Alumnae Cantabrigienses* (London 1974); Hornby Castle, depositions of John Airey, Marmaduke Ball, Joseph Bell, John Camm, Dr Campbell, Thomas Casson, Ambrose Cookson, Thomas Cookson, William Coulston, Mary Denny, James Foxcroft, Thomas Hall, John Halton, Jane Hill, Peter Hodgson, Nicholas Holme, Robert Humber, Anne Lambert, John Langshaw, George Mashiter, the Reverend Robert Procter, Thomas Robinson, Anne Seward, Robert Sharp, John Tatham, Anne Thompson, Thomas Townson, William Wakefield.

Chapter 2: George Wright

1. Hornby Castle, 11.6.12, deposition of Ellen Millar, once of Aughton.
2. Hornby Castle, 11.6.12, deposition of James Dean of Lancaster, once of Aughton.
3. Hornby Castle, 5.3.3, deposition of George Wright.
4. Hornby Castle, 11.6.12, deposition of Thomas Rowlandson of Over Kellet, farmer.
5. Hornby Castle, 11.6.12, deposition of Ellen Millar.
6. Hornby Castle, 6.4.15, deposition of George Mashiter, husbandman of Prestwich, ex-servant to Henry Marsden.
7. Hornby Castle, 6.3, deposition of Betty Sedgwick, ex-kitchen maid at Wennington Hall.
8. Hornby Castle, 6.3, deposition of Mary Denny of Wray, foster sister of Henry Marsden.
9. Borthwick Institute of Historical Research, York, administration bond of Henry Marsden, 17 April 1780.

Other sources for this chapter: Hornby Castle, 11.7.2, Sandford Tatham's MS; parish registers of Caton, Colton, etc.; *Rolls of the Freemen of the Borough of Lancaster*, ed. T. Cann Hughes, Record Society of Lancashire and Cheshire, 87, 90; Hornby Castle, 11.6.2, undated letter of John Lingard to Sandford Tatham, quoting evidence of Robert Herst, farmer, of Aughton; Hornby Castle, 6.4.14, 6.4.15, 11.6.12, depositions of Robert Humber of Kendal, ex-gardener at Wennington Hall; Hornby Castle, depositions of Ambrose Cookson, Joseph Gardner, Mary Higham, Robert Hindley, Rose Leeming, Ann Lowther, John Miller, Thomas Parker.

Chapter 3: Sarah Cookson

1. Hornby Castle, 6.1.2, deposition of Joseph Lambert, attorney, of Bradford.
2. Hornby Castle, John Marsden's account book.
3. Alexander Fraser, *A Verbatim Report of the Cause doe dem. Tatham v. Wright: Tried at Lancaster Assizes 1834* (Lancaster 1834), i, pp. 207–20; evidence of Giles Bleasdale. The 1834 trial was the third. Some of the witnesses from the first trial at York (Bleasdale among them) were by then dead, so their earlier evidence was read out in court.
4. Hornby Castle, 11.4.2, 11.4.4, 11.4.7, correspondence of Thomas Greene, some of which was used in the trials.
5. Fraser, *A Verbatim Report*, i, p. 369, evidence of Dr Campbell (deceased).
6. Ibid., ii, p. 50, evidence of John Rutherford of Heysham, ex-servant to Reverend Mr Croft of Gargrave.
7. Ibid., ii, p. 5, evidence of Robert Humber (deceased).

Other sources for this chapter: Hornby Castle, 11.7.2, Sandford Tatham's MS; Hornby Castle, depositions of William Barker, Mary Denny, Jane High, Robert Humber, Thomas Parker, Ann Robinson, Elizabeth Sedgwick.

Chapter 4: Admiral Tatham

1. Carlisle Record Office, DRC 3/16, Carlisle Consistory Court records.
2. Hornby Castle, 11.7.2, Sandford Tatham's MS.
3. Hornby Castle, 11.7.23, copy of will of Elizabeth Tatham 1778.
4. Carlisle Record Office, probate records, will of Reverend Sandford Tatham 1777.
5. Hornby Castle, 11.7.2, Sandford Tatham's MS.
6. Ibid.
7. Hornby Castle, 11.6.2, deposition of James Robinson.
8. Hornby Castle, 11.7.2, Sandford Tatham's MS.

Other sources for this chapter: Hornby Castle, depositions of Robert Bracken, Mary Denny, Robert Humber, Elizabeth Kitson, Margaret Pattinson.

Chapter 5: Wennington Hall

1. Hornby Castle, 11.7.2. Information concerning Elizabeth Tatham is mainly from Sandford Tatham's MS.

2. Alexander Fraser, *A Verbatim Report of the Cause doe dem. Tatham v. Wright: Tried at Lancaster Lammas Assizes 1834* (Lancaster 1834), i, p. 364, evidence of Miss Dorothy Butler of Boughton, near Chester.
3. Ibid., ii, p. 62, evidence of John Hayes of Caton, labourer.
4. Ibid., ii, p. 54, evidence of Thomas Bleazard, porter, of Preston.
5. Hornby Castle, 6.4.15, deposition of Robert Humber, gardener, of Kendal.
6. Hornby Castle, 7.3.4, deposition of William Humber of Lancaster.

Other sources for this chapter; Hornby Castle, 11.7.2, Sandford Tatham's MS; Hornby Castle, depositions of Francis Beck, Thomas Cookson, Peter Hodgson, John Nickson, Thomas Parker, the Reverend Robert Procter, Ann Robinson, Thomas Robinson, James Sawrey, James Tatham, Bryan Townson, John Walker, Edward Willan.

Chapter 6: Hornby Castle

1. *Hornby Castle Survey and Year's Accounts*, ed. W.H. Chippindall (Chetham Society, 1939).
2. *Gentleman's Magazine*, April 1732.
3. Thomas Gray, quoted in *Victoria County History of Lancashire*, ed. William Farrer and J. Brownbill (London 1913), viii, p. 198.
4. *Lonsdale Magazine*, 30 November 1822.
5. Alexander Fraser, *A Verbatim Report of the Cause doe dem. Tatham v. Wright: Tried at the Lancaster Lammas Assizes 1834* (Lancaster 1834), ii, p. 47, evidence of Jane Hill.
6. Ibid., i, p. 121, Sir Frederick Pollock, leading counsel for Wright.
7. Ibid., i, p. 87, letter signed by John Marsden.
8. Ibid., i, p. 87, letter signed by John Marsden.
9. Ibid., i, pp. 88–89, letters of Thomas Greene, attorney.
10. Hornby Castle, 6.1.2, deposition of Elizabeth Kitson.
11. Hornby Castle, 11.5.3, Captain Robert Barrie to Sandford Tatham, 1 December 1826.
12. Fraser, *A Verbatim Report*, ii, p. 35, evidence of John Hartley, attorney of Settle.
13. Hornby Castle, 6.1.2, deposition of William Housman, magistrate of Lancaster.

Other sources for this chapter: *Dictionary of National Biography*; Lancashire Record Office, DDX/147/1, sale document of Hornby Castle Estate, 1786. Information concerning the financing of the Hornby Castle purchase is drawn from Fraser, *A Verbatim Report*.

Chapter 7: Wright in the Ascendant

1. Alexander Fraser, *A Verbatim Report of the Cause doe dem. Tatham v. Wright: Tried at the Lancaster Lammas Assizes 1834* (Lancaster 1834), i, pp. 52–53.
2. Ibid., ii, pp. 23–24, evidence of John Smith, ex-servant at Wennington Hall.
3. Ibid., i, p. 52, letter signed by John Marsden.

4. Lancashire Record Office, probate records (WRW), will of Sarah Cookson, 1791.
5. Hornby Castle, 11.5.1, Henry Tatham's appointment as Clerk of the Peace for Westmorland, 1792.
6. Hornby Castle, 6.1.2, deposition of Robert Bracken of Manchester, commission agent.
7. Hornby Castle, 6.1.2, deposition of William Thompson of Caton, labourer.
8. Hornby Castle, 6.1.2, deposition of Jane Hill of Rossendale.
9. Hornby Castle, 6.1.2, deposition of Agnes Hogarth of Lancaster.
10. Lancaster Record Office, RCHy 6958, April 1831, letter of John Lingard to John Higgin.
11. Hornby Castle, 6.1.2, deposition of Ann Robinson of Totteridge, former housemaid at Wennington Hall.
12. Hornby Castle, 6.1.2, deposition of John Croudson of Lancaster, joiner.
13. Hornby Castle, 11.4.7, correspondence of Thomas Greene and C. J. Lefevre with John Marsden.
14. Fraser, *A Verbatim Report*, i, p. 368, evidence of Miss Dorothy Butler.
15. Hornby Castle 7.3.5, deposition of the Reverend Thomas Butler of Poulton-le-Sands.

Chapter 8: Friends and Neighbours

1. Alexander Fraser, *A Verbatim Report of the Cause doe dem. Tatham v. Wright: Tried at the Lancaster Lammas Assizes 1834* (Lancaster 1834), i, p. 154, evidence of William Sharp, attorney of Lancaster.
2. Ibid., ii, p. 139, evidence of John Clarke, ex-gardener to the Reverend Thomas Clarkson of Heysham.
3. Lancaster Record Office, DDX/147/1, 'A Particular of the Estates of the Honourable Francis Charteris' (July 1786).
4. Lancaster Record Office, RCHy 6958, letter of John Lingard to John Higgin (undated).
5. Fraser, *A Verbatim Report*, i, pp. 72–81; Hornby Castle, 8.3.18, correspondence of William Dawson and John Marsden.
6. Ibid., i, pp. 83–84; Hornby Castle, 8.3.18, correspondence of Alexander Marsden and John Marsden.
7. Hornby Castle, 11.5.18, deposition of Jane Procter.
8. Hornby Castle, 9.1.7, deposition of Mary Walling (née Procter).

Other sources for this chapter: Hornby Castle, 11.7.2, Sandford Tatham's MS: Hornby Castle, 6.1.1, 6.3.4, 8.3.2, various depositions of the Reverend Robert Procter. As for many years he dined every Sunday at the Castle, and was visited almost daily by John Marsden, he was also one of John Lingard's most prolific sources of information.

Chapter 9: Dr Lingard

1. Martin Haile and Edward Bonney: *The Life and Letters of John Lingard* (London

n.d. [1910?]), p. 138, quoted in the preface to first octavo edition of John Lingard, *The Antiquities of the Anglo-Saxon Church* (Newcastle, 1806).

2. Haile and Bonney, *The Life and Letters of John Lingard*, p. 19, letter of John Lingard, 30 September 1847.
3. *Catholic Registers of Robert Hall and Hornby*, ed. William Wrennall, p. 322, Miscellanea 4, Catholic Record Society (London, 1907)
4. Haile and Bonney, *The Life and Letters of John Lingard*, p. 26, letter of John Lingard to the Reverend E. Price, 10 January 1847.
5. Ibid., p. 88. quoted preface to Lingard, *The Antiquities of the Anglo-Saxon Church*.
6. Ibid., p. 111, letter of John Lingard to Bishop Poynter, 26 February 1817.
7. Hornby Castle, 5.5.4, deposition of John Lingard.
8. Hornby Castle, 7.1.2, schedule of George Wright's property.
9. Hornby Castle, 11.7.6, deposition of James Worthington; 11.6.2, deposition of Mary Williamson; 6.1.2, depositions of Robert Park and William Thompson.
10. Alexander Fraser, *A Verbatim Report of the Cause doe dem. Tatham v. Wright: Tried at the Lancaster Lammas Assizes 1834* (Lancaster 1834), ii, p. 152, evidence of Joseph Hetherington, plumber of Garstang.

Haile and Bonney's work is still the only full-length biography of John Lingard. Unfortunately it gives very few references to the sources of their material.

Chapter 10: The Will

1. George Smith, diary (unpublished, in private hands): the source of most information in this chapter concerning John Marsden's illness, death and funeral.
2. Alexander Fraser, *A Verbatim Report of the Cause doe dem. Tatham v. Wright: Tried at the Lancaster Lammas Assizes 1834* (Lancaster 1834), ii, pp. 346–56. John Marsden's will and codicil printed in full.
3. Hornby Castle, 11.5.18, John Lingard to Sandford Tatham, undated.
4. Hornby Castle, 11.7.7, John Lingard to Pudsey Dawson, 11 October 1831.
5. Hornby Castle, 11.5.18, John Lingard to Sandford Tatham, 28 October 1828.
6. Lancashire Record Office, RCHy 6958, John Lingard to John Higgin, undated.
7. Hornby Castle, 6.1.2, deposition of Thomas Cookson of Thorp Arch.
8. Hornby Castle, 11.3, correspondence of George Wright and William Sharp, 1 July 1826.
9. Hornby Castle, 11.3, Sandford Tatham to William Sharp, 1 July 1826.
10. Fraser, *A Verbatim Report*, i, p. 113; ibid., p. 190, evidence of Giles Bleasdale and William Sharp.
11. Ibid., ii, pp. 346–56, John Marsden's will and codicil.
12. Hornby Castle, 11.5.18, John Lingard to Sandford Tatham, 1 November 1829.
13. Hornby Castle, 11.7.22, William Dawson to Sandford Tatham, 1826.
14. Hornby Castle, 11.7.2. Sandford Tatham's MS.
15. Hornby Castle, 11.7.6, John Higgin to Sandford Tatham, 30 October 1826.

Chapter 11: Towards a Trial

1. Hornby Castle, 11.6.2, Sandford Tatham to John Higgin, 28 July 1829.
2. Hornby Castle, 11.7.6, Sandford Tatham to John Higgin, 16 July 1826.
3. Hornby Castle, 11.6.2, correspondence of Sandford Tatham and John Higgin, 1826.
4. Hornby Castle, 11.5.3, correspondence between Francis Pearson, John Higgin and others concerning the search for proof of the marriage, and the question of Sandford Tatham's legitimacy.
5. Hornby Castle 11.5.1, correspondence and memoranda, various, concerning William Mears.
6. Hornby Castle, 6.3.2 and 6.3.3, correspondence and memoranda, various, in support of Sandford Tatham's claim to be heir at law.
7. Hornby Castle, 11.5.18, John Lingard to John Higgin, undated.
8. Hornby Castle, 11.6.2, I. Gell to John Higgin, 31 July 1826.
9. Hornby Castle, 6.5.6, opinion of Samuel Duckworth, barrister.
10. Hornby Castle, 11.6.2, Sandford Tatham to John Higgin, 2 February 1827.
11. Hornby Castle, 11.7.22, correspondence of William Dawson to Sandford Tatham, 1826–29.
12. Hornby Castle 11.6.2, correspondence of William Askwith, Proctor of York, the Reverend Ambrose Dawson and E. Pate of Chester with Sandford Tatham and John Higgin, October to November 1826.
13. Hornby Castle, 11.3, George Wright to William Sharp, 30 November 1826.
14. Hornby Castle 11.3, William Sharp to George Wright, 10 January 1827.
15. Hornby Castle, 11.6.12, deposition of Robert Park of Lancaster, ex-servant of Giles Bleasdale.
16. Hornby Castle, 6.1.1, deposition of William Batty of Kirkby Lonsdale, surgeon apothecary.
17. Hornby Castle, 11.7.18, John Lingard to Sandford Tatham, 30 December 1828.
18. Hornby Castle, 11.5.18, John Lingard to Sandford Tatham, July 1829.
19. Hornby Castle, 11.5.18, John Lingard to Sandford Tatham, 27 February 1830.
20. Hornby Castle, 11.7.18, John Lingard to Sandford Tatham, 13 March 1830.

Other sources for this chapter: George Smith, diary (unpublished, in private hands); *Victoria County History of Lancashire*, ed. William Farrer and J. Brownbill, viii (London, 1913); Hornby Castle, 11.7.2, Sandford Tatham's MS; Tunstall parish registers.

Chapter 12: The Trial at York

1. Hornby Castle, 11.6.2, Sandford Tatham to John Higgin, 14 February 1827.
2. Hornby Castle, 11.3, Thomas Cuvelje to William Sharp, 22 January 1827.
3. Hornby Castle, 11.6.2, John Higgin to Samuel Duckworth, n.d. [1828].
4. Hornby Castle, 6.5.6, Samuel Duckworth's opinion.
5. Hornby Castle, 11.5.3, correspondence from and concerning Captain Robert Barrie, including a letter from the Admiralty permitting him to come to England for the trial.
6. Hornby Castle, 11.7.16, John Lingard to Sandford Tatham, 26 March 1838.

7. Alexander Fraser, *A Verbatim Report of the Cause doe dem. Tatham v. Wright: Tried at the Lancaster Lammas Assizes 1834* (Lancaster, 1834), ii, p. 238. Quotation from Frederick Pollock's speech at Lancaster.
8. Ibid., i, pp. 107–20, evidence of Giles Bleasdale.
9. Hornby Castle, 6.3.4, evidence of William Sharp, quoted by Judge James Alan Park.
10. Hornby Castle, 6.3.4, summing-up of Judge James Alan Park.

Other sources for this chapter: George Smith, diary (unpublished, in private hands); Hornby Castle, 11.5.18, 11.7.18. Many details of the build-up to the trial at York are drawn from undated letters of John Lingard to Sandford Tatham, filed under these numbers; Hornby Castle, 8.1.1, list of witnesses called; Hornby Castle, 5, 6, depositions of the witnesses called; Hornby Castle, 8.2.3, notes of Judge James Alan Park; Hornby Castle, 6.3.4, summing-up of Judge James Alan Park.

Chapter 13: The Trial That Failed

1. Hornby Castle, 11.5.6, Sandford Tatham to Pudsey Dawson, 9 April 1830.
2. Hornby Castle, 11.5.5, Sandford Tatham to Pudsey Dawson, 19 April 1830.
3. Hornby Castle, 11.7.29, John Bush and Matthew Gardner to Sandford Tatham, April 1830.
4. Hornby Castle, 11.5.5, Pudsey Dawson to John Higgin, 12 April 1830.
5. Hornby Castle, 11.5.5, Sandford Tatham to John Higgin, April 1830.
6. Hornby Castle, 11.5.6, Sandford Tatham to Pudsey Dawson, 22 August 1830.
7. Hornby Castle, 11.6.5, Mrs William Dawson to Pudsey Dawson, n.d.
8. Hornby Castle, 11.5.7, Sandford Tatham to Pudsey Dawson, 18 February 1831.
9. Hornby Castle, 11.5.8, Sandford Tatham to Pudsey Dawson, 4 February 1832.
10. Hornby Castle, 11.7.20, John Higgin to Sandford Tatham, 7 February 1832.
11. Hornby Castle, 11.5.8, Sandford Tatham to Pudsey Dawson, 3 April 1832.
12. Hornby Castle, 11.5.10, Sandford Tatham to Pudsey Dawson, 26 January 1833.
13. Hornby Castle, 11.7.4, Pudsey Dawson to Sandford Tatham, 21 August 1831.
14. Hornby Castle, 11.2.1, William Sharp to George Wright, 6 November 1830.
15. Hornby Castle, 11.2.1, William Sharp to George Wright, 8 November 1830
16. Hornby Castle, 11.5.5, John Lingard to John Higgin, 18 November 1830.
17. Hornby Castle, 11.7.16, John Lingard to Sandford Tatham, 29 March 1831.
18. Hornby Castle, 11.5.8, Sandford Tatham to Pudsey Dawson, 7 March 1832.
19. Hornby Castle, 11.5.8, Sandford Tatham to Pudsey Dawson, 3 September 1832.
20. Hornby Castle, 11.5.8, Sandford Tatham to Pudsey Dawson, 2 November 1832.
21. Hornby Castle, 11.7.16, John Lingard to Sandford Tatham, 27 September 1832.
22. Hornby Castle, 11.7.17, Pudsey Dawson to Sandford Tatham, 23 February 1833.
23. Hornby Castle, 11.7.17, Pudsey Dawson to Sandford Tatham, 3 April 1833.
24. Hornby Castle, 6.4.9, William Sharp to George Wright, 12 March 1833.
25. Hornby Castle, 11.5.10, Sandford Tatham to Pudsey Dawson, 13 April 1833.

Other sources for this chapter: further letters of the named correspondents; Lancaster Reference Library, Z10/PT853, *The Great Will Cause, doe dem Tatham v. Wright: Tried before Mr Baron Gurney and a Special Jury on April 2–5 1833* (anonymous pamphlet published by W. Helme of Lancaster).

Chapter 14: The Trial at Lancaster

1. Hornby Castle, 11.7.16, John Lingard to Sandford Tatham, 13 April 1833.
2. Hornby Castle, 11.5.10, Sandford Tatham to Pudsey Dawson, 13 July 1833.
3. Hornby Castle, 11.7.17, Pudsey Dawson to Sandford Tatham, 12 August 1833.
4. Hornby Castle, 11.7.17, Pudsey Dawson to Sandford Tatham, 12 April 1833.
5. Hornby Castle, 11.7.17, Pudsey Dawson to Sandford Tatham, 13 June 1833.
6. Hornby Castle, 11.7.17, Pudsey Dawson to Sandford Tatham, 17 May 1833.
7. Hornby Castle, 11.7.17, Pudsey Dawson to Sandford Tatham, 19 August 1833.
8. Hornby Castle, 17.7.17, Pudsey Dawson to Sandford Tatham, 14 November 1833.
9. Hornby Castle, 11.5.10, Sandford Tatham to Pudsey Dawson, 19 November 1833.
10. Hornby Castle, 11.7.17, Pudsey Dawson to Sandford Tatham, 14 November 1833.
11. Hornby Castle, 11.5.12, Sandford Tatham to Pudsey Dawson, 26 January 1834.
12. Hornby Castle, 11.7.7, John Lingard to Pudsey Dawson, 17 February 1834.
13. Hornby Castle, 11.2, George Wright to William Sharp, 3 November 1834.
14. Alexander Fraser, *A Verbatim Report of the Cause doe dem. Tatham v. Wright: Tried at the Lancaster Lammas Assizes 1834* (Lancaster, 1834), i, p. 181.
15. Ibid., i, p. 337.
16. Ibid., i, p. 339.
17. Ibid., i, p. 345.
18. Ibid., i, p. 7.
19. Ibid., i, p. 347.
20. Ibid., ii, p. 294.

Other sources for this chapter: further letters of the named correspondents; Fraser, *A Verbatim Report*.

Chapter 15: The Last Trial

1. Hornby Castle, 11.5.30, memorandum of Matthew Atkinson, 16 August 1834.
2. Hornby Castle, 11.5.10 and 11.5.12, Sandford Tatham to Thomas Gorst, 7 September 1834, 27 September 1834.
3. Hornby Castle, 11.2, William Sharp to George Wright, 3 November 1834.
4. Hornby Castle, 11.5.10, Edward Dawson to Pudsey Dawson, 5 October 1834.
5. Hornby Castle, 11.7.28, Pudsey Dawson to Sandford Tatham, 18 February 1835.
6. Hornby Castle, 11.5.4, Thomas Gorst to Pudsey Dawson, 17 March 1835.
7. Hornby Castle, 11.5.4, Thomas Gorst to Pudsey Dawson, 24 October 1834.

8. Hornby Castle, 11.5.11, Sandford Tatham to Pudsey Dawson, quoting John Lingard, 25 October 1835, 24 December 1835.
9. Hornby Castle, 11.2, William Sharp to George Wright, 28 October 1835.
10. Hornby Castle, 11.2, John Sharp to George Wright, 19 October 1835.
11. Hornby Castle, 11.2, William Sharp to George Wright, 11 January 1836.
12. Hornby Castle, 11.2. William Sharp to George Wright, 9 February 1836.
13. Hornby Castle, 11.7.7, John Lingard to Pudsey Dawson, 27 June 1836.
14. Hornby Castle, 11.7.7, John Lingard to Sandford Tatham, 4 July 1836.
15. *Lancaster Gazette*, 3 September 1836.
16. Ibid., 10 September 1836.
17. *Mr Justice Coleridge's Summing Up*, anonymous pamphlet printed Lancaster, 13 September 1836, p. 6.

Other sources for this chapter: George Smith, diary (unpublished, in private hands); *Dictionary of National Biography*; *Lancaster Gazette*, 3 September 1836; further letters of the named correspondents.

Chapter 16: Lord of the Manor

1. George Smith, diary (unpublished, in private hands), 12 September 1836.
2. Hornby Castle, 11.5.14, Sandford Tatham to Pudsey Dawson, 4 January 1837.
3. Hornby Castle, 11.7.8, Pudsey Dawson to Sandford Tatham, 27 October 1836.
4. Hornby Castle, 11.7.8, Pudsey Dawson to Sandford Tatham, 22 November 1836.
5. Hornby Castle, 11.7.8, Pudsey Dawson to Sandford Tatham, 18 November 1836.
6. Hornby Castle, 11.7.8, Pudsey Dawson to Sandford Tatham, 29 December 1836.
7. Hornby Castle, 11.7.8, Pudsey Dawson to Sandford Tatham, 24 June 1837.
8. Hornby Castle, 11.7.8, Pudsey Dawson to Sandford Tatham, 2 December 1837.
9. Hornby Castle, 11.5.14, Sandford Tatham to Pudsey Dawson, 1 May 1837.
10. Hornby Castle, 11.5.2, Sandford Tatham to Pudsey Dawson, 2 February 1838.
11. Hornby Castle, 11.5.14, Sandford Tatham to Pudsey Dawson, 13 March 1837.
12. Hornby Castle, 11.5.15, Sandford Tatham to Pudsey Dawson, 13 May 1837.
13. Hornby Castle, 11.5.15, Sandford Tatham to Pudsey Dawson, 14 September 1837.
14. Hornby Castle, 11.5.2, Thomas Gorst to Pudsey Dawson, 22 May 1838.
15. Hornby Castle, 11.5.16, Sandford Tatham to Pudsey Dawson, 8 June 1838.
16. Hornby Castle, 11.7.25, Pudsey Dawson to Sandford Tatham, 7 June 1838.
17. Hornby Castle, 11.7.16, John Lingard to Sandford Tatham, 21 June 1838.
18. Hornby Castle, 11.7.25, Pudsey Dawson to Sandford Tatham, 14 November 1838.
19. Hornby Castle, 11.5.16, Sandford Tatham to Pudsey Dawson, 15 June 1838.
20. Hornby Castle, 11.5.2, Sandford Tatham to Pudsey Dawson, 25 March 1838.

Other sources for this chapter: other letters from the named correspondents; legal reports in *The Times*, *Lancaster Guardian* and *Lancaster Gazette*, August 1838.

Chapter 17: Summing-Up

1. Hornby Castle, 11.5.16, Sandford Tatham to Pudsey Dawson, 16 March 1839.
2. Hornby Castle, 11.7.11, Pudsey Dawson to Sandford Tatham, 29 September 1838.
3. Hornby Castle, 11.7.25, Pudsey Dawson to Sandford Tatham, 24 January 1839.
4. Hornby Castle, 11.5.17, Sandford Tatham to Pudsey Dawson, 18 November 1838.
5. Hornby Castle, 11.5.17, Sandford Tatham to Pudsey Dawson, 30 March 1839
6. Lancashire Record Office, probate records (WRW), will of Admiral Sandford Tatham dated 27 October 1825, codicil dated 15 August 1838.
7. Hornby Castle, 11.7.25, Pudsey Dawson to Sandford Tatham. 27 October 1838.
8. Hornby Castle, 11.7.11, Pudsey Dawson to Sandford Tatham, 1 June 1839.
9. Martin Haile and Edward Bonney, *The Life and Letters of John Lingard* (London n.d. [1910?]), p. 293, John Lingard to Reverend John Walker (n.d.)
10. Ibid., pp. 308–9, John Lingard to the Reverend John Walker (n.d.)

Other sources for this chapter: *Victoria County History of Lancashire*, ed. William Farrer and J. Brownbill, viii (London, 1913); *Dictionary of National Biography*; George Smith, diary (unpublished, in private hands); Lancashire Record Office, probate records (WRW), will of George Wright 1848; further letters of the named correspondents; local and family information; parish registers; monumental inscriptions.

Index

Illustrations are shown in bold